The Author:

Leo Lowenthal is a professor at the University of California in Berkeley. Previously he conducted courses in the sociology of literature at Columbia, and before that was a member of the Institute of Social Research at the University of Frankfort. He is co-author of *Prophets of Deceit* and author of many articles in various learned journals, here and abroad.

LITERATURE
AND THE IMAGE OF MAN

Sociological Studies of the European
Drama and Novel, 1600-1900

By Leo Lowenthal

The Beacon Press   *Beacon Hill*   Boston

For Max Horkheimer

Library of Congress catalog card number: 57-6528

Printed in the United States of America

Preface

The theme of this book is the changing image of man in relation to society as revealed in some of the great literature of the Western world from the end of the sixteenth century to the beginning of the twentieth. Its method is frankly unorthodox. As a social scientist I am here dealing with materials traditionally allocated to the humanities; and I have employed techniques of analysis other than those commonly expected in the social sciences. Against the risk of attack from both scholarly camps, I can only hope to contribute to some rapprochement between them.

My interest in such an investigation dates from my joining the Institute of Social Research at the University of Frankfurt in 1926, and since then it has been stimulated greatly by my close association with Max Horkheimer, director of the Institute, and Theodore W. Adorno. I have also profited from many lively discussions with students in my courses in the sociology of literature at Columbia University during the last two decades and at the University of California since 1955.

The book was written in 1955 and 1956 while I was a Fellow of the Center for Advanced Study in the Behavioral Sciences at Stanford, California. No atmosphere could have been more conducive to my task than that of the Center. Under its generous policy, judiciously administered by the Director, Ralph W. Tyler, I enjoyed a unique opportunity to submit my research to the constructive criticism of scholars working in the same, or related, or even seemingly unrelated fields. I am particularly indebted, among the many Fellows who assisted me in this undertaking, to the historian Merle Curti, the sociologist Seymour M. Lipset, the psychologist Daniel Miller, and the novelist and critic Wallace Stegner.

In addition, the manuscript was read by a number of other friends and colleagues, and I wish to express gratitude to Siegfried Kracauer, Daniel K. Lowenthal, Hereward T. Price, Philip Rieff, David Riesman, Gertrude Jaeger Selznick, Philip Selznick, and Allan Temko. I owe special thanks to my wife, Marjorie Fiske Lowenthal, whose patience was surpassed only by the substance of her advice.

For editorial assistance I am grateful to Bennett Berger, Miriam Gallaher, Lester Hawkins, and Edgar Rosenberg. Maria Paasche's secretarial competence and perseverance were outstanding.

Wherever possible, inexpensive and readily available editions in English have been quoted in this study. Learned references have been kept to a minimum since this book is intended as much for the general reader as for the scholar.

Permission to quote from coyprighted works was graciously granted by Dover Publications; E. P. Dutton and Co.; Alfred A. Knopf; Random House; Charles Scribner's Sons; The Viking Press; and Mr. William Rose.

LEO LOWENTHAL

Berkeley, California

Contents

CONTENTS

Introduction: SOCIAL MEANINGS
IN LITERATURE

Creative literature conveys many levels of meaning, some intended by the author, some quite unintentional. An artist sets out to invent a plot, to describe action, to depict the interrelationships of characters, to emphasize certain values; wittingly or unwittingly, he stamps his work with uniqueness through an imaginative selection of problems and personages. By this very process of selection—an aspect of creativity that is most relevant to the theme of this book —he presents an explicit or implicit picture of man's orientation to his society: privileges and responsibilities of classes; conceptions of work, love, and friendship, of religion, nature, and art. Through an analysis of the works included in this volume, an image may be formed of man's changing relation to himself, to his family, and to his social and natural environment, from the beginning of the seventeenth to the threshold of the twentieth century.

The writer indeed develops believable characters and places them in situations involving interaction with others and with the society in which they live. He must present what he considers to be the essentials of the individual largely through the behavior of particular characters as they face concrete situations. Of course, the historian does not neglect such considerations. But he often depersonalizes the reaction of the individual to other individuals and to society in order to reveal the broader political, economic, and social forces at work. At the other extreme, memoirs, autobiographies, diaries, and letters might be offered as sources of data at least as personal and specific as the contents of imaginative literature. In such personal documents, however, rationalization and, particularly, self-justification often blur or distort the image of social reality. It is the artist who portrays what is more real than reality itself.

One of the concerns which the creative writer shares with the theoretician is to describe and name new experience. The artist's desire to re-create the unique and the important often leads him to explore hitherto nameless anxieties and hopes. He is neither an articulate recording machine nor an inarticulate mystic but a specialized thinker, and it is often only after his creative tasks have been performed that society recognizes its predicaments. The specific treatment which a creative writer gives to nature or to love, to gestures and moods, to gregariousness or solitude, is a primary source for a study of the penetration of the most intimate spheres of personal life by social forces. It is the task of the sociologist of literature to relate the experience of the writer's imaginary characters and situations to the historical climate from which they derive. He has to transform the private equation of themes and stylistic means into social equations.

Certainly, other sources describe the occupations and preoccupations of the bourgeois at the time of Molière; but only Molière reveals what it was like to live this experience. Similarly Goethe depicts the social and occupational problems which faced the sensitive bureaucrat or white-collar worker of his time. But the writer not only reports how the individual reacts to the pressures of society; he also offers a picture of changing views about the comparative importance of psychic and social forces. Corneille, the spokesman for the French absolute monarchy, viewed man as naturally incapable of imposing order on himself and his affairs without the guidance of a powerful state authority. Ibsen, on the other hand, living in the heyday of a competitive society, portrays individuals who are highly competitive in all their affairs, both public and private, and who ascribe their conduct to their innate natures. In fact, most generalized concepts about human nature found in literature prove on close inspection to be related to social and political change.

In the late sixteenth and early seventeenth centuries, the values of the national state and the monarchy were almost universally accepted by authors who saw in them not only a cure for the evils of the remnants of feudalism, but also a delimiting framework for the boundless aspirations characteristic of the time. It was only later that republican ideals appeared in literature, and later still that the elaborate social critique of an Ibsen could make its debut.

Authors may look forward or backward to a different age, but they tend to do so within the confines of an existing or foreseeable reality. Because the writer is not so much concerned with objects, events, or institutions as with attitudes and feelings which his characters have about them, any social or political "bias" he may have is far from the severe handicap that it would appear to be at first sight. Man is born, strives, loves, suffers, and dies in any society, but it is the portrayal of *how* he reacts to these common human experiences that matters, since they almost invariably have a social nexus. Precisely because great literature presents the whole man in depth, the artist tends to justify or defy society rather than to be its passive chronicler.

All literary materials, including those hitherto considered beyond the province of the sociologist, therefore assume social meanings. The idea of "nature," for example, at different moments of history has had these very different connotations: the non-human world to which one goes for relaxation from the human scene; a Utopia which idealizes an extra-historical space as opposed to society in corruption; the sanctuary for those in flight from a frustrating situation. Sometimes the style of the artist provides significant clues, as when Ibsen's people use almost identical terms to describe competition between husband and wife and competition in the professional world. Or again it may be the emotions which assume social relevance. Thus, for example, Cervantes displays a number of sentiments and actions denoting extreme personal insecurity, ranging from worry about professional status to moral and philosophic doubts. Such fears in turn can be related, more or less directly, to the unprecedented social mobility which followed the disintegration of the feudal world, and they indicate how profoundly the individual was affected by this dramatic change.

The literature of any period gives its audience meaningful portraits of human types. The Spaniards to whom Cervantes spoke, the Englishmen who saw Shakespeare's plays, and the French audiences of Corneille, Racine, and Molière had no difficulty in identifying their dramatis personae or in recognizing their nuances. Because of this representational quality, all literature, whether first or second rate, can be subjected to social analysis. But the works of a Cervantes or Ibsen present problems quite different from those of the hack.

The writer achieves greatness because of the depth of his insight into the human condition. The fact that literary genius is rare and its audience small, presents in itself a sociological problem, but this in no way detracts from the writer's role as interpreter. More important is the question of his relation to various population groups, as a participant or observer. For if a group has no opportunity to express its own emotional or intellectual experiences, and is isolated from the literate sector of society, it may lie beyond the artist's range of observation. To the Greek tragedian, for example, the feelings and thoughts of slaves were of little significance. The contemporary American writer, on the other hand, has almost unlimited access to behavior on all social levels, from the industrial tycoon to the migrant farm laborer. The problem here is simply to be as clear as possible about the scope of the author's view. For most of the periods studied, members of the lower classes of the European population rarely appear as fully drawn characters in works of literature. There are exceptions; Cervantes and Shakespeare both went to considerable pains to create individuals from the lower classes, and Cervantes surely had unusual opportunities to observe them closely. But the bulk of the fictional characters considered here are from the middle and higher levels of society.

This analysis of three centuries of European literature begins with the breakdown of feudalism and the rise of absolutist governments, then turns to the growth and consolidation of the middle classes, and ends with the fore-shadowings of modern totalitarian orders. As social history, it suggests an arc, curving upward in the first tentative gropings toward modern individualism, rising to a plateau of confidence in the individual, and finally declining at the point where the individual feels threatened by technological and social forces. Each end of the trajectory marks a period of stress.

The breakdown of the feudal order forced man to fall back upon himself; he had to learn how to cope with count-less problems and decisions that were once taken care of by worldly and spiritual hierarchies. But together with the anxieties generated by this new autonomy he sensed a great promise, for in the period of the formation of the national state and the development of a mercantile economy his own future seemed to have infinite possibilities. At the end of the curve, in our own century, he begins to feel threatened by the encroachment of powerful social forces emanating not only from his own corner of the earth but from every part of a contracting world.

This curve, as illustrated in the works studied here, also describes the context of the individual's growing aware-ness of his own history and of the social conditioning of his roles. In Shakespeare's day, men tended to be aware of society mainly through face-to-face encounters with others; human bonds, whether of pity or sympathy, were felt to be freely assumed. From the time of Corneille onward, how-ever, the individual learned to see himself as irrevocably involved in a social order, whether he subjected himself to it or revolted against it in the name of a different order. After Molière, social awareness increased to the point where the problem of adaptation to organized society became a central theme of literature; Goethe and Ibsen were both concerned with the price this adaptation exacted from the individual, and at times each writer went to great pains to reveal the social determinants of private problems. Ibsen's works explicitly portray persons as they experience the all-pervasive force of their society.

For the beginning of the period, Lope de Vega, Cervantes, and Calderon represent Spain; Shakespeare, England; and Corneille, Racine, and Molière, France. Strict chronological sequence has been sacrificed for the sake of preserving national groupings. The Spanish writers are dealt with first, since Spain remained closest to feudalism and did not succeed in developing a viable national state or a successful capitalist economy.

The effect on Spain of its conquests in the New World was dramatic; and the three writers considered display three different ways of facing the social changes brought about by this development. Calderon accepted the *status quo* with a kind of fatalism, while Lope de Vega adopted a more dynamic social orientation in glorifying the benefits of an absolute monarchy; Cervantes rejected it.

The Spain of Cervantes' novels is a highly mobile and competitive society. Man has become the measure of a world which is losing its theological determinants; he can now judge what he sees in strictly human rather than theological terms. He rejects much of his society, particularly those deformations of character that are the result of competition and insecurity, but he does so in the name of a man-made ideal. Despite the obvious fact that Don Quixote is presented as a feudal knight, the ideals and observations of Cervantes are too modern, too secular, and too close to the Renaissance concept of the individual for us to call him a sentimentalist. Unlike Cervantes, Lope de Vega is very much the successful and active man of his times, and very much at home in his world. He is intoxicated, in a sense, by the splendor of Spanish power at its peak. But by the middle of the seventeenth century only the deluded could maintain a glorious image of the declining empire: Calderon no less than Lope endorses monarchism; his allegiance, however, is colored by nostalgia for medieval values, caused perhaps by his awareness of diminishing Spanish strength.

Shakespeare in *The Tempest* presents a paradigm of the condition of man at the beginning of the modern era. Shakespeare's age was still characterized by the spirit of an adventurous, mercantile economy which preceded the consolidation of the middle class. He provides the most complete picture of the Renaissance individual who interprets the world almost exclusively in the light of his own needs and to whom outward events appear as tests of an inward adequacy and dynamism. While Shakespeare advocated the importance of competent rulers, he simultaneously perceived their subjects enmeshed in a new pattern of social mobility which could push the individual downward as well as up.

The French writers, too, reacted to the radical social changes of their times. Their viewpoints, however, are focused on a progressive state where the monarchy is firmly established and the middle classes have begun to flourish. Corneille's individual stands in need of a powerful state authority for guiding his acts—a dependency on outside authorities that would have been alien to Shakespeare. Racine rebels against all authority in favor of the individual, whom he sees as frustrated by submission to the powers that be. Molière sees man feeling his way through the new order to individual autonomy. The French dramatists thus represent three stages in the middle of the development of increasing social control: the bourgeois ethos is more apparent in Racine than in Corneille, and in Molière it is virtually all-pervasive.

Sociologically, Goethe is Molière's direct successor. His work is a progression from the revolt of the Storm and Stress period to his acceptance of middle-class responsibility in *Wilhelm Meister's Travels*. His final view is that the individual is worthy of the name only if he performs a useful social task. Goethe knew the price of adaptation, however, and in his old age became particularly concerned with the growing problem of the alienation of the artist from society at large.

The curve ends with Ibsen and Hamsun. Ibsen was an incisive critic of middle-class society, and the main question he posed was whether society has lived up to the claims of its apologists. His answer was almost invariably negative. In every sphere of life he found the results of competition and specialization to be pernicious. In all of their personal and social encounters, his characters emerge as losers. The institutions and façades of public life become incompatible with individual needs, and man is torn by this conflict. Ibsen explores the classical image of the autonomous individual found in Shakespeare and Cervantes, only to see him break apart under the impact of the very forces that were supposed to help him to realize his potentialities.

If Ibsen presents the dilemma of liberalism, Knut Hamsun implies its authoritarian resolution. There is, in all his novels, an anticipation of the Nazi ideology. He rejects modern, urban, industrial society with its frustrations and responsibilities. His solution is a flight to nature in the form of submission to forces beyond human control, with which he combines admiration of "blood, race, and soil." Such values led him finally into the Nazi movement.

It is striking that in the works of all these periods—underneath the fashions of classicism and romanticism, of rationalism and empiricism in taste and thought—there is a certain continuity in the changing relationships of the individual to his society. Studied separately, the works of each writer yield impressive insights into seemingly timeless universals. Considered together, they testify that man, as he has grappled with the ever-changing problems of his adaptation to society, has become increasingly preoccupied with his own integrity and increasingly aware of the forces which threaten it. The Western ideal of freedom that emerged in the late Renaissance was at first thought to be boundless. That this ideal was found to be subject to the manifold limitations of economic laws, social pressures, and the vagaries of political history may in part account for the fact that pain and anxiety are predominant themes of creative literature. The question the artist asks of mankind is whether pain and anxiety are necessary elements of human destiny, or whether they are mainly a consequence of social conditions.

Chapter I: THE SPANISH WRITERS

Paradoxically, the nation that more than any other inaugurated the modern age did not long enjoy the fruits of this era but fell rapidly into economic and political decline. Spain is closely linked to the discovery of North and Central America, to the ensuing importation of colonial products, and, above all, to the increase of precious metal in Europe. But Spain's brief period of unprecedented expansion was badly mismanaged; neither the court nor the nobility recognized that only the creation of strong national industries and a firmly centralized government could guarantee her continuance as a major world power. The ruling strata had developed a type of economic parasitism which found ample nourishment in the wealth of the old and new worlds. But with the devaluation of precious metals, what had for a brief period been a comfortable over-abundance for parasites now became a ruinous over-abundance of parasites.

Although Spain played an ever more negligible role in the new order, the three most eminent Spanish writers of the sixteenth and seventeenth centuries represent the three social points of view prevailing in the Europe of that time. The chronology of their appearance is, however, the reverse of what one would expect. The oldest, Cervantes, is the most critical and the most forward looking of the three while the youngest, Calderon, looks to a society that has already been superseded. Lope de Vega, as spokesman for the absolute monarchy, looks neither backward nor forward but tries to adjust to the prevailing conditions. Of the three, Cervantes is the most rewarding for the purpose of our analysis, namely, to trace the social origins of individual expectations and anxieties.

I.

LOPE DE VEGA (1562-1635)

Background

Lope's life might be described as that of an intellectual entrepreneur. He was born into a family of the metropolitan aristocracy, with excellent connections at court. Educated by the Jesuits, he enjoyed the special tutelage of an uncle who, as Inquisitor, belonged to the upper bureaucracy of the Church of Spain. Then, in quick succession, Lope became active as a soldier, bishop's page, and secretary to the Duke of Alba, a most influential political figure of his time. In early middle age he suffered the sole setback of his career when scandals about his love affairs resulted in a few years' exile from the capital. This trouble, however, seems to have cast no shadow on Lope's future; he returned to Madrid neither sadder, wiser nor more chaste, and there he comfortably spent the last forty years of his life still pursuing his erotic activities. After two marriages, terminated by the death of both wives, Lope was ordained a priest and assigned to one of the fashionable metropolitan churches. His deviations from the moral code did not prevent his earning many honors; he enjoyed the favor of the current power cliques, and the Pope bestowed upon him an honorary doctorate for having extolled Mary Queen of Scots as a Catholic martyr in one of his innumerable plays.

Lope participated in the proceedings of the Inquisition, and was able to reconcile his religious activities with the colorful private life to which seven illegitimate children bore witness. His literary production, too, was nearly inexhaustible. More than two thousand plays came from his pen, of which a third have been preserved. Cervantes

(whom Lope snubbed all his life, only to eulogize him four-
teen years after his death) with some justice called him "a
monster of nature." Lope died in 1635, in his seventy-third
year. His funeral was as spectacular as his life had been;
the obsequies lasted nine days, with three bishops in attend-
ance.

Lope's work portrayed the ambiguities in the social position of the Spanish ruling groups in his time. The Spanish
monarchy and the worldly and ecclesiastical aristocracy
bound up with it were able to maintain their luxuries for a
while on the proceeds of the great Spanish explorations,
especially on the proceeds of colonial wealth and the booty
acquired in victorious campaigns. This prosperity was
bound to be frustrated sooner or later, if only because the
mode of production which was beginning to replace feudalism demanded not luxury but industriousness—that is,
industry in both senses of the word. The internal inconsistency between the medieval and modern ways of social
life which characterized the Spanish aristocracy—its attempt
to subordinate essentially capitalistic types of production
and consumption to an antiquated feudal system—furnishes
Lope with his underlying theme.

The Maintenance of Order: Authority

For an understanding of this inner contradiction as it
manifests itself in Lope and in the group of which he was a
part, the reader might refer to almost any one of the dramas. Consider, for example, *The Duke of Viseo*. The play
begins with the triumphant return of a general of the
army from his successful African campaign. He is wel-
comed by the king in a manner somewhat less than friendly,
however, for he and his brothers have been accused by the
favorite courtier of high treason. The courtier plans to
marry a lady attached to the court, who makes the mistake
of asking the general's advice on the desirability of the

match. The courtier's grandmother having been discovered to be a Moor, the general thinks the marriage ill-advised, and swears the lady to secrecy in the matter of the African grandmother. Of course, the lady talks; the court circles teem with gossip and internecine quarrels break out. In these intrigues, the Duke of Viseo, brother-in-law to the king and the epitome of loyalty to his in-laws, becomes unhappily involved. The outcome for the duke is death; the king has him destroyed, along with the general who began it all, as well as the general's brothers. A young lady, in love with the duke, dies of sorrow at his bier. The denouement, however, is the king's acknowledgment of the duke's innocence; to mend matters as best he can, he confers the honors due to the unjustly condemned duke upon the duke's brother and, in fact, pronounces him heir-apparent to the throne. It is taken for granted that the king has behaved with propriety and justice and, in his eleventh-hour restitutions, has shown an ample degree of forbearance and good sportsmanship.

The play is typical of Lope, its authoritarian structure reconciling social values of the medieval type with the emerging values of monarchical absolutism. At no point is there doubt that Lope sides with the principle of absolute authority. The matter could not be pinpointed more specifically than it is in a conversation between the duke and one of his peers, a member of the duke's camarilla, both of whom are eventually put to death by the king whose praises are being sung:

> *Guimarans:*   Viseo,
> Such honorable thought in you's the issue
> That we and you in war and peace were both
> Restrained by law, and by the law impell'd
> To hold in high esteem our king, for that
> He stands for God in our country. As for ourselves,
> We princes are on earth what in the heavens above
> The Angels are unto God's countenance.
> Therefore we owe him all obedience
> And thanks for aught he does.[1]

And the duke takes it up from there:

Viseo: It is a lofty and a noble thought
That you observe in our earthly hierarchy
An image of the heavenly.[2]

Sublime or banal, the observation is commonplace enough to the Renaissance with its highly schematic system of analogues. But what is of interest is that this respect for the traditional order, for authoritarian force, is an absolute for Lope; the king is respected even when he is transparently in the wrong. Once he has his grandees murdered, he need only appoint the murdered man's brother to be his successor to set everything straight again. Similarly, in another of Lope's dramas, the well-known *Jewess of Toledo,*[3] a Spanish king falls in love with a beautiful young Jewish girl; the innocent heroine is put to death and, although the king causes her downfall, the murder is justified because it recalls the king to his duties as ruler and father.

One need only compare, for instance, Viseo's ethos with Don Quixote's to recognize the degree of Lope's conformism. Don Quixote symbolizes a conflict in which the individual is finally shattered by the authority of social facts. This conflict is to become a pervasive motif in literature throughout the ensuing modern era. But Lope's theme is one which plays on the potential compatibility of the individual's private and public life; in case of doubt, however, it is society that has the final say. When the Jewess is put to death, the state benefits by her removal; and what is the death of one Jewess, no matter how innocent, when measured against the welfare of the state?

In Lope's glorification of the absolute monarchy we do not find any longer the moralistic compulsion of the Middle Ages, nor do we, on the other hand, find the artist a spokesman for individual freedom. Like Corneille in France, Lope is a poet of the new nationalism. The medieval sense of inner duty is replaced by an attitude of dependence on a secular power from without. In another of Lope's plays, *The Sheep Well,* the king is shown as coming to the aid of the people against the depredations of a feudal lord. Here, as elsewhere in the plays, we get a picture of a society in which almost anything can happen, and it is the will of the king that imposes a pattern on events, insures order and, occasionally, promotes justice. It has been thought by some that Lope was indirectly giving lectures to kings on justice and on reparations for injustice. However that may be, it is just as certain that he was equally concerned with absolute allegiance to the monarch.

But while Lope raises the issue of conformism, he at the same time obscures the conflict between individual wishes and the claims of the state. He persistently portrays victory as on the side of the ruler in the struggle between good and evil, right and wrong, honor and caprice, virtue and vice. With the dice thus loaded, we can do no more than infer the price of conformity to his protagonists; Lope is too rigid a monarchist to display it at any length.

The Threat to Order: Passion

The concern of Lope's protagonists is to placate the powers-that-be in order to stave off complete destruction. The realities of the social world, however, tend constantly to be veiled by metaphysics. The essential characteristics of the modern era—industriousness, professional concerns, the conflict between rich and poor, the importance of private property and competition in trade and industry—all are absent, or appear only incidentally, in his work. All those aspects of social observation which in Cervantes' novels are so rich are either left out of account or made part of an inscrutable human destiny. Accidents of every description, even miracles and magic tricks, recur repeatedly.

Lope's fatalism was a response to the mobility of seventeenth-century society, with its chance meetings and its possibilities for accidents, including sudden downward movements on the social ladder; it is a fatalism that has more in common with Calvin's doctrine of predestination than medieval Catholic dogma. Yet Lope's fatalism prov markably inconsistent. At times, tragic human even viewed as the unforeseeable results of destiny but, on occasions, they are viewed as springing from human passions. At one point we get the lines:

> Even if fate's intent could be discovered
> Its reach no human being could escape.
> So soon as man has found his enemy in fate
> Not even the firmest will can then withstand it.[4]

But in the same play we read this interchange:

King: Elvira then is dead?
Don Luis: Aye, cold, my lord.
There's not a breath upon her to be felt.
King: Why, has she killed herself?
Don Leonardo: My lord,
She did not.
King: What, then, was the cause?
Leonardo: Immeasurable love.[5]

Lope portrays love as a force that cannot be brought into harmony with the existing social order—a motif which, as we shall see, will frequently form the point of departure for an implied social critique, e.g., in Racine and in the Goethe of *Werther*. In Lope's plays the idea of absolute monarchy, the principle of the existing order, always wins out; nevertheless such an expedient resolution, as, for instance, in *The Jewess of Toledo*, must have been pale in comparison with the dramatic effect of the passion with which the king loves first his wife and later the Jewess. This passion engulfs him to such a degree that he is ready to discard all obligations. Once the Jewess has been brought to him he renounces all thought of a campaign against the Moors. In the conflict between his duty as a commander and his desires as a lover, the lover—until duty conquers all—is victorious. An unbridgeable gulf opens between social order and the individual.

Pessimism

Thus for Lope, society is formalized into a value in itself, against which passion is viewed as a fateful, if not fatal, accident. Cervantes, on the other hand, makes a clear distinction between a bad society and one which is beneficial to human beings. The world which mocks Don Quixote is in many respects a useful world; only insofar as it stunts human morality does it deserve to be rejected by Cervantes and the Knight alike. But behind the hilarity of the Knight's adventures, Cervantes has managed to express the hope that there may some day emerge a society in which people will no longer laugh at Don Quixotes, and in which individual freedom and the collective good may be maintained side by side. In this sense, *Don Quixote* is not only a non-conformist but also an optimistic document, the more optimistic in that it provides a framework within which right action and wrong action are clearly distinguishable from each other.

Far otherwise with Lope. Basically he distrusts the individual's capacity for self-discipline and right social action, and he implies the need for a rigidly binding relationship between governor and governed. What he demands is ready submission to the will of the ruler who, once having been designated to keep peace in the social body, must be inviolable. Since man is incapable of self-government, the only reasonable solution is for him to abdicate the task to the state. Lope, like Hobbes and Machiavelli, begins with an assumption of innate disorder in human nature.

However sympathetic he is to the *status quo,* Lope nevertheless registers the bewilderment of the man of his century in a way that is more bleakly sad than that of either Cervantes, with his bagful of Utopian possibilities, or Calderon, with his strong religious ties and his (even if deceptively) firm medieval moorings. And at times a genuinely desperate note can be caught in Lope; it is heard

quite distinctly in such lines as the following, from
monologue of a young gardener (Belardo) in *The Jew*
of Toledo:

How foolish is the world, and how ridiculous
Are the illusions to which it surrenders.
All is delusion and hypocrisy,
Stupidity or else presumptuousness.
God in His Heaven is addressed as "thou,"
Base man is titulate' "Your Highness,"
A wife sans shame and honor's now a courtesan;
Depravity may pass for youthful folly,
Thieving's misnamed dexterity; poverty, dishonor,
Honorable he alone who's rich and fortunate.
Foolhardiness assumes the name of bravery,
And vulgar cunning's likened to discretion.
Madness and avarice take on ambition's name . . .
Thus have all designations been confounded,
But death alone cannot be altered by this world,
For he alone does level all whom he encounters.[6]

The feeling of futility in Lope's distress is sharpened if we
contrast the lines with another work of the same period:
Lope's theme is sufficiently similar to that of Shakespeare's
Sixty-sixth Sonnet to justify their analysis side by side:

Tir'd with all these, for restful death I cry
As to behold desert a beggar born,
And needy nothing trimm'd in jollity,
And purest faith unhappily forsworn,
And gilded honour shamefully misplac'd,
And maiden virtue rudely strumpeted,
And right perfection wrongfully disgraced,
And strength by limping sway disabled,
And art made tongue-tied by authority,
And folly—doctor-like—controlling skill,
And simple truth miscall'd simplicity,
And captive good attending captain ill:
Tir'd with all these, from these would I be gone,
Save that, to die, I leave my love alone.[7]

It will be noticed that in Belardo's monologue the world's madness is characterized by a confusion and corruption of terminology. The uses of language have been perverted and defiled; distinctions have broken down; coherence is gone; anything can be made to equal anything else; meanings can be reversed at will; language has become an instrument of deception, hypocrisy, falsification, disguise. Death alone can neither be changed as a reality, nor can it be falsified by language. It remains the sole safeguard and certainty to which man has access in a world gone mad. It has literally "gone" mad; for there is a certain dynamic quality in Belardo's words which allude to a time when the world was neither absurd nor insane, and the suggestion, though undeveloped, is very strong that things have not always been this way.

While Belardo's words bear a highly generalized impress, in Shakespeare's sonnet the entire atmosphere is to a very marked degree personalized. Shakespeare's "I" is in the foreground of the recital continuously. Moreover, the defects which the sonnet stigmatizes are not corruptions of language but corruptions of institutions, attitudes, actions. In other words, Shakespeare deals with a more or less specific historical development into which the individual is thrown and in which something happens to him. It is not, as in the case of Lope, a phenomenon of general misorientation which is being indicted, a case of linguistic aberration, the perversion of speech as the genuine tool of truth, but rather the corruption of a way of life. Insofar as the abuse of language is at all criticized in Shakespeare's verse, the criticism really sidesteps language in order to get at something else: the wicked reality. Lope's words betray a certain desperate explosiveness; they might almost be interpreted as the outburst of a man at his wit's end. Shakespeare's words—raising the truisms of contemporary tavern philosophers to artistic consciousness—sound a very articulate protest indeed against conditions that have overwhelmed the individual; they are capable, however, of being changed—they are historical phenomena, societal facts and tendencies that contain their own possibilities for change.

The two excerpts reveal the difference not only between two poetic temperaments but between two social situations as well. Lope de Vega typifies a transitional period. His philosophy still shows the influence of the medieval brand of realism, according to which the essence of reality consists in universal concepts which are, as creations of God, fixed and static; the world does not change.

Shakespeare, on the other hand, stands in the more advanced position of the nominalist. For him such names as honor, virtue, fame—although they may temporarily have no phenomena to which they can be related—denote human attributes which can again become part of reality. One might say that for Shakespeare man's measure—the very definition of man—lies in his ability to change. And change is brought about by the force of love. Lope's ultimate lines aver only the invincibility of death; Shakespeare's project the individual toward life. To the man of the Renaissance the concept of love bears distinctly revolutionary aspects. It indicates uniqueness, specificity, particularity; it can neither be inherited nor transmitted. It is no more grounded in tradition than it can be taught for future use: in short, it is the very essence of individuality.

2.

CALDERON (1600-1681)

Background

Calderon's life spans the final stages of Spain's decline as a world power, her loss of supremacy to France and England and the economic decay that followed the first phases of colonization. Calderon neither gave his endorsement to this state of affairs, nor, since he was a loyal servant of

the Crown, did he attack it. Of the three possible positions
—to sympathize with the existing order, to criticize it, or to
withdraw from it—Calderon's was the latter, an escape into
the past; to all intents, his is the viewpoint of medieval man.

Like Lope, Calderon was educated by the Jesuits. His
family enjoyed intimate connections at court, his father having served as under-secretary in two successive reigns.
After his military service, Calderon became poet laureate to
the court and like the glamorous Lope, who befriended him,
was knighted in due time, became a priest, and spent the
last years of his life in increasingly eminent positions assigned to him by the Crown. Unlike Lope, however, he
seems to have led a personally honorable life and to have
confined himself to the pattern of the well-behaved courtier.

The idea of monarchy which Calderon exalted had little
in common with the modern power-state as Lope conceived
it. What Calderon portrays is, in substance, the feudal
state, now prolonged in the Inquisition, in league with the
Church. The concept of honor that lies at the center of his
reaction has an artificial character: it means not merit but
a prestige like that of the Spanish Empire itself, backward
looking and without intrinsic strength. There are two
classes: the feudal lords, and the rest who are their sub-
ordinates. Only among the former do we find pure passion,
excellence of conduct, bravery, and virtue. In the lower
strata nearly everybody is vulgar, cowardly, and dissolute.
Nothing could more pointedly mark the contrast between
Calderon and Cervantes: Cervantes at times places his final
truths in the mouths of gypsies and robbers; Calderon
would shrug off these dregs of humanity as unworthy candi-
dates for prestige and honor.

The Concept of Honor

Calderon has occasionally been described as an author
who glorified emerging middle-class values, and his play,
The Mayor of Zalamea, has been cited in support of this

interpretation. A close examination of the drama will not, however, bear out this view. The play portrays the infatuation of a captain, who is a member of the gentility, for the daughter of the mayor of Zalamea, a wealthy farmer in whose house the captain is billeted. When the affair comes to light, the father insists that the captain restore his daughter's violated honor by marrying her—an unusual request because of the social distance between the gentry and a peasant, however wealthy and respected he may be in his community. Since the captain rejects this request the peasant has him murdered and petitions the king to sanction this avengement of his daughter.

A superficial analysis of the play might suggest that Calderon's intention was to take the part of the mayor and his class against the gentry. If nothing else the mayor's request to the king to approve his drastic action rules out this view. It also becomes increasingly clear that the model of "honor" in this case is not middle-class virtue, but a concept that originates in and chiefly refers to the highest feudal circles, from which the subsidiary orders derive their *raisons d'être*. In a conversation between the mayor and the captain's commanding officer, the peasant raises the point of honor three times in quick succession in an atmosphere heavy with tension; he has made up his mind not to stop short of the most drastic measures if his demands are ignored:

> *Crespo:* And I tell you, whoever points his little finger at my honour, I'll cut him down before hanging.
> *Lope:* Know you not, you are bound by your allegiance to submit?
> *Crespo:* To all costs of property, yes; but of honour, no, no, no!
> My goods and chattels, aye, and my life—are the king's;
> But my honour is my own soul's . . .[8]

What enables these two people, miles apart socially, to communicate with each other is the commonly understood reference to a traditional hierarchy of values that is impervious to any practical exigencies. They both know what "honor" entails, and this keeps the conversation going. At the same time—though so faintly as to be just audible—a new concept of man is caught in the peasant's remonstrances: his readiness to relate honor to his private individuality, to his "soul." But it would be too far-fetched to interpret this passing allusion as the same attitude as that which found expression in the paeans to the individual and his soul, and which was developed in the philosophies of Cervantes and Shakespeare. The most Calderon is saying is that honor belongs to any one, given the sanction of higher authority. He is not having the peasant formulate a new insight, as Cervantes might have done. The peasant is, on the contrary, merely repeating lessons about honor he has learned and that have been passed down to him from on high.

Calderon and Lope

In Calderon's play, the peasant's son, conversant with the devices for attaining upward mobility in the decaying years of the bankrupt and money-hungry Spanish monarchy, suggests to his father that he might easily avoid the discomforts of having his house used for billeting army personnel by simply buying a title of nobility. But the father says:

> A patent of gentility; upon thy life now dost think there's a soul who doesn't know that I'm no gentleman at all, but just a plain farmer? I should only prove I was worth so many thousand royals, not that I had gentle blood in my veins, which can't be bought at any price . . . If a fellow's been bald ever so long, and buys him a fine wig, and claps it on, will his neighbors think it his own hair a bit more? . . . They know his bald pate is safe under it all the while. That's all he gets by it.

Still the son objects:

> Nay, sir, he gets to look younger and handsomer, and keeps off sun and cold.

Whereupon the father says:

> . . . I'll have none of your wig honour at any price. My grand-father was a farmer, so was my father, so is yours, and so shall you be after him.[9]

Quite obviously, the father's argument is extra-rational and depends solely for its persuasiveness on identification with the concepts of those who have the highest prestige.

Literary historians have suggested that the peasant's speech may have been inspired by the following passage in one of Lope's plays:

> He that was born to live in humble state
> Makes but an awkward knight, do what you will.
> My father means to die as he has liv'd
> The same plain collier that he always was;
> And I too must an honest ploughman die.
> 'Tis but a single step or up or down;
> For men there must be that will plough or dig,
> And when the vase has once been fill'd, be sure
> 'Twill always savour of what first it held.[10]

Although it is obvious that Lope and Calderon are like-minded in their benevolent view toward the *status quo*, as opposed to Cervantes who of the three stands alone as its critic, nevertheless between the former two we find significantly different motivations. Lope's argument for things as they are is based on considerations of utility: "for men there must be that will plough or dig." He is not unaware of the factor of upward (or, for that matter, downward) mobility, but in justifying the division of labor in his own society he sidesteps the issue by pointing to the quite honorable, concrete social tasks of the peasant. For Calderon, however, social mobility is something beyond the pale; a man's station and role in life is transcendentally determined: "gentle blood . . . can't be bought at any price." The different reasons for supporting the social order may perhaps be explained by the contrast between a social climate of confidence in the future of the *status quo*, as Lope had known it in earlier years, and that of a power system in rapid decline, which was the heritage of Calderon.

The difference between the two writers emerges most clearly when we consider the over-all qualities of their works. Lope wrote countless plays with a contemporary setting (though his social observations were far less rich and realistic than those of Cervantes). Calderon, on the other hand, was attracted by feudal settings. When he does deal with a contemporary theme, the language seems stilted and codified.

In *The Great World Theater* (*El Gran Teatro del Mundo*), Calderon shows God assigning people their professional status before placing them on earth. Quite naturally, only the king is satisfied with the role given him; all the others strongly object. Their objections are pointless because the will of God cannot be contradicted. The beggar, in particular, finds it hard to accept his status, but he is assured that it is not the role itself that matters but how well it is played. In the end, the conclusion is that life on earth will, in any case, be brief and will be followed by an eternity in heaven for those who play their parts well. The drama makes quite apparent that no one can change his role without incurring divine wrath; the beggar can only hope to be a good beggar, the king a good king. The rewards, if there are any, spring from acceptance. The play exemplifies the formalism, rigidity and, at the same time, the dreamlike quality of the decaying Spanish empire.

Artificial Traditionalism

In *The Physician of His Honour* Calderon has an impetuous prince lose his dagger in the bedroom of a noble lady. The prince is being impetuous to no great purpose; the woman retains her innocence. But the dagger having been discovered, the intrigue must be resolved and honor restored. The transparent fact that no honor has been lost to begin with is quite beside the point; the rite must go on.

The husband is denied the possibility of a duel with the prince, for it is not within the rules of the game for a grandee to take bodily revenge on a son of the royal house. Instead, the husband restores his honor by opening the veins of his sleeping wife; and he does so with the complete approval of the king, whose son has thus in effect murdered the one innocent party in the cabal.

The play reads like an indictment; the very absurdity of the murder speaks of the meaninglessness of the traditional code. But the over-all character of Calderon's works testifies to the fact that no irony is intended (although the phantastic element in his plays suggests that he himself may have been, at some level, aware of the hollowness of the social system he was glorifying). One's role may be absurd; nevertheless the advice is to accept it and to play it well. The situation reminds one of Lessing's *Emilia Galotti,* written roughly a hundred years later. In the German writer's drama, a patrician kills his own daughter rather than allow the tyrant of a petty Italian state to dishonor her. But Lessing's temperament was critical and his message revolutionary. In his drama the rising middle class indicts the arbitrariness of absolute monarchy; there could not have been any doubt in the minds of the audience that the dagger which struck Emilia should have been aimed at the prince. Calderon's play, on the other hand, inadvertently depicts the decay of a once respectable value system that is degenerating to the status of a private ritual. To paraphrase a well-known *mot:* in Lessing's world the situation is serious but not hopeless; in Calderon's it is hopeless but not serious.

The social position of Calderon may perhaps be illuminated by a comparison of the moral values expressed in *The Mayor of Zalamea* with those which prevail in a story by Cervantes, wherein a rich peasant boy dishonors a young girl and refuses to marry her. In the former, as we remember, the stubborn Crespo has the captain executed because the captain, equally stubborn, refuses to marry the peasant's daughter. In *Don Quixote,* however, the claims of restitution of honor as a traditional moral value lose out to the prerogatives inherent in the possession of private property: the lord of the region is unable to force the rich peasant's son to marry the girl—because the lord is the peasant's debtor. Calderon's peasant, on the other hand, where honor is involved, imitates to an almost grotesque degree the professed ideologies of medieval chivalry in words like these:

> You shall forthwith take all my substance, without reserve of a single farthing for myself or my son, only what you choose to allow us; you shall even brand us on back or forehead, and sell us like slaves or mules by way of adding to the fortune I offer you—all this, and what you will beside, if only you will with it take my daughter to wife, and restore the honour you have robbed. . . . And what is my demand? But that you should restore what you have robbed: so fatal for us to lose, so easy for you to restore . . .[11]

The reactionary character of the speaker is further underscored by the way in which he refers to the new social order, the rule of law, the protection of certain rights enforced by sane and solid magistrates. He will not violate the traditional hierarchy by taking recourse to orderly procedures of law, so as to have redress

> . . . which I could myself now wrest from you by the hand of the law but which I rather implore of you as a mercy on my knees! [12]

The unbending rigidity with which a privileged group tries to cling to antiquated concepts may be noted again in the captain's evasive and impertinent reaction to the old peasant's plea:

> As to the wrong you talk of, if you would avenge it by force, I have little to fear. As to your magistrate's stick there, it doesn't reach my profession at all.[13]

The final sanction of the mayor's act of retribution is unequivocal. The king himself forgives the peasant, because he has, "if unusually, not unjustly," acted in the spirit of the Spanish monarchy. As a parting symbol of a mentality which abhors nothing more than change, the king appoints Crespo "perpetual Mayor of Zalamea. And so fare well." [14]

Calderon's greatness as a literary artist is not, of course, under question here. But it may be interesting to note in this context that Goethe, who had the highest respect for Calderon's art, in the end repudiated him. According to Goethe, the audience was forced into an attitude of total passiveness, obliged to accept the contents, spirit, characters, and morals of Calderon, as if they were ingredients of so much spoon-fed medicine.[15] Goethe speaks here for the progressive middle-class critic, who rejects not only the reactionary authoritarian values of Calderon but also, in the last analysis, the rigidity of the art forms through which they are manifest.

In some of Calderon's plays, ironically enough, there is a quixotic element of doubt about reality, and wherever we encounter it even the courtly pomp with which in his own life he was surrounded seems to take on a dream-like quality. But such ambiguity with regard to reality is far removed in its social meaning from the phantasy of Cervantes, whose idealism does not prevent him from acutely observing the world around him.

Chapter II: CERVANTES
(1547-1616)

Don Quixote is read today primarily as a collection of humorous adventures. Its author nevertheless experienced the bitter uncertainty of the small man in post-medieval society. Cervantes attempted perpetually, and in vain, to shake off the conditions of poverty into which he was born. His father, coming from the lowest ranks of gentility, was a man of somewhat obscure professional qualifications, part lawyer, part physician; he was both deaf and destitute. Cervantes wavered for a time between attempts to make a career in the papal bureaucracy of Rome and efforts to hew out a place for himself in the military by enlisting in the Spanish Navy, which just then was readying to engage the Turkish fleet at Lepanto. During this battle the poet all but lost his life.

After a partial recovery, Cervantes again joined the fleet, only to be captured by Algerian pirates; the next twelve years he spent in captivity. His various attempts to escape brought him near to hanging, burning, and impaling. When finally his widowed mother scraped together the needed ransom, Cervantes returned to his homeland and found a modest position as collector of taxes and procurer of military provisions. At this time he married, and it seems that for the next few years he was able to support his growing family (though barely) by various additional jobs, some of them literary. The last twenty years of his life were spent trying to survive on the meager proceeds from his writing and from occasional government posts, none of which he was able to hold for any length of time. This was his routine, interrupted periodically by imprisonment for debt, for unsubstantiated charges of civil disorder or embezzlement. On one of these occasions (he was then under suspicion of murder) he had to take his entire family to jail with him. He died in a state of utter destitution the same year Shakespeare died—tradition has it that they died the same day.

Cervantes' life, in a way, symbolizes the plight of the non-aristocratic individual in a society that is no longer bound by the fixed relationships of the medieval worldly and ecclesiastical hierarchy, but has become impersonal and abstract. Fundamentally the themes of his novel are those of an old way of life being replaced by a new order. Cervantes stresses the resulting conflicts in two ways: through the struggles of the Knight, and through the contrast between him and Sancho Panza. Don Quixote lives in a phantasy world of the vanishing feudal hierarchy; the people with whom he deals, however, are merchants, minor functionaries in the government, unimportant intellectuals —in short, they are, like Sancho, people who want to get ahead in the world and, therefore, direct their energies to the things which will bring them profit.

But common sense, this altogether correct answer to the challenge of organized society, tends to obscure a quality which Don Quixote possesses in ample degree—humaneness, which always protests injustice. It is from Don Quixote's humaneness that certain tendencies, anti-authoritarian and, for his time revolutionary, derive. The protest takes the form of an ironical twist: Don Quixote is always wrong, the others always right. A shaving bowl is not really a helmet, nor is a windmill a dragon. The wineskins are no more giants than the innkeeper is a knight. It is absurd to want to free the galley slaves, because they will only commit more crimes and finally take their liberty out on their liberator. The people are "right" in protecting their belongings against the onslaughts of a Don Quixote and in guarding against his interference in their private affairs. Common sense has a higher authority than his absurd pretensions.

This is not to say that Don Quixote is not a hero, any more than it is to say that Cervantes is nostalgically oriented toward the past. If we examine the novel closely, we see that Cervantes' concept of man is in every way contrary to the medieval concept. True, Don Quixote does pay lip service to obsolete structures—the hierarchy of the Church and the feudal social system, together with the conceptions of virtue and chivalry associated with them. But he does not accept them in their old meanings; he recasts them to suit his own purpose. One might say that Don Quixote is the first figure in Renaissance literature who seeks by action to bring the world into harmony with his own plans and ideals. Cervantes' irony lies in the fact that while overtly his hero battles against the new (the early manifestations of middle-class life) in the name of the old (the feudal system), actually he attempts to sanction a new principle. This principle consists, basically, in the autonomy of individual thinking and feeling. The dynamics of society have come to demand a continuous and active transformation of reality; the world must be perpetually constructed anew. Don Quixote recreates his world even though he does so in a phantastic and solipsistic fashion. The honor for which he enters the lists is the product of his thinking, not of socially established and accepted values. He defends those whom he considers worthy of his protection and assails those he believes to be wicked. In this sense he is a rationalist as well as an idealist.

Despite his feudal accouterments the Knight shares another attribute with the new post-medieval character—solitude. His opponents, too, are isolated, but for a quite different reason: their atomization is a consequence of the fact that each is pursuing his own selfish motives. Don Quixote is isolated because what he wants to accomplish is impossible: he wants to suppress those who are evil, to do away with force, to free men, to realize his feeling of devotion for humankind in his love for Dulcinea. He runs head-on into conflict with all authority as soon as he begins to put such good intentions into effect.

His idealism has two sides, metaphysical and moral. The world as he sees it, he sees on the basis of his own ideas, and his ideas reside simply, sometimes simple-mindedly, in his impressions. The world, as he reconstructs it, is in truth his private property. The peasant is not a peasant but an Arab; the windmill and the wine-skins are dragons and giants; the innkeeper is a lord of the castle; the peasant girl a noble lady. This world, which he has created, he then evaluates by his own moral ideals. The outcome for him personally can only be failure, since his adversary is no less than the expedient relativism of the common-sense world.

But while *Don Quixote* ends on a note of sad resignation, this solution seems not to have reflected the author's convictions. Cervantes had in fact a practical, first-hand knowledge of the forces of hunger, of money, of private property. In some instances he raised quite specific demands for reform; in this he may have been stimulated by manifestoes on natural rights to be found in Catholic literature, which not only traced the authority of the king to that of the people but enunciated more or less outspoken demands for radical economic change. (For example, statements may be found in these broadsides which appear to call for cooperative farms.) Whether Cervantes was directly familiar with the writings of Mariana and Suarez, we have no way of ascertaining; but we do know that he envisioned a Utopia roughly along the lines indicated by these writers. As already noted, his critique of the *status quo* was essentially cloaked in images of artistic irony. Thus, he stressed in many variations the society of the poor as the only place where genuine human feelings still exist, because there people remain uncorrupted by interests in worldly goods. In the "exemplary" tale of *Rinconete and Cortadillo*, he even allowed himself the extended jest of picturing a society of robbers and thieves as exemplars of true human solidarity.

I.

MOBILITY: SANCHO PANZA

The New World Picture

Midway through *Don Quixote,* the noble Knight takes
it into his head to reward Sancho Panza, the peasant servant whom his errant mind has transformed into a medieval
squire, by conferring upon him the governorship of an
island. The island is, of course, imaginary. For some time
Don Quixote and Sancho have gone their separate ways,
but the expectation of the good fortune of the governorship
brings the servant back to his master. He tells his wife that
he has been offered the job of running an entire island by
himself and that, although the job entails his separation
from his family, it would be criminal to turn it down on
that account. It is quite "necessary" that he take the job,
he says,

> . . . and then, too, I like to think that I may be able to come
> upon another hundred crowns to take the place of those we've
> spent, although, naturally, it makes me sad to have to leave you
> and the young ones. . . . I can tell you one thing, wife, said
> Sancho, that if I did not expect to see myself the governor of an
> island before long, I would die right here and now.[1]

By implication, Sancho is raising an issue that will later
become a fundamental one in middle-class society, the issue
of social mobility. Granted that the peasant's phantasies
about the extent of his mobility are extreme—the possibilities open to a peasant at the turn of the sixteenth century
certainly did not range from utter destitution to high political positions—they nonetheless serve to reveal areas of
feelings and perceptions which are real enough despite the
rather absurd event that occasions them.

It is difficult for us today to imagine and to reconstruct
the uncertainties to which Western man was exposed during

the century-long revolution which marked the transition to middle-class life. The feudal society of the late Middle Ages had brought its own vicissitudes; but uncertainty had not been notably one of them. The peasant, for better or worse, was no more than a subunit of the feudal pyramid—born into it and replaced in it by his offspring. His position was both specifically defined and predictable. But with the waning of the closed system of an agricultural society people found themselves increasingly freed from the securities as well as the bondages that inhere in an unchangeable social location.

By the turn of the sixteenth century most of the former touchstones—social, cultural, religious, and economic—had become questionable or entirely useless. Man had to begin, again, from scratch: he had to learn to orient himself to a situation in which he was increasingly thrown back upon his own resources. He found himself between two worlds, "one dead, the other powerless to be born." John Donne was to formulate this sense of frustration in a famous passage from his *Anatomie of the World:*

And new Philosophy calls all in doubt,
The Element of fire is quite put out;
The Sun is lost, and th'earth, and no man's wit
Can well direct him where to look for it.
And freely men confess that this world's spent,
When in the Planets and the Firmament
They seek so many new; they see that this
Is crumbled out again to his Atomies.
'Tis all in pieces, all coherence gone;
All just supply, and all Relation:
Prince, Subject, Father, Son, are things forgot,
For every man alone thinkes he hath got
To be a Phoenix, and that then can be
None of that kind, of which he is, but he.
This is the world's condition now.[2]

Everything seemed, in Cervantes' day, to be possible at every moment; catastrophe impended, but so did success. The notion that *"tout est dangereux ici-bas"* had all the force of an ever-present, acutely-felt state of mind although the other half of Voltaire's observation, *"et tout est néces-saire,"* had not yet been added. And it is precisely this inner reflection of mobility which Sancho Panza's words convey: failure or glory, far beyond the normal expectation of a peasant's career, both seem accessible, perhaps equally accessible to him.

Now this upward or downward mobility (for which the phantasy knows no limit) has certain decisive consequences for human relationships. Consider first the peasant's attitude toward his employer, the Knight. Sancho's words betray the fact that he can no longer quite clearly separate motives of personal loyalty from motives of self-interest. Even while he stammers a trifle defensively about some felt "necessity," his acquisitive mind is drawn toward the possibility of a monetary windfall. This is no longer the feudal peasant who unquestioningly surrenders his life to the tasks and purposes of the person one step above in the hierarchy; he is instead a being who must rely on an entirely new set of motivations. It is, suddenly, the motivation of modern man, in whom self-interest and friendly feeling are often closely allied. The relationships among individuals are now determined by uncertainties and ambiguities, and private decisions must be based on a relativist concept of social reality.

Mobility penetrates even the intimate sphere of family relations. In the peasant's ruminations the drive for success and the concern for wife and children are at once separate and complementary forces. While Sancho, in his chatter about having to leave Teresa and the little ones, pays lip service to family responsibilities, this emotional drive is quite clearly subordinated to the drive for acquisition and success, the means for obtaining luxury as well as security for the family unit. The lines between the egoism of the thriving middle-class individual and the altruism of the family man have become blurred in Sancho's declaration— but in case of doubt he will defend the governorship against the claims of his wife.

Secularization of Family and State

Turn now to the wife's answer to Sancho's argument:

No, not that, my husband, Teresa protested. Let the hen live even though she may have the pip, and in the same way you should go on living and to the devil with all the governorships in the world. Without a governorship you came out of your mother's belly, without a governorship you've lived up to now, and without a governorship you will go, or they will carry you, to your grave when God so wills. There are plenty of folk in this world who manage to get along without being governors . . . but [they] are still numbered among the living. The best sauce in the world is hunger, and since this is something they never lack, the poor always have an appetite.[3]

The passage reveals a number of added features characteristic of post-medieval society; we may confine ourselves briefly to three.

First, the secularization of feelings. There is no pious traditionalism in Teresa's reply, which is directed toward individual needs and pragmatic ways to gratify them. The casual reference to the Deity is hardly more than a stock response; but while the identification of man and animal is not uncommon in medieval literature, Teresa's opening sentence inaugurates a new theme: she avails herself of a private metaphor which is all the more convincing for being part and parcel of her whole outlook. The goal of life is survival, not transcendental salvation. What matters are the hens, not God. Teresa's points of orientation are not the great powerful institutions of society, or religious convictions, but rather are to be found in concrete and cogent life situations which must be maintained and possibly bettered, if the improvement can be brought about on a realistic, sensible level.

Second, the passage tells us something about woman's role in the society of Cervantes' day. Teresa's reaction is conservative; social mobility frightens her. She foreshad-

ows the dual role of the wife in the middle-class family: exclusion from social processes outside the family while remaining a touchstone for the husband's ability to assert himself in his role of breadwinner. When Sancho works up
the anticipation of grandiose personal success, the woman
acts as the representative of common sense, which seems to
be required for the survival of the family unit. Even as she
considers the unlikely event that her husband should realize
his dreams, her attitude remains one of down-to-earth reasonableness:

> But look, Sancho, if by any chance you do fall in with a gov-
> ernorship, don't forget me and your children. Remember that
> little Sancho is already turned fifteen, and it is only right that
> he should go to school. . . . Remember, too, that your daughter,
> Mari-Sancha, would not drop dead if we married her off.[4]

Sancho immediately toys with the idea of marrying the
children into high society, but the wife, true to form, ad-
vises him to stick to his own station: "You bring home the
money, Sancho, and leave the marrying of her to me." The
wife acts throughout as manager of the family, which in
turn functions as the only stabilizing element in the turmoil
social mobility has created among the Panzas. The family
is conceived of as having its own norms, in line with the
mores and conventions of the social group for which the
husband qualifies; for the wife the bonds of the family
guarantee stability and serve as a counterforce to the
dangers inherent in both upward and downward mobility.
Teresa warns Sancho that their daughter might make blunders in marrying

> . . . some great count or high and mighty gentleman who every
> time he happened to feel like it would call her an upstart . . .
> she will be a stranger to others and to herself.[5]

The third issue raised by Teresa's reply to Sancho is a
suspect view of government. Her remark takes place in the
context of the social condition in which the national state
has replaced the feudal order. It was largely tradition that
had bound the individual to the feudal hierarchy, but the

new national state must enforce its claims to power. Not since the time of the late Roman Emperors had Europe experienced to such a degree the force and strength of the state apparatus—its magistracy, its military, its police—in a series of harsh and demanding laws that regulated work and possession. This new political milieu was experienced simply as harshness and toil by the broadest stratum of the population, who were almost always its victims and seldom its beneficiaries. We need only consider how, even in a lenient democracy, the attitude of the ordinary citizen toward the state is compounded of a certain ambivalence in order to infer that the first centuries of modern history must have been a time of extreme uneasiness and aversion toward a rigid monarchy.

Sancho's attitude toward the organs of government is identical with his attitude toward society as a whole. He wants to get on; he wants to be part and parcel of the small group of masters. By masters he more or less unconsciously means people who have a lot of money, and he is inclined to identify a high office of government with money. Teresa's attitude, on the contrary, reflects a wife's skepticism of these risky schemes and stratagems, and an acute anxiety lest the head of the family drift away from home and lose himself in dubious adventures. Cervantes merely hints at these tensions, as he merely hints at all social topics, but they are present in his work in germinal form.

2.

CREATIVITY: DULCINEA

Illusion or Reality?

An intriguing scene occurs in the thirty-second chapter of the second part of *Don Quixote*. Here we are introduced to a social rank far above that of Sancho Panza and his wife as the Knight argues politely with his hosts, the Duke and Duchess. When the conversation turns to Don Quixote's relationship to his beloved, the Lady Dulcinea del Toboso, the Duchess observes:

> . . . if we are to believe the tale about Senor Don Quixote that was recently published in these parts and that won the praise of all—we are to gather from this tale, if I remember rightly, that your Grace has never seen the lady Dulcinea, that there is, in fact, no such lady in existence, or, rather, that she is a purely fanciful one, created in your Grace's own mind, whom you have endowed with all the charms and perfections that you chose to give her.[6]

The Duchess thus ceases to talk as a fictitious character may be expected to, within the story; instead, she talks about the story (by virtue of which she exists at all) and discusses *Don Quixote* with Don Quixote. Today, we are not so startled as Cervantes' contemporaries must have been by the device; it is a kind of irony that has been used often since, although his must certainly be a very early example.[7] In any case, enough of the mood of ambiguity survives to give us a sudden feeling of uncertainty. For a moment, we no longer know whether we are inside the novel or out of it, and the demarcation between existence and phantasy becomes problematic, as indeed it is in the Knight's world. The question: does Dulcinea exist? points to the heart of Cervantes' ambiguous philosophical position, a position that betrays the fundamental uncertainty of his time.

In the Middle Ages, the world and everything in it had been viewed as created and guaranteed by God. The hierarchy of society, perceptions of the "real" and even the imagination of man, all had their fixed places in this ordering. The figure of Don Quixote arises in a world that has lost this theological compass, a world in which man must create his own ordered meanings so that he can locate himself, others, and the external world. Don Quixote does this by embracing two seemingly irreconcilable philosophies— those of sensualistic empiricism and rational idealism—but the two complement each other as orientation courses in

the new order. To Don Quixote, Dulcinea exists. She represents the Knight's perception as well as her own (after
all, she is his creation), and the Knight's and her own
rational and moral criteria. Don Quixote is man placed at
the center of things after the fall of the feudal hierarchy.
To him, only that exists which man creates, perceives, im-
agines, or anticipates.

The evaluation Cervantes makes of Don Quixote (and of
himself) is also one he applies to others, in a moral sense:
man is the offspring of his own works. The Knight, in a
conversation with a peasant boy at a strategic point early in
the novel, asserts "the fact that every man is the son of his
works." [8] The same words are used by the Knight's servant
when, much later in the story, Sancho Panza reminds himself that "each one is the son of his own works, and being
a man I may become to be pope, not to speak of being
governor of an island; for my master may win so many that
there will not be people enough to give them to." [9] Similarly, all the love of a Don Quixote would not be enough
to create the shining image of Dulcinea if she did not herself act out the infinite potentialities of her inner being, if
she were not "the daughter of her works." [10] There is
hardly a concept more generic to the modern style of life in
the Western world than this which burdens the individual
with the responsibility for his own life and for the life of
man.

The ideal of man as the center of his acts brings us
close to modern concepts of democracy. The social world
comes into being by virtue of the individual's creative acts;
and it is in this recognition, morally, that the foundation of
human equality resides. Man, any man, contains a creative
potential, although his condition, his social role, may not
allow him to realize it.

Two basic concepts of human nature run through modern
moral beliefs. The one, represented by Machiavelli, Lu-
ther, and Hobbes, endows the human being with innate
qualities of evil—or, at least, brutishness—and prescribes
rigid coercive measures. The other, whose chief spokesmen

are artists, endows man with the primary quality of innocence. Of course, the Christian dogma of Original Sin was
taken seriously by artists of the Renaissance and it was
often a potent factor in their lives; indeed, if there is one
commonplace of which the schoolboy in Cervantes' or
Shakespeare's time was daily reminded, it was:

> In Adam's fall
> we sinnèd all.

But it may be laid down that for Cervantes and such artists
as Shakespeare, Racine, Schiller, and Ibsen, the original
kindness and benevolence of man shines through all his
manifestations—his acts as well as his attributes. Cervantes, nevertheless, while he believes human beings are by
nature good, admits that they often are not. The original
kindness is constantly jeopardized.

The Jeopardy

It is society at large that confronts the idealism of the
creative individual with the reality of competitiveness. In
place of the egoism of the creative artist, or of a Don
Quixote, it imposes the egotism of private gain. It is no
mere coincidence that Cervantes, the highly fanciful literary
artist, was also an excellent reporter of the social realities
of the Renaissance. If he was interested in the individual
who was the "son of his own works," he was also an observer of the conditions that threatened him. In *The Man
of Glass,* a crazy young student expatiates at length on the
professions, specifically on laborers, lawyers, and physicians.
Repeatedly he emphasizes instances of human coldness and
competitiveness that result in spiritually and materially
damaging others.

In speaking of "lads with mules for hire," for example,
the student says:

> All you lads have in you something of the pimp, something of
> the thief, and something of the mountebank. If your masters

(for such is the name you give to those you carry upon your mules) chance to be simpletons, you play more tricks on them than this city has known for many years past; if they are foreigners, you rob them; if they are students, you curse them; if they are religious, you blaspheme against them; and if they are soldiers, you tremble from fear.[11]

The carter comes off no better:

Half the time he is singing and the other half he is cursing or yelling "Get behind there!" when someone tries to pass him. And if by any chance he has to stop to get one of his wheels out of a rut, two good round oaths are of more use to him than three mules.[12]

The sailors

. . . are a fine lot, though unversed in city ways, and they know no other language than that which is used aboard ship. In fair weather they are diligent, but they are lazy in a storm. In a tempest they give many orders and obey few. Their god is their seaman's chest and their grub, and they find amusement in watching the seasick passengers.[13]

And the carriers, finally, are indicted in language scarcely less restrained:

They have been divorced from sheets and have married packsaddles. They are so industrious and have such an eye for business that they would lose their souls rather than a day's haul. Their music is that of hoofs, their sauce is hunger, their matins consist in speaking their mind, and they go to mass by hearing none.[14]

All of these Theophrastian characters are drawn from the growing class of transport workers who had arisen with the revival of European trade and were now in evidence on a vast scale as the economy of Europe expanded. All show traits of rudeness and indifference to fellow men. Anxious to counter the exploitations to which they are subjected, these people respond by exploiting others in turn—in ways that are petty and limited, certainly, for that is all their depressed station in society allows. Moreover, they share another dehumanizing trait: a shrunken capacity for speech.

The mule drivers "blaspheme"; the carters are "cursing or yelling"; the sailors speak only in the crude language "which is used aboard ship"; the carriers substitute "speaking their mind" for prayers. Language, the principal tool of human communication, is being used only to convey aggression and hostility. These socially useful working men have reduced language to a point where they, as social men, are silent.

No less interesting are the student's remarks about a second vocational group peculiar to the new society: the free professions—the physicians and lawyers, both of whom are inseparable from the basic features of the emerging social picture. The physicians come to the fore as practitioners of the natural sciences, the lawyers as the executors and administrators of the law with jurisdiction over substantial areas of land—counties, states, even international areas—a jurisdiction that makes possible and facilitates the mechanics of a commercial economy. The Man of Glass ironically acknowledges their respectability, at the same time indicting them for concealing ignorance and self-interest behind the masks of expert knowledge.

> The judge may pervert or delay justice; the man of law may in his own interest plead an unjust cause; the merchant may drain off our property—in short, all those with whom we must necessarily deal may do us some wrong, but there is none of them other than the doctor who is in a position to deprive us of life itself, without punishment. Physicians may and do kill without fear or running away and without unsheathing any other sword than that of a prescription; for there is no means of discovering their crimes, since they at once bury them underground.[15]

It should be noted that the Man of Glass speaks in one and the same sentence of "the merchant" and the learned professions. What they have in common is the self-seeking monetary drive:

> He charged lawyers and solicitors with being negligent and ignorant, comparing them to doctors who, whether or not the patient recovers, collect their fee; these gentlemen of the legal

profession did the same regardless of whether they won or lost their case.[16]

But there is one group of professions of which the Man of Glass has only good things to say—authors and actors. In the course of the story, someone remarks that "there are many actors who are well-born and sons of somebody"; to this, the Man of Glass replies with his customary lucidity:

> That is true enough, but what the stage stands least in need of is individuals of gentle birth. Leading men, yes, who are well mannered and know how to talk, that is another matter. For it might be said of actors that they earn their bread by the sweat of their brows, with an unbearable amount of labor, having constantly to memorize long passages, and having to wander from town to town and from one inn to another like gypsies, losing sleep in order to amuse others, since their own well-being lies in pleasing their public. Moreover, in their business, they deceive no one, inasmuch as their merchandise is displayed in the public square, where all may see and judge of it.[17]

And as for authors, they

> . . . too, have an incredible amount of work to perform and a heavy burden of care; they have to earn much in order that by the end of the year they may not be so far in debt that they will have to go into bankruptcy; yet for all of that, they are as necessary to the state as are shady groves, public walks, and parks, and other things that provide decent recreation.[18]

Cervantes, if anyone, knew the artist's calculated risks, the constant threats of economic disaster; but that is by the way. What is very much to the point is the defensiveness, even the defiance, of Cervantes' attitude. From the very beginning of the new era the artist finds himself socially and economically—and thus psychologically—in a position of jeopardy, which forces him to articulate and to press his claim, not merely for toleration but for recognition of his unique role. The nature of the argument is transparent: art is as important to the maintenance of the social equilibrium as are all other public institutions and activities.

Above and beyond that, the artist has something to bring to society which neither the tradesman nor the professional brings. His task is to serve men by giving them pleasure; thus his function is not one of exploiting his fellows but, on the contrary, of socializing them. And he is continuously creative. Wherever he goes—if he is an actor—or whatever he achieves—if he is a writer—he helps men to maintain their identity and integrity in this strange new world.

And yet, at the same time, no other professions had to fight so persistent a battle for respectability and recognition as did the actor and the free-lance literary artist.

Who Is Dulcinea?

With this background in mind, we can appreciate the serious side of the otherwise comic conversation between the Knight and his hosts, the Duke and Duchess. According to Don Quixote, something has happened to Dulcinea; some baffling and awful metamorphosis has taken place in her:

> I found her under a magic spell, converted from a princess into a peasant girl, from a beautiful creature into an ugly one, from an angel into a devil, from a fragrant-scented being into a foul-smelling wench, from a fine-garbed, dignified lady into a rustic clown, leaping in the air—in short, from Dulcinea del Toboso into a Sayago country woman.[19]

He goes on to say that certain terrifying influences that can be neither accurately named nor controlled are the cause of this kind of sudden downward fate of a human being. But, unlike the explanations provided in the old fairy tales, such causes as the Knight assigns can scarcely be interpreted as supernatural in origin; if anything, they are social. "Who is it," asks the Duke, "could have done such a wrong to the world?"

> Who? Don Quixote repeated. Who could it have been except some malign enchanter of the many envious ones who perse-

cute me? That cursed race of beings was born into the world
to darken it, to frustrate the achievements of the virtuous and
exalt those of the wicked.[20]

Thus enter the anonymous forces of reality, thinly veiled
in poetic symbols. These are the threat to human creativity,
these as yet indefinable and hence all the more troubling
agents—"some malign enchanters." Sancho can dream of
upward mobility, but he can all too easily fail disastrously
—and so can the Knight. The world teems with unknown
enemies, with accidents and unaccountable misfortunes,
with human injustice, expediency, and greed.

On the other side of the ledger is the infinite power of
creativity. A human being develops his own fulfillment out
of his own activity. Who is Dulcinea? She is never completely real since there are always possibilities which must
remain latent: neither is she completely unreal since some
possibilities have been realized. As Don Quixote puts the
matter:

> God knows whether or not there is a Dulcinea in this world or if
> she is a fanciful creation. This is not one of those cases where
> you can prove a thing conclusively. I have not begotten or given
> birth to my lady, although I contemplate her as she needs must
> be, seeing that she is a damsel who possesses all those qualities
> that may render her famous in all parts of the world, such as:
> a flawless beauty; dignity without haughtiness; a tenderness that
> is never immodest; a graciousness due to courtesy and a courtesy
> that comes from good breeding; and, finally, a highborn lineage,
> for beauty is more resplendent and more nearly perfect in those
> of lofty extraction than in creatures of a humbler origin.[21]

The last lines in this passage might sound like a refuta-
tion of democratic philosophy, since the Knight takes recourse to such issues as "highborn lineage" and "lofty ex-
traction." He introduces them, however, merely to dis-
parage them in what follows. Part of Cervantes' genius is
that he invites the reader's participation in the creative
process: Don Quixote, seeming suddenly to realize that he
has allowed himself to relapse into the prejudices of an

obsolete social order, stops and catches up with himself by observing:

> I can say only that Dulcinea is the daughter of her works, that virtues shed luster upon the bloodstream, and that a person of low degree who is possessed of them is more to be esteemed than the vicious one who has risen to high station. Moreover, Dulcinea has qualities that well may bring her to a crown and scepter; for a woman who is at once beautiful and virtuous may by her merits come to work miracles, and has locked within her, potentially if not actually, a higher fortune than the one she knows.[22]

The argument is now restated: a person of low degree deserves high praise if he develops his capacities; "high station" in itself is not a mark of virtue.[23] The figure of Dulcinea as she finally emerges symbolizes the new concept of man: the question of Dulcinea as real "in this world" or as "a fanciful creation" is resolved when the Knight describes her as "the daughter of her works," thus tipping the scale in favor of man's fulfilling his meaning by activity. Man becomes the creator of his world rather than a mere creature in it. This is true of Don Quixote and his Dulcinea, as well as of Cervantes himself, who has entered the scene by way of the Duchess' remarks and who is the creator of them both. But the reliability of one's own constructs is precarious, and so is the moral desire to recreate the world in a genuine human image. Hence, the philosophical ambiguity that arises at the beginning of the modern era. The artist as the prototype of the idealist takes this risk of ambiguity.

By the time of the Renaissance the world has come to be viewed as an immense *tabula rasa*. It has no prior and accepted guarantees. Intellectuals, philosophers, belleletrists, as well as geographers and explorers, all tried to begin *ex nihilo* and to discover the very nature of the universe, both inside and outside the human realm. When Pascal enunciated his famous confession of terror, *"les silences éternels de ces espaces infinis m'effraient,"* he may have been thinking along cosmological lines, but he also gave utterance to the fears of the late Renaissance individual. The infinite spaces needed replenishing. The historical absurdity in which Don Quixote engages and revels replaces all factual concreteness with a world made new by him.

Cervantes, in sum, is in all his works on the road to the discovery of human nature. The process is critical and non-conformist, realistic in method and idealistic in intention. This journey toward the discovery of the individual takes place in two stages: the first seeks to observe reality; the second defines the ideal. The concluding sections of this chapter will deal with these two stages respectively.

3.
PROPERTY: THE GYPSIES

Beset by economic uncertainties, haunted by accident and misfortune, Cervantes speaks for the little man of his time when he says in one of his prefaces to *Don Quixote*: "I will have profit, for without it fame is not worth a farthing." Repeatedly he describes private property and particularly money as the new regulators of social relationships which had once been determined by feudal fealty. In the second part of *Don Quixote,* he tells the story of "a most dignified duenna" who has fallen on hard times and whose daughter has been disgraced. Here is a story that must have happened many times over:

> The son of a very rich farmer, in a village not far from here that belongs to my lord the duke, fell in love with her. How it happened I do not know, but they came together and, under promise of marrying her, he made a fool of my daughter and now is unwilling to keep his word.[24]

Formally, the feudal order shows itself in such passages as this. Ostensibly, the farmer owes loyalty to the lord of the region, but, in reality, the impoverishment of the landed aristocracy has destroyed the validity of an artificially maintained social system. The duenna, steeped in the tradition of mutual responsibility, has pleaded her cause with the lord, but in vain:

> My lord the duke is aware of this, for I have complained to him not one but many times, imploring him to order that farmer's son to marry her, but he turns a deaf ear and scarcely listens to me. The reason is that the young deceiver's father is so rich; he lends the duke money and goes security for his debts from time to time, and so my lord does not wish to offend him or give him trouble of any sort.[25]

What hitherto had been a binding personal relationship has become a cold, anonymous, impersonal dealing, rooted in monetary property. The reiteration of the theme in Cervantes shows the impact of the rapid social change on the ways people looked at the world.

Marginal Man

Cervantes' view of property relations reminds one of the apothecary's speech in Shakespeare's *Romeo and Juliet* and the experiences of Timon and Lear. In the works of both these artists the nature of man comes to the fore when the protagonists are placed in situations of material scarcity; this is true not only of Don Quixote but of a number of lesser figures in the *Novellas,* just as it is true of Timon and Lear in the solitude of nature, and of Prospero, Ferdinand and Miranda on their remote island in *The Tempest.* It is an element of the quasi-Utopian idyl of *As You Like It* that the society which surrounds the exiled duke should be free from the cares and conspiracies attending the larger context of propertied society from which he has been banished.

These incidents of material deprivation point to the function of such marginal situations. A number of writers have, like Cervantes, introduced marginal figures as true representatives of human concerns and as standards for understanding (and criticizing) the central features of their society. One might almost say that the prevailing philosophy of human nature since the Renaissance has been based on the conception of each individual as a "deviant case" whose existence consists very largely in his efforts to assert his personality against the restrictive and leveling claims of society.

Very quickly after the downfall of feudalism, the literary artist developed a liking for figures who look at society not from the viewpoint of a participant but from the vantage point of an outsider. The further these figures are removed from the affairs of society, the greater is likely to be their social failure (which is almost, but not quite, a tautology) ; they are also more prone, as a result, to display unspoiled, uninhibited, and highly individual characteristics. The conditions—whatever they may be— that remove them from the affairs of society are viewed as the conditions that bring them closer to their inner natures. The more primitive and "natural" the setting into which they are cast, the better are they able to develop and maintain their humaneness.

Cervantes presents an array of such marginal figures and situations. There are, first, the mad people—Don Quixote and the Man of Glass—who though still operating in the social world are in continuous conflict with it by word and deed. Then in *Rinconete and Cortadillo,* we meet petty crooks and beggars who live parasitically off the social world. One step farther from the center we find the gypsies presented in *The Little Gypsy* (*La Gitana*) ; they are completely outside the main stream of affairs. Finally, we have the situation wherein Don Quixote, the marginal Knight, speaks to the simple goatherds about the Golden Age in which the unity of man and nature reaches its fulfillment.

To this catalog of marginal types and situations, we add the figure of woman, who almost throughout the entire course of modern literature from Cervantes to Ibsen has been treated as an individual closer to her own nature and truth than are men, since man is indissolubly bound up with the competitive processes of work, in contrast to the enforced removal of woman from professional activities. Not accidentally does Cervantes use Dulcinea as a symbol of human creativity.

The Morality of the Marginal Man

There are two, not mutually exclusive, ways of looking at the marginal figures of Cervantes; they are the refuse of a society that has cast them aside, and they are, in their own right, moralists.

In a world in which man is taught common sense and skills leading to wealth and position, those devoid of property or common sense have no place; they are actually or potentially outside the social limits. They might just as well not exist. But since, manifestly, they do exist (though somewhat *in absentia*), society protects itself against them by an elaborate system of controlling devices, above all by punishing those who do not respect property and isolating those who do not respect common sense. The latter provide the basis for a large range of comedy (as we shall find in our analysis of Molière).

All these marginal creatures, the beggars, the crooks, the gypsies, the insane, constitute "overheads" of society, to which they are either unwilling to belong or from which they are forcibly cast out. But while they are accused, indicted, and confined, they themselves in turn are accusers. Their very existence denounces a world they never made and which wants no part of them. The artist, in giving these people a voice, may seek to inspire uneasiness on the part of those who have profited by the prevailing order. The artist's voice, in sum, is most often not the voice of the victors who arrogate their spoils. His is the voice of the losers.

The other aspect in which the marginal figures may be viewed leads us back to the concept of idealism. The marginal figures not only serve the negative function of indicting the social order; they also positively demonstrate the idea of man. They all serve to show the possibilities of Utopia, where everyone has the freedom to be his own deviant case—with the result that the very phenomenon of deviation disappears. The outcast society of robbers and thieves who are plying their trade on the fringes of Sevilla, and the society of gypsies encamped on the outskirts of Madrid, are grotesque Utopian prototypes: everybody works according to his talents, and everything is shared by everybody. Paradoxically enough, the robber, whom we would expect to place a high valuation on possession, displays only indifference to worldly goods. Money as such has no meaning for him; the principles which govern his life are honor among thieves and responsibility to his fellows. The highest moral law he recognizes is that of solidarity. The society of the robbers calls itself a "brotherhood"; the society of the gypsies obeys the "law of friendship." The acting chief of the "brotherhood" describes two older members of the club as if he were recommending them for membership to some respectable alumni group: "very truthful and upright individuals, God fearing and conscientious; they led model lives and enjoyed a good reputation." [26] Add the quality of "leadership," and you have all the customary prerequisites.

The meaning of Cervantes' critical idealism is even clearer in *The Little Gypsy*. During a performance in Madrid, a young man with an unimpeachable social background falls in love with a gypsy girl. He follows the tribe to its camp outside the city. Like Shaw's young idealist in *Major Barbara,* he plans to join the gypsies in order to be united with his beloved. The tribal chief teaches the young aspirant the code by which the group lives.

> We observe inviolably the law of friendship; no one solicits the object of another man's affection; we live free from the bitter curse of jealousy.[27]

By implication, human traits are conceived of as unchangeable: if man is left to himself, the *lumen naturale* is

bound to shine forth, and its rays are as self-evident as all
other natural phenomena. Friendship derives from human
nature itself. Jealousy is a symptom of property coveted;
it may operate in the "normal" world where private property rules, but it should have no place in human relationships. Implied is the view that each person possesses his
own inviolable individuality; he makes choices freely—in
this case, of the other sex. (We shall see presently how
Cervantes provides a corrective for masculine superiority,
the remaining defect in an otherwise egalitarian society.)

Later the gypsy chief describes to the young man the
means of livelihood available. They fall roughly into two
categories, spoils gained from nature, and those acquired
from the civilized world. As for the natural spoils:

> We are lords of the plains, of the crops, of the woods, of the
> forests, of the wells, and of the streams. The forests supply
> us wood free of cost, the trees fruit, the vine grapes, the gardens
> vegetables, the fountains water, the streams fish, and the pre-
> serves game, the rocks shade, the hills fresh air, and the caves
> houses. For us the inclemencies of the weather are breezes, the
> snow a refreshment, the rain baths, the thunder music, and the
> lightning torches. For us the hard clods of earth are feather
> beds.[28]

The means for satisfying human needs are detailed here
in a spirit completely removed from the anxious concern
for survival and self-assertion which is everywhere evident
in the conversation of Sancho Panza and his wife. The
gypsies experience their intercourse with nature as pleasures, "breezes," "refreshment," "music." In contrast, all
the paraphernalia of civilization, whether they be respectable values like honor or mere devices of conspicuous living,
appear as so many infringements on the freedom of man:

> We are not harassed by the fear of losing honour, nor are we
> kept awake by the desire to increase it, nor do we keep up parties,
> nor do we rise before daybreak to present memorials, or accom-
> pany grandees or solicit favours. We esteem these shanties and
> movable encampments more than gilded ceilings and sumptuous
> palaces.[29]

As for the livelihood acquired from the "inside society" of the civilized world, it is gained by illegal means. But again, the very way in which their thievery is described mocks the concept of private property which they neither practice nor respect.

> For us the beasts of burthen are reared in the fields; and pockets are cut in cities. There is no eagle or other bird of prey which swoops down more speedily on the victim that it spies than we on the opportunities that hold out to us any prospect of gain. And in conclusion we have many talents that promise us a fortunate end. In prison we confess, and in the pillory we are silent; by day we work, and by night we steal, or, to express it better, we warn everyone not to be careless in seeing where he places his property.[30]

The old man sums up the state of affairs in the private Utopia of the gypsies: "We have what we want since we content ourselves with what we have." [31]

Cervantes' marginal figures have in common integrity and responsibility in their human relationships and the serenity and self-reliance with which they cling to their convictions. Don Quixote does what he believes to be right; the Man of Glass speaks out what he believes to be true; the city thieves will not betray each other, and the gypsies are fully at peace with their lot. None of them adjust themselves to social expediency; their very existence is a protest against a mode of life in which the peasant runs after riches, the peasant's wife after desirable mates for the children, the rich farmer after greater riches and yet more desirable mates, and the lord of the mansion after expedient measures by which to satisfy his creditors. Thus at the threshold of the new society Cervantes describes the laws by which it operates and confronts it with its professed measure: the autonomous and morally responsible individual. And behold, this responsible and independent man is to be found only on the margin of society, which at once produces and expels him.

The Soul as Private Property

We might by this time reasonably assume that the highest degree of freedom has been announced with the happy society of the gypsies. But Cervantes has a still more compelling voice at his command. The woman who does not accept so much as the bare minimum of legal authority, who rejects the conventions and conformities even of this quasi-liberated world, is yet more emphatic than the manifesto of the chief. The last word remains the gypsy girl's. The chief of the tribe having set down his principles, the young inamorato declares his intention of permanently attaching himself to the tribe and marrying the girl. The male council has given consent; but now the girl has her say:

> Although these legislators have found by their laws that I am thine, and have handed me over to thee as thine, I have found by the law of my will, which is the strongest of all, that I do not choose to be so, except it is on those conditions that, before thou camest hither, were concerted between us two. Two years hast thou to live in our company before thou enjoyest mine, in order that thou mayest not lightly repent, nor I from haste be deceived. Conditions over-ride laws: those that I have made with thee, thou knowest. If thou dost care to observe them, it may be that I shall be thine, and thou mine. . . . These gentry can quite well hand over my body to thee, but not my soul, which is free and was born free, and has to be free as long as I wish.[32]

What here comes to the fore is a Renaissance concept which the literary artist will keep alive until the era of Romanticism and well into it; an individual is to be defined by his possession of himself. The soul, ironically, is used here as a quasi-legal term for this inviolable and inalienable property right. The possessor can divest himself of this innermost property-title only at the price of losing his identity. Such a concept of the soul is not formal, but substantial; it has content, and the content is love. And love, in turn, must not be misconstrued to mean some irrational, accidental and therefore ephemeral quality (as we encountered it in Lope's concept of passion); it is indeed the very essence of freedom. The lover makes his decision; the decision once made, its consequences are no longer accidental or irrational.

In a way, the gypsy girl, for all her verbal lucidity, is quite mad. She has no say in the male world, she is young and powerless. The group to which she claims membership has stipulated her course of action; still she says "No." "No, the law of my will is the strongest of all; my soul is free." This attitude is the attitude displayed by Don Quixote. His craziness has its very wellspring in his persistent independence: he will not be bribed by expedient measures; he will not be diverted from realizing his innermost convictions and ideals.

4.

JUSTICE: DON QUIXOTE

Next Year in Utopia

It is not only fitting that Don Quixote should be the one to tell the story of the Golden Age, it is equally appropriate that his audience should be composed of a group of goatherds very much akin to the Utopian gypsies—an audience fit in no ordinary degree for anticipating "the happy age and happy centuries to which the ancients gave the name of golden . . . because those who lived in that time did not know the meaning of the words 'thine' and 'mine' " :

> All then was peace, all was concord and friendship; the crooked plowshare had not as yet grievously laid open and pried into the merciful bowels of our first mother, who without any forcing on man's part yielded her spacious fertile bosom on every hand for the satisfaction, sustenance, and delight of her first son.[33]

This is a description of Utopia, certainly, and Don Quixote exalts it as the yardstick for human life which, bafflingly and inexplicably, "as time went on and depravity increased," brought about the exploitation of nature by man, of man by man, of female by male. Don Quixote regards himself as the guardian of this dream—realized once long ago, and to be realized again long hence; it will be up to him to right whatever wrongs time and depravity have wrought; and so . . .

> It was for the safety of such as these, as time went on and depravity increased, that the order of knights-errant was instituted, for the protection of damsels, the aid of widows and orphans, and the succoring of the needy. It is to this order that I belong, my brothers, and I thank you for the welcome and the kindly treatment that you have accorded to me and my squire. By natural law, all living men are obliged to show favor to knights-errant, yet without being aware of this you have received and entertained me; and so it is with all possible good will that I acknowledge your own good will to me.[34]

One might regard these words as a mere plot paraphrase of the novel or merely as self-summary: to be sure, the Knight is engaged in the deeds he describes. But placed in the context of the episode—the depiction of the Golden Age for the benefit of the goatherds—the Knight's words may be interpreted as a succinct symbol of his age. The psychological and economic uncertainties which in Cervantes' day afflicted the European nations are well known: the sharp upward turn in competitive struggle for primacy in the professions, the trades, the political administrations, the ordinary labor market; the intellectual, moral, and emotional anxieties of the average person in an era of bloody encounters between loyalist states and rebellious states, of struggles between the Mother Church and her dissident offspring, and struggles among the offspring themselves.

At the same time, the ideals of Don Quixote contain germinally the elements of which the new concept of man is to be constituted. They illustrate first of all that triumphant concept of the Renaissance to which Alexander Pope gave the name "the great chain of being": the notion of the universal escalator on which each individual occupies a definite place, the whole continuously engaged in the process of ascension toward the *summum bonum*. To be sure, Don Quixote strikes some important variations of the concept; what he describes is not a continuously upward line but a process that extends from a golden past to a golden future over a deep abyss of depravity. But the golden age is no less a reality for all that, and it guides Don Quixote's every action: at any given moment in the time continuum the golden life is as possible as a continued life of injustice. Moreover, the inner nature of man is so universal and so constant that a leader such as the Knight may speak to the lowliest of his fellow creatures with complete assurance of being understood by them; and he can refer to generations in the dimmest past with the certainty that their behavior and ideas will be comprehended by his contemporaries. Finally, the ideal of the Golden Age is not to be passed off as nostalgic self-indulgence; the universals in man are viable in every individual, and are fulfilled in Don Quixote himself. In his parting words, in which he pledges himself to the cause of justice among men, he takes on a specific responsibility. And there is no principle involved which would prevent any one of these goatherds from becoming a Don Quixote.

The Conditions of Justice

We may call this twofold responsibility of the individual for his own self and for the world the *credo* of the democratic idea. Don Quixote's memorable speech instructing Sancho in the basic rules of government on the eve of the peasant's taking over the long-coveted governorship of the island spells it out clearly:

> Remember, Sancho, that if you employ virtue as your means and pride yourself on virtuous deeds, you will have no cause

to envy the means possessed by princes and noble lords; for blood
is inherited but virtue is acquired, and virtue by itself alone has
a worth that blood does not have.[35]

In other words, men are basically equal; Sancho has
hardly more education than have the goatherds, the gypsies,
the pastoral citizens of the Golden Age. Whatever Don
Quixote can do, Sancho can do as well. To govern does
not mean to dominate but to apply insight. The term
virtue is decisive in this context. Machiavelli, the arch-
proponent of the pessimistic concept of human nature, had
used it merely to indicate rational efficiency and skillful
application of the rules by which the majority of men are
to be manipulated, domesticated and forced to submit.
Cervantes takes virtue far more literally; to him it denotes
the human and the manly, and becomes the expression
of the inseparability of insight and action.

The very touchstone by which to test the concept of
equality among men is to be found in the administration
of justice, for the very essence of justice lies in the distribu-
tion of power among the parties involved. The legislator,
the statesman, and the judge are, as decision-makers, endowed with symbolic and factual power: they occupy a
position which by its very function is *de facto* superior to
the positions of those to whom their jurisdiction extends.
The relationship is here necessarily one between supplicant
and grantor; and it is therefore crucial to Don Quixote
that Sancho Panza should refrain from abusing the powers
which he is about to confer upon him.

We have already seen that Cervantes' critical idealism
tends always to be of a very realistic sort; and while it
becomes most clear in its intentions whenever it alights on
marginal and quasi-Utopian situations, it asserts itself quite
as forcibly when dealing with issues central to society,
such as property relations and administrative super-
structures. The island for which Sancho Panza is about to
embark is part and parcel of the contemporary Spanish
society which Cervantes describes, and which the Knight

wants to bring back to the fold of the human ideal. Don Quixote's parting instructions illuminate the process of reasoning by which a nonconformist intellectual at the threshold of our era undertakes to improve the reality of a middle-class society by an ideal conception of man. We have already considered the Knight's preamble; the rest of the speech follows:

Never be guided by arbitrary law, which finds favor only with the ignorant who plume themselves on their cleverness. Let the tears of the poor find more compassion in you, but not more justice, than the testimony of the rich. Seek to uncover the truth amid the promises and gifts of the man of wealth as amid the sobs and pleadings of the poverty-stricken. When it is a question of equity, do not bring all the rigor of the law to bear upon the delinquent, for the fame of the stern judge is no greater than that of the merciful one. If the rod of justice is to be bent, let it not be by the weight of a gift but by that of mercy. When you come to judge the case of someone who is your enemy, put aside all thought of the wrong he has done you and think only of the truth. Let not passion blind you where another's rights are concerned, for the mistakes you make will be irremediable, or only to be remedied at the expense of your good name and fortune.

If some beautiful woman come to you seeking justice, take your eyes from her tears, listen not to her moans, but consider slowly and deliberately the substance of her petition, unless you would have your reason drowned in her weeping and your integrity swept away by her sighs. Abuse not by words the one upon whom punishment must be inflicted; for the pain of the punishment itself is enough without the addition of insults. When a guilty man comes under your jurisdiction, remember that he is but a wretched creature, subject to the inclinations of our depraved human nature, and insofar as you may be able to do so without wrong to the other side, show yourself clement and merciful; for while the attributes of God are all equal, that of mercy shines brighter in our eyes than does that of justice.

If you observe these rules and precepts, Sancho, your days will be long, your fame will be eternal, rewards will be heaped upon you, indescribable happiness shall be yours, you will be able to marry off your children as you like, your children and

your grandchildren will have titles to their names, you will live
in peace with all men, and in your last days death will come to
you amid a ripe and tranquil old age, and the gentle, loving
hands of your great-grandchildren will tenderly close your
eyes.[36]

In the passage cited, we find three recurring areas of
concern. These may be classified—without any particular
regard for the logic of parallelism—as *truth, mercy* and
emotionality. To begin with the last-named class: no less
than six times within the relatively brief context of the
passage do we encounter the mention of tears or emotional
correlates—"tears of the poor," "sobs of the poverty-
stricken," "tears of a beautiful woman," "her moans,"
"her weeping," "her sighs." The category of truth finds expression in the following five variations: "uncover the
truth," "think only of the truth," "your reason," "substance
of a petition," "human nature." The category of mercy,
finally, occurs six times: "compassion in you," "merciful
judge," "the weight of mercy," "show yourself clement,"
"show yourself merciful," "the attribute of mercy."

The configuration of these categories constitutes in almost complete form the philosophy of modern idealism—
morally as well as epistemologically. The world in which
Sancho has to act is perceived as consisting of people who
are rich and poor, beautiful and ugly, tearful and stubborn,
ignorant and clever; but all these social and psychological
specificities are the mere trimmings of human nature of
whose virtue, as well as verity, the judge must be constantly aware. This holds true, for example, with respect
to the display of emotions, genuine or simulated, by which
the supplicant might turn disadvantage into advantage.
Human communication depends upon language which is
oriented toward commonly shared experience and insight;
tears would substitute accidental, transient, unreflective,
and quasi-biological responses for the exercise of reason,
and Sancho will do well to make the necessary reduction.

The Knight is the Chief Justice who passes on to Sancho the responsibilities of the legal office. The ultimate function of this office lies in the inseparably related tasks of finding out the truth and following up the new insight by suitable action. Perhaps above all the rule of law, with its underlying egalitarian concept, asserts itself as the most important single manifestation of the secularized order—even of greater weight than the Baconian concept of science. According to the scientific mode, theory and knowledge are potentially the instruments of power, but the theories and experimental findings of the natural scientist merely admit the possibility of practical application. Usefulness is by no means a necessary component of science itself; the scientist may satisfy himself by mere contemplation. But the rule of law is the measure of man's capacity for rational behavior both in theory and in practice. The guarantee for the presence and the perpetuity of the rational mode in human relations resides in legal institutions, and any change in their substance or form presupposes findings on a higher plane of rationality than those which are presently available. The Knight's instructions emphasize this aspect of modern rationality; he wants to safeguard the realm of reason against any form of irrational intrusion, whether it be the arbitrary laws of tyrants and ignoramuses or the emotional outbursts of lovely women. Thus the recurrent appeals to reason are calculated to reinforce the very foundations on which human life is built. The exaltation of the judge's office testifies to the confidence in man's rationality, a faculty which enables him to discover truth unaided by those higher powers that have lately departed.

Needless to say, Cervantes has his hero describe an experiment in government which is a good deal closer to the enlightened monarchies of the eighteenth century than anything before or after. It remains uncertain how the laws, which the governor is supposed to apply in his dual function of administrator and judge, actually come about. What is certain and important is the recognition that the evident and necessary differences in political status within such a body politic in no way detract from the essential equality among all members of the commonwealth.

The Appeal to Mercy

While the confident search for applicable truth shows the optimistic integration of man's thinking and feeling into the strange new world that he is about to recreate, the burdensome aspects of secularized existence also get their due in the Knight's Magna Charta of justice. True, man is endowed with reason; but he is also endowed with mortality. In deference to this, Cervantes, like Shakespeare, exalts the unrestrained quality of mercy that former centuries had experienced only as a promise of life after death. Now it gains the features of a solace, not in the hereafter, but in the here-and-now. Man is alone, and as an autonomous, rational individual must assume responsibility for his own mortal fate and for the welfare of others. To overcome the feelings of aloneness, one need only become aware of his identification with all mankind in the commonly shared experience of aloneness. The exhortation to mercy as the highest of human attributes may be looked upon, in a way, as the initial phase of the existentialist view: there is positively nothing beyond the human realm; reason can never be absolute and can at best serve as an ever-threatened, precarious weather vane.

The recognition that the other person stands as much in need of certainty as one's self and the acknowledgment that certainty is ultimately impossible lead to another aspect of democratic beliefs. Although it is true that every individual is endowed with reason, by which he is enabled to survive, he is also endowed—and equally endowed—with the ever-present possibility of social or biological catastrophe, with the impending loss of fortune or health. The quality of mercy thus enters as a constituent element of man's rationality; it is in no way opposed to reason but complements its potential power by the acknowledgment of weakness, for this acknowledgment, in turn, strengthens the cohesiveness of man. Recognizing themselves to be both rational and mortal, men must discover in themselves that moral or emotional agency which prevents reason from becoming a new tyrannical force; and in the last analysis they make common cause by confessing to themselves and to each other a condition of need to which the confession itself brings its own gratification. The voluntary tempering of rational prerogatives out of respect for one's own frailty, and out of humility in the face of it, transforms acts and protestations of mercy from a symptom of human weakness into a symbol of man's greatest strength.

Cervantes' conception of mercy as complementary to reason is paralleled in Shakespeare. The rule of law as the manifestation of reason may be circumvented if the circumvention is closer to virtue than is compliance, however "rational" in appearance. In *The Tempest,* Miranda, the most obedient as well as the most dedicated of daughters, tries to induce Ferdinand to disobey her father's orders out of pity for her lover; similarly the Knight does not discourage the tempering of justice with mercy.

Consider the very architecture of the Knight's speech. It begins with the principles by which justice is to be applied; it introduces a number of relevant social and psychological factors; it then balances the merits of truth and mercy; and culminates in a reference to the soul. The speech reduces human relations to their core: the social world is concretely described; the rule of law is justified by the essential equality of all human beings; and the soul is exalted as the central and archetypical concept of man.

The Knight's speech is very much a document of the Renaissance intellectual. The whole orientation is so exclusively toward life in this world, so entirely concerned with filling every moment of life with meaning, that it would be unthinkable on the basis of it to distinguish between pleasure and morality. The dichotomy between moralism and hedonism, which will become one of the most contested issues in the history of middle-class ideologies, has no validity for Cervantes. If Sancho Panza observes the precepts of reason and mercy—the rule of virtue—he will reap the harvest of "indescribable happiness."

Chapter III: SHAKESPEARE'S
THE TEMPEST

The process of secularization in the Renaissance has intimate connections not only with an emerging individualism but with the problem of authority. This problem is, in turn, closely identified with a typical Renaissance concept of history—an interpretation of events in terms of the passions, drives and inner conflicts of leading historical figures: we can understand Roman history if we know what kind of man Coriolanus, or Caesar, or Anthony was, and we can understand English history by studying the characters of the English kings. This psychologizing was a natural response to secularization; in a sense, no other kind of interpretation was possible, since "society" had not yet come to be viewed as a body of changing institutions. The problem, therefore, was to legitimize secular authority by finding moral guarantees for those who exercise it.

In *The Tempest,* irrational and rational authority are pitted against each other: the one is authority based on social position, property and power; the other is authority that is exercised and submitted to on the basis of mutually recognized attributes and responsibilities, which embody the qualities of virtue and reason. These types of authority are represented most clearly in the figures of the two brothers, Antonio the scheming and dissolute usurper, and the wise and virtuous Prospero, rightful Duke of Milan. The moral guarantees for those who exercise authority are explicitly stated: learning and power are to be combined in the Baconian sense and are to be applied to the affairs of men rather than to the search for God's will.

I.

THE CONCEPT OF HUMAN NATURE

With the wavering of theological certainties during the Renaissance, the prevailing doctrines of human nature became subject to considerable doubt. The concomitant decline of the hierarchized society of the Middle Ages and the advent of a society with a high degree of social mobility made the question of the essential qualities of human nature truly crucial. The evidence to be found in everyday life was conflicting and untrustworthy. Men did not consciously look to organized society for their norms; the explicit appeal to custom and common sense that later developed with the solidification of middle-class control had little drawing power for the adventurous individualists of Elizabethan England.

The urge to seek out the basic elements of human nature led primarily in two directions: to the study of exemplary situations of the past, particularly as recorded by Plutarch, and the observation of contemporary individuals in marginal situations which would free them from the demands of conformity and ordinary practicality. As we have seen, Cervantes found revelations of human nature among gypsies, robbers, and other outcast groups. *The Tempest* constitutes a marginal phenomenon of an extreme kind, since in it men are removed from a socially predetermined environment and are cast back upon themselves and the elements.

Because of its island setting, reflecting the Elizabethan enthusiasm for the distant corners of an expanding world, *The Tempest* presents what we may look upon as an experimental situation. By its remoteness from organized society human nature is reduced to essentials—allowing Shakespeare's characters to display their deepest and most intimate reactions. Paradoxically, it is their removal from

society that makes their behavior an ideal source for sociological interpretation.

The Tempest then is a play of man alone, or rather of
man confronted by nature, without the help or interference
of social institutions. Its miniature company lives outside history, responding only to the exterior challenges of nature
and the interior attributes of man himself. These two sets
of influences are symbolized in the stage settings: the first
scene shows men facing a storm at sea; the remainder of
the play takes place on a small island unaffected by the
historical and social exigencies of the milieu.

The play is not, however, a vision of an Utopia, as the
setting might suggest. It is more on the order of a "laboratory" experiment, demonstrating the true nature of man as
Shakespeare had conceived it. The few people on the
island live outside the protection of institutions, law or
power—whether feudal or monarchical. In many respects,
The Tempest reminds us of the Robinson Crusoe story.
Prospero's island is as isolated as Crusoe's, and both situations pose the problem of man's survival apart from normal
life conditions. Shakespeare's and Defoe's heroes both are
thrown back to primitive natural conditions (although, due
to Prospero's magic, in radically different ways) and everything has to be created anew. In both instances man,
against his own volition, has to contend with nature in a
raw state.

Ever since the Renaissance, modern man has perpetuated
the idea that he carries an infinity of possibilities within
himself; their realization is always within reach, at least
in his phantasies and dreams. His potentialities are such
that, if need be, he could live apart from the rest of society; he could return to nature. Moreover, once Western
man gave up the idea that his true life began only with
death, once his nervous system no longer was inscribed with
hope for eternal life or fear of eternal condemnation, his
expectations came to be centered on the natural and the
human. Nature supplants God, in a sense, but, unlike God,
its ways have not been defined with certainty and finality;

once the experiments of *The Tempest* and *Robinson Crusoe* are concluded, the people can return to society with the new knowledge they have gained.

Both stories are dramas of individualism, but with this decisive difference: Shakespeare's play does not deal with the *homo economicus* but with the *homo moralis*. Inherent in the struggles of Robinson Crusoe is the earnest conviction that man's true goal lies in the social, economic, and political institutions of an individualistic and competitive society. Inherent in the moral stubbornness of Prospero is the eschatological dream that man can, by continuous introspection, by listening to his soul, achieve harmony for himself and others. When the tempestuous seas have washed away the jetsam of history and society, the people on the island can remake a world from their own essential humanity.

Thus, while *Robinson Crusoe* is oriented to social themes, *The Tempest* is concerned with the nature of man. Although Crusoe is alone, except for Friday, he still remains an eighteenth-century man who is imbued with the desirability of a freely competitive society. The specifically economic focus of the story is the product of a mind that thinks in social terms, the issue is *laissez faire* versus state interference in economic activities. *The Tempest*, on the contrary, is the product of a mind that locates the drama of human existence within the soul of individual man; it is the innermost victory or defeat that determines the success or failure, triumph or tragedy, of man's life. Prospero learns how to reform himself, and it is only by reforming himself that he will make a better duke.

The Tempest presents a wide range of attitudes of Renaissance man. If we keep in mind the given historical setting of the play, it supplies abundant examples of individuals reacting to their environment in the transitional period between feudalism and middle-class society. Indeed, the abundance is such that one is tempted to interpret the play word by word. But since there is no space here for such an enterprise, and since an appendix[1] contains an interpretation of a single scene—the incident of the ship-wreck that opens the play—the following analysis is limited to a number of motifs that run throughout the entire play.

We have suggested that *The Tempest* may be looked upon as a "laboratory" experiment to which the characters of the play are exposed. It opens aboard a ship that represents, both literally and symbolically, the last ties to organized society for the group that is destined for the island.

The storm takes place while the established chains of command are still firmly retained. The mariners go about the business of meeting the challenge of the storm in an orderly manner. The captain details his strategy to the boatswain, who then passes on orders to the crew, in an entirely friendly, workmanlike fashion. The noble lords, who are their passengers, are meanwhile anything but calm. They curse out the crew, falsely accuse the boatswain of drunkenness and generally act out of fear and impatience.

For the time being, it is sufficient to note here that the boatswain by his good sense and his workmanlike command of the situation emerges as the hero of the scene. Gonzalo, the counsellor of Alonso, King of Naples, is shown as a man of calm understanding. Although at first sight he does not appear to be much more than a noble who shows conventional loyalty, he is a professional civil servant; he is thus distinguished from the lords, who are merely persons of high status, neither acknowledging any responsibility to, nor having any function in, society. In the behavior of these aristocratic passengers, we find totally lacking the industriousness, humanity, or knowledge that became the progressive values of the Renaissance individual in Shakespeare's day. We see them rather as reminders of the old order, just as Gonzalo and the boatswain personify the new.

2.

FIVE THEMES ON THE ISLAND

After the shipwreck, we are introduced to the island where Prospero—who has magic powers at his disposal—is telling his daughter Miranda that many years ago he had lost his dukedom to an usurper, how after his exile he had found refuge on the island, and how he now had caused the shipwreck that would put his enemies into his hands. Presently other voices emerge from behind these two: the deformed and treacherous Caliban and the ethereally beautiful Ariel respectively trudge and fly about. We learn that the ship's survivors have now reached the island, and that most of them are in a state of despondency; Alonso's son Ferdinand wanders alone in a state of complete despair until he meets Prospero and Miranda. Here, then, is a handful of people living on what is to all intents and purposes a naked planet. But extreme as the situation may be, their biological, psychological, and social needs continue to exist and must be satisfied; they, therefore, must become increasingly socialized. Soon an embryonic society is apparent.

Five aspects of this emerging society on the island are of interest to us here: work, learning, language, sleep, and sex. In the process of examining how the individuals who make up this small society deal with these five human concerns, we shall discover the degree of their success or failure in living up to the image of man which was being developed in Renaissance society.

A. WORK

There is no doubt concerning Prospero's role on the island nor of his ability to rule it and assign tasks to its members. He is a wise man, completely at peace with himself and fully aware of the ways of his fellow men after years of introspection into his own nature. By following only his own inner voice he has attained an authority similar to that of the master of the ship in the course of his professional career. Although Prospero no longer has the external trappings of his former power, he emerges as a real "duke," in the literal sense of "leader." Without question he is entitled to be the initial organizer and supervisor of the people on the island.

The person who has reached the highest degree of rationality becomes by this very achievement the maker of decisions. No one but Prospero makes decisions. That they turn out to be the "right" decisions is further evidence of his qualifications. Prospero's mistakes lie in the past; like Lear at the end of the second act, he is now throwing off his self-destructive indifference to the world. His mission is to work out his own salvation, and instead of taking revenge on his enemies, to provide for their safe survival as well as for the welfare of all others for whom he takes responsibility.

Caliban and Ariel: Torpor and Frivolity

As the gods do in Homer, the extra-human creatures in Shakespeare's works—such as the ghosts of Banquo, Caesar, and Hamlet's father—function as visible manifestations of psychic processes. Like Prospero's magic power, Caliban and Ariel are not essential to the plot in *The Tempest;* they are in fact entirely supererogatory. Although such extra-human types may generally symptomize a tedious conscience, in sociological terms they help to round out the image of man by demonstrating outwardly and visibly his interior conflicts and phantasies.

The relationship of Prospero to his helpers may be illuminated by the psychoanalytic schema of the personality.

Caliban represents untamed, uncivilized urges and desires. He is the *Id,* as expressed in a number of ways:

(1) his primary concern with nourishment—see, for example, his irrelevant introjection of the topic of food into a conversation with Prospero (Act I, Scene 2);

(2) his continual resistance to the performance of useful work;

(3) his propensity for sexual promiscuity and rape as demonstrated, for example, by his offer to deliver Miranda to the bed of the scoundrel Stephano (III,2);

(4) his irrational conduct in general—for example, his drunken stupor once Stephano has given him a bottle, or his serving notice on the values and mores associated with his master (II,2);

(5) his view of biological pleasure as an expression of freedom, and his tendency to equate the two. The word freedom is one he loudly parades when all inhibitions are gone (II,2):

Freedom, highday! highday, freedom! highday, freedom!

Ariel is his direct counterpart. His realm is the *Super-Ego* phantasy. In contrast to Caliban, he is continually engaged in considerate acts: he puts the tired seamen to sleep (I,2); he intercedes with his master in behalf of Prospero's enemies, who have now been sufficiently punished, professing that these would be his own actions "were I human" (V,1). Whereas Caliban is all brute instinct, Ariel connotes the moral and esthetic aspirations that are potential in every human being.

Finally, Prospero himself may be viewed as assuming the role of the *Ego,* perpetually engaged in striving to reconcile the two basic psychic forces for the purpose of mastering reality on all levels.

Seen from this viewpoint, Caliban and Ariel help us to visualize the deeper level of that secularized, human-centered new world, the Empire of Man which is in the process of replacing the City of God. At the same time, however, they are individualities in their own right, and it is from this point of view that we look at them now, particularly in regard to their attitude toward work.

Caliban, sometimes called by Prospero a "slave," has not achieved the transition from mere biological sensationism to the sphere of sensibility specific to man. He represents the animal in man that must be tamed, and forced by threats of punishment (I,2):

> If thou neglect'st or dost unwillingly
> What I command, I'll rack thee with old cramps,
> Fill all thy bones with aches; make thee roar,
> That beasts shall tremble at thy din.

Caliban exemplifies the condition from which man must be freed if he is to find salvation (for even a Caliban can be ennobled). The new, secular salvation comes from man's rising to a reflective rationality, by which he recreates the natural world about him and, in the process, discovers his own nature. Caliban's notion of "useful" work is the most perverted imaginable: to kill Prospero and act the part of procurer to Stephano, the drunken butler.

Ariel symbolizes a more affirmative and agreeable aspect of natural man. Playful, imaginative relaxation is to him a well-earned reward for "worthy service," honestly performed; he has "made no mistakings, served without or grudge or grumblings" (I,2). Still it is clear that Ariel's service, though lovable, is performed with a minimum of personal exertion; he wants to enjoy without paying for enjoyment by toil. He would as soon not "work" at all, though he is glad to put the sailors to sleep or move Prospero to pity, and to render whatever service can be rendered easily and enjoyably. With him, too, Prospero must resort to threats (I,2):

> If thou more murmur'st, I will rend an oak,
> And peg thee in his knotty entrails till
> Thou hast howl'd away twelve winters.

Thus, Ariel and Caliban symbolize two disparate pitfalls of the new autonomy of the individual: escape into the lethargy and apathy of unproductive behavior, or escape into the illusion of complete independence without responsibility or exertion. Both Ariel and Caliban would perish without a Prospero.

Ferdinand and Miranda: The Volunteers

As part of his experiment, Prospero has kept Ferdinand in bondage and has imposed on him, as on everybody else, burdensome tasks. In the beginning of the third act we find Ferdinand hard at work with heavy logs (III,1):

> There be some sports are painful, and their labour
> Delight in them sets off; some kinds of baseness
> Are nobly undergone and most poor matters
> Point to rich ends. This my mean task
> Would be as heavy to me as odious, but
> The mistress which I serve quickens what's dead
> And makes my labours pleasures . . .

Ferdinand's response to the test to which Prospero has subjected him (in order to discover the degree of his devotion to Miranda) is a telling example of one who finds within his own soul the meaning of life. Discovering the key to his individuality in his love for Miranda, Ferdinand sees the whole world in terms of this love; the chains of slavery melt away under the sun of a human relationship which transforms labor into "pleasures." Once work is accepted as not merely a means to one's own survival but as a service to those one loves, it becomes a value in its own right, part and parcel of the individual's integrity.

Miranda epitomizes this idea. Untrained for manual labor, a demure young girl, brought up with care and delicacy by a wise father, she nonetheless identifies with Ferdinand to such a degree that she wishes not only to share his harsh task but to take it from him (III,1):

> If you'll sit down,
> I'll bear your logs the while. Pray, give me that:
> I'll carry it to the pile.

Neither tempted by the escapism of Caliban and Ariel, nor forced into a working situation as Ferdinand is, Miranda formulates the virtues of work as a voluntary and free expression of herself and her love (III,1) :

> It would become me
> As well as it does you: and I should do it
> With much more ease; for my good will is to it,
> And yours it is against.

She does not mean that Ferdinand is unwilling to work, but that he is performing forced labor and is thereby prevented from exercising free choice. She alone is in a position to "volunteer," unhampered by her father's beneficent strictures.

The Noble and the Vulgar Drones

It is noteworthy that Alonso the King of Naples, Sebastian his brother, and Antonio the usurper of the throne of Milan, are as idle socially as they are contemptible morally. This is equally true, despite their menial stations, of Trinculo the jester and Stephano the butler. Ariel says to the first three (III,3) :

> You are three men of sin, whom Destiny . . .
> Hath caused to belch up you; and on this island,
> Where man doth not inhabit; you 'mongst men
> Being most unfit to live.

All five are ghosts of the past, parasites from the upper and lower rungs of the feudal ladder. They are unrelated to the productive affairs of men; the nobles do not know how to administer or supervise such affairs, and the two underlings do not know how to execute them. On the possibility of their doing any work themselves, they are all conspicuously silent. On the possibility of utilizing the labors of others for their own ends, they are a bit more articulate. When Stephano first encounters Caliban in the wilderness of the island, he thinks at once of a way to improve his station in life by exploiting Caliban once he is safely back in Milan (II,2):

> . . . I will give him some relief, if it be but for that: if I can recover him and keep him tame and get to Naples with him, he's a present for any emperor that ever trod on neat's-leather.

B. Learning

The Renaissance concept of work as it appears in seventeenth-century literature is far removed from the theoretical concept of good works performed in the service of God; work becomes the very act of creation, and without it there would be no human world but only Caliban's atavistic chaos. The meaning of learning has gone through a corresponding transformation. In *The Tempest*, certainly, schooling is no longer conceived as a step toward the experience of the infinite wisdom of a heavenly power, but as a prerequisite for the transformation of the world by productive labor. The post-medieval era does away, at a very early stage, with the traditional exaltation of *vita contemplativa* at the expense of *vita activa*.

The Tempest bears witness to this view that man's life centers around productive labor with learning an essential correlate: labor and learning together make possible the discovery of one's own productive potentialities (one's nature), and are basic to the transformation of natural phenomena into a man-controlled and man-centered world.[2]

Learning and Power

In the first scene of *The Tempest*, the skilled manual experts as well as Gonzalo, a skilled intellectual, go about their business on the basis of acquired knowledge. To these men, the application of learning to the task of resisting the forces of nature brings about a state of equanimity—one is almost tempted to say happiness. Performing their duties

by the precept of rational decision, they live in harmony
with themselves and with their fellow men.

In the experimental context of the island, Prospero may
be said to rediscover and reconstruct out of his own reasoning the essentials of the educational process. His first words
in the play, in the opening lines of I,2, are words of instruction to Miranda whom he is at pains to inform further on
the responsibilities of adulthood:

> I have done nothing but in care of thee,—
> Of thee, my dear one! thee, my daughter!—who
> Art ignorant of what thou art, nought knowing
> Of whence I am; nor that I am more better
> Than Prospero, master of a full poor cell,
> And thy no greater father.

It is noteworthy that nowhere else does Prospero show such
signs of pride; only when telling his daughter that he is
living up to the task of passing on knowledge to the next
generation does he boast:

>   . . . and here
> Have I, thy schoolmaster, made thee more profit
> Than other princes can, that have more time
> For vainer hours and tutors not so careful.

For Prospero, the gentleman scholar, the search for truth
is not a leisurely pastime but the most serious business of his
life. Prior to his exile, however, he had been unable to relate theory and practice, unable to apply his learning to the
conduct of the affairs of state. When he describes to his
daughter the injury inflicted on him by his brother Antonio,
whom he had deputized to "manage the state," he admits
that he had prized his "library" above his "dukedom" and
that he was "reputed"

> In dignity, and for the liberal arts,
> Without a parallel . . .

But by living as a secularized monk, lost in books, abandoned to the *vita contemplativa,* he had actually invited his
brother's outrageous behavior:

I, thus neglecting worldly ends, all dedicated
To closeness and the bettering of my mind
With that, which, but by being so retir'd,
O'er priz'd all popular rate, in my false brother
Awak'd an evil nature . . .

He who is not aware that knowledge includes the responsibility for its application, or, to quote Bacon, its "power," has not fully learned the human lesson. Prospero as administrator of the island is trying to make up for what he had neglected when he was Duke of Milan. He, too, is now in an experimental situation, and the test he must pass is his ability to connect learning and doing.

The Utopian and the Caveman

Gonzalo understands and explains the role of learning on different levels, and counsels accordingly. He reminds us of Kent in *Lear,* who functions essentially as the rational norm by which the excesses, passions, and imbecilities of the others may be measured.

In the first scene of the first act, Gonzalo shows great respect for the social usefulness of manual skills. In addition, we learn later that it was Gonzalo who, when he had the distasteful assignment of shipping Prospero and his daughter into exile on an unseaworthy bark, had managed surreptitiously to provide them not only with the physical requirements of life but with some intellectual necessities as well. As Prospero reports it (I,2):

Some food we had, and some fresh water that
A noble Neapolitan, Gonzalo,
Out of his charity,—who being then appointed
Master of this design,—did give us; with
Rich garments, linens, stuffs, and necessaries,
Which since have steaded much; so, of his gentleness,
Knowing I lov'd my books, he furnish'd me
From mine own library with volumes that
I prize above my dukedom.

On the island, Gonzalo proves himself by helping people
who would not otherwise survive. His head and heart are
instantly awake to situations that threaten life. It seems
perfectly natural that Ariel should single him out to awaken
Alonso to the Antonio-Sebastian conspiracy. In other
words, Gonzalo displays that practical ability to apply his
knowledge which Prospero has had to learn so painfully.

The Baconian doctrine that man fulfills his mission by
functioning both as *ego cogitans* and *ego agens* is demonstrated in *The Tempest* by Gonzalo's draft of an Utopian
"commonwealth." What Prospero, the unworldly philosopher, was driven by necessity to create, Gonzalo conjures
up in a spirit of playful phantasy. To counter the melan-
cholic apathy of the shipwrecked nobles, as well as his own,
he volunteers a daydream of ideal life. This New Atlantis
Gonzalo describes is not the dream of a scientific mind, as
was Bacon's, but that of a critical moralist, who, like Cervantes, conceives the absence of domination as a condition
for the fulfillment of the potentialities of the individual
(II,1) :

> I' the commonwealth I would by contraries
> Execute all things; for no kind of traffic
> Would I admit; no name of magistrate;
> Letters should not be known; riches, poverty,
> And use of service, none; contract, succession,
> Bourn, bound of land, tilth, vineyard, none;
> no use of metal, corn, or wine, or oil;
> No occupation; all men idle, all;
> And women, too, but innocent and pure;
> No sovereignty.[3]

In the play of his imagination, he bans not only institutionalized weapons for the domination of man over man, but
also the technical instruments for the domination of man
over nature:

> All things in common nature should produce
> Without sweat or endeavor: treason, felony,

Sword, pike, knife, gun, or need of any engine,
Would I not have; but nature should bring forth,
Of its own kind, all foison, all abundance,
To feed my innocent people.

While the feudal parasites can understand his dream only
as an opportunity for Caliban-like behavior, whereby each
of them "would be king" and everyone else "whores and
knaves," what Gonzalo is really envisioning is shedding the
privileges of his office in favor of a society in harmony
with nature and in which the state has "withered away."

Caliban's phantasies, at the other extreme, may be looked
upon as those of a man for whom the old order of life has
lost its meaning, and who has not yet found his way in the
new. He is like the eighteenth-century machine wreckers,
who, ground down by history, blamed the machines for
their misery rather than the factory system itself. When
Caliban, plotting to imitate Antonio's perfidious plans, ad-
vises his two provisional masters—the drunken butler and
the crude jester—to murder Prospero and dishonor Miranda, he advocates what three centuries later is to become
a well-known practice:

Why, as I told thee, 'tis a custom with him,
I'the afternoon to sleep: there thou may'st brain him
Having first seiz'd his books . . . (III,2)

And in order to make certain that the scoundrels have not
missed the point, he repeats his advice in the middle of the
same speech:

. . . Remember
First to possess his books; for without them
He's but a sot . . .

And again:

. . . Burn but his books;
He has brave utensils,—for so he calls them—
Which, when he has a house, he'll deck withal.

Thus he advocates, so to speak, a pre-literate, indeed a pre-
historic, stage of man.

C. LANGUAGE

The dominant approach to language in the Middle Ages was that of scholastic realism, according to which concepts and existence were identical; both were regarded as manifestations of one and the same supernatural act of creation. During the Renaissance the emphasis shifted to the tenets of the nominalist school, that concepts denote things, physical as well as non-physical. Words now become the property of man—tools which help him to assume his responsibility in the human-centered world—and great literature begins to create the signposts by which man can recognize himself and his environment. Language becomes the instrument of self-identification, as well as of orientation. And, as we observed in our analysis of Cervantes' writings, the more firmly a person commands words, the higher is the degree of his self-realization.

The language of Caliban as well as that of Antonio and Sebastian is a kind of perverted scholastic realism. When they speak forthrightly, they curse. Enter Caliban; he enters cursing (I,2):

> As wicked dew as e'er my mother brush'd
> With raven's feather from unwholesome fen
> Drop on you both!

and thereafter he hardly opens his mouth without giving vent to similar barbarisms. The curses accomplish nothing, but like children the cursers attempt to give their objects the predetermined reality of names. Caliban, Antonio and Sebastian are remote from the world of human interaction; their curses are not viable in human affairs. What they accomplish is entirely negative: they limit the cursers to the confines of their under-developed and regressive personalities. When Prospero reminds Caliban (I,2):

> . . . I endow'd thy purposes
> With words that made them known . . .

Caliban retorts:

> You taught me language; and my profit on't
> Is, I know how to curse: the red plague rid you
> For learning me your language!

Prospero gives us the meaning of productive "nominalistic" language when he tells Caliban that while

> thou . . . wouldst gabble like
> a thing most brutish . . .

or has, in other words, only instinctual sounds at his disposal, he Prospero

> Took pains to make thee speak, . . .

so that he (Caliban) would

> Know thine own meaning.

The dynamic interconnection of work, learning, and language is apparent in the dispirited jesting among the lords that initiates the second act. The courtiers make conversation, but it is empty word play, a desperate dragging out of small talk and gossip to while away tedious hours and to conceal their fears. The artifice of their conversation has nothing of the deliberate decorative intent that we find in the courtly scenes of Shakespeare's early romantic and satirical comedies, in which the language is often as stiff and sometimes quite as silly. There, true enough, the ladies and gentlemen engage in a sterile type of repartee; they are not really making conversation with each other, but are tossing words back and forth as if engaged in a cunning boy's game.[4] But that is all convention and high artifice, whereas to call scoundrels such as Sebastian and Antonio "artificial" would be to compliment them. Antonio and Sebastian mock the very function of language. Their impertinent jokes constitute a play within a play—an anticipation of Restoration comedy to which the gentry came flocking in order to see the re-enactment of their depravity on the public stage. Until middle-class society finally consolidated its triumph over obsolete court cliques, the language of the latter continued to survive as a testimony to their parasitism.

Gonzalo's use of language is rational, affirmative, and humane. His age and profession have brought him a certain degree of stolidity and patience which permit him to repay insolence with solace; he tries to humor King Alonso, who thinks his son lost in the storm, by persuading him that after all there are still chances for survival; only wait, and the king will see Ferdinand alive again. But Gonzalo might have spared himself the trouble; as his king puts it (II,1):

> You cram these words into mine ears, against
> The stomach of my sense . . .

Nor does Gonzalo fail to chide Sebastian, the king's unsavory brother, for abusive language when the situation calls for words of comfort and hope. "Sir," Sebastian maliciously remarks, "you may thank yourself for this great loss"; naturally Alonso would prefer not to be thus reminded, and asks to be left alone, "prithee, peace." Sebastian will not leave him in peace; most certainly not:

> . . . We have lost your son,
> I fear, for ever: Milan and Naples have
> More widows in them of this business' making
> Than we bring men to comfort them; the fault's
> Your own.

Gonzalo tries (in vain) to improve the situation by a lesson in humaneness:

> My lord Sebastian,
> The truth you speak doth lack some gentleness
> And time to speak it in; you rub the sore,
> When you should bring the plaster.

In short, Gonzalo is at pains to use language reasonably. For the rest, his task is to serve his king, more so than ever in a situation of emergency. He avows his loyalty—not ritualistically but sensibly, pragmatically even—whenever such avowals will do the king some good. Now, for example, he appeals to the king's own duty to bear up, lest his

subjects, taking their cue from his own conduct, be cast
down with him:

> It is foul weather in us all, good sir,
> When you are cloudy.

His Utopia oration (which comes next and which he designs
to keep the king's mind off the loss of his son) has no effect.
Gonzalo finally gives up with an inward shrug. His next-to-
last lines very neatly, if somewhat self-disparagingly, sum
up the whole scene:

> I do well believe your Highness; and did it [talked to his king]
> to minister occasion to these gentlemen, who are of such sensible
> and nimble lungs that they always use to laugh at nothing.

The function of language as a means of self-identification
finds its most precise expression whenever a person is under
stress. When Ferdinand, while looking for his father,
meets Miranda this is how he tries to identify himself
(I,2):

> My language! heavens!—
> I am the best of them that speak this speech,
> Were I but where 'tis spoken.

His opening speech reveals his essential qualities as surely
as do Caliban's beginning lines. The one curses, the other
appears musing in the wake of Ariel's ditty:

> Where should this music be? I' th' air, or th' earth?
> It sounds no more;—and sure, it waits upon
> Some god o' th' island . . .
> This music crept by me upon the waters,
> Allaying both their fury, and my passion,
> With its sweet air . . .

It should be noted that Ariel and Caliban both sing—
Ariel lightly and continuously, Caliban once only and in a
drunken stupor, when he stumbles over his own name:

> 'Ban, 'Ban, Ca-Caliban.

And it may be said in behalf of Caliban that he is not in-
sensitive to beautiful sounds. Shakespeare endows him with

one speech which might well be spoken by a worthier character. When Caliban (II,2) tries to persuade Stephano that there is nothing to be afraid of, he describes the charming noises on his island with a lyrical power as unexpected as Mercutio's Queen Mab recital.

> Be not afeard: the isle is full of noises,
> Sounds and sweet airs, that give delight, and hurt not.
> Sometimes a thousand twangling instruments
> Will hum about mine ears; and sometime voices,
> That, if I then had wak'd after long sleep,
> Will make me sleep again: and then, in dreaming,
> The clouds methought would open and show riches
> Ready to drop upon me; that, when I wak'd,
> I cried to dream again.

Still the receptivity to music in itself tells us nothing of Caliban's humanity or lack of it. Caliban is receptive to lovely sounds, but then so are animals.[5]

D. SLEEP

Sleep comprises one of the dominant metaphors in *The Tempest*. As we explore the extent to which the portrayal of this biological function varies with the social roles and personalities of the major figures in the play, it becomes apparent that even so extra-social a phenomenon as sleep is related to the image of man, to his potentialities for self-discovery, or for the loss of the self.

To put a character to sleep may be thought of as one means of reducing him to his essential nature, shorn of worldly prerogatives and unencumbered by extrinsic frailties. During sleep all social processes—work, learning, communication with the outside world—appear to have been suspended. Since the substances of the little sleeps which occur in *The Tempest* are not revealed, we may assume that in them all activity has ceased. The problem then, in the context of the metaphor, is to discover why a character falls asleep, the manner in which he falls asleep, and the manner in which he wakes up again.

They Fall Asleep

To begin with the situation as we find it in the first scene of the first act, we note that the crew of the ship, so ubiquitous in this scene, does not turn up again until the very end of the play; then a little reception committee, consisting of the master and the boatswain, expresses pleasure at finding the passengers safe and sound. In between, for five long acts, we are not once reminded of them. As it turns out, they have been asleep. They went to sleep almost immediately after the catastrophe, sung to their rest by the kind intercession of Ariel, who dutifully reports the event (I,2) :

> The mariners all under hatches stow'd;
> Who, with a charm join'd to their suffer'd labour,
> I have left asleep . . .

This is a group of people who on a manual level have worked exceedingly hard, whose job is finished for the time being, and who are now rewarded for their physical strain with hours of well-merited rest. Shakespeare here has almost totally forsaken the anti-populism which frequently erupts in earlier plays, as in the great soliloquy of Henry V on the eve of Agincourt (Act IV, Scene 1).

Those who operate on a more complex level of rationality than do the skilled workers have different sleep habits. Theirs is the privilege of comfortable naps after intellectual exertion. Gonzalo has no difficulty in falling asleep once he has tried as well as he can to comfort Alonso. His sleep is as much an expression of inner peace as are the early afternoon naps of Prospero, the diligent scholar, who breaks up the strenuous mental labors of his day by a short after-dinner sleep.

It is during this respite from bookish pursuits that Prospero becomes more easily prey to Caliban's stratagems (III,2):

> Why, as I told thee, 'tis a custom with him
> I' th' afternoon to sleep: there thou may'st brain him.

In his primitive fashion, Caliban senses the connection between Prospero's scholarship and his resting habits. One might almost feel that the picture of Prospero asleep adds to Caliban's hatred; his outbursts gain momentum as he becomes emboldened by the thought of Prospero helpless:

> . . . I'll yield him thee asleep,
> Where thou may'st knock a nail into his head.

Could it be, one might ask, that the serf experiences a kind of dread before the knowledgeable eyes of the intellectual —that he feels he can free himself from this dread only by putting out the "vile jelly" forever?

Now let us glance at Miranda as one who achieves, in the course of the play, a personal autonomy. Still between childlike innocence and full awakening to the experience of love, she falls asleep early, overpowered by the wealth of exciting information about the curious ways of humanity which her father has just given her (I,2). So much is "beating in my mind," she tells him, that she needs a pause before she can accept any more; for the time being she has absorbed all her consciousness can take. Her father gives his blessings:

> . . . Here cease more questions;
> Thou art inclin'd to sleep; 'tis a good dulness,
> And give it way;—I know thou canst not choose.

And so too for Miranda sleep harmonizes with her personality, just as the sleep of the intellectual and the manual worker accords with theirs.

Two Who Stay Awake

The high lords, embodiments of anti-rational amorality and physical sloth, do not fall asleep easily. Alonso, who is not quite so abominable as are his brother and Antonio, has difficulty in getting rest but he succeeds eventually, though only after Gonzalo has already begun to snore. Sebastian and Antonio do not go to sleep at all.

We are aware again here of the essential unimportance of magic procedures in the play. True, Ariel has flown on-stage, "invisible, playing solemn music," but the lullaby has different effects on different people—which after all must mean that the nature of the respective sleeps is determined not by the lullaby but by the sleepers. Gonzalo reacts to Ariel's singsong by slipping off to sleep immediately; Alonso finally drifts off after a period of moaning and jeering by turns; and Sebastian and Antonio, who no more deserve sleep than does Macbeth who "hath murdered sleep," are immune to Ariel's soporific ariettas. They remain very much awake indeed, hatching plots for their own benefit, which include a scheme to kill Alonso in his sleep.

The implication in their sleeplessness seems clear: their motives, their language, their type of reasoning, are directed toward goals the very opposite of those which are conducive to life-renewing sleep. Their solution to the dilemmas which face them is, like Caliban's, murder. While others sleep to restore their energies, which will be expended in rational and productive tasks, Sebastian and Antonio remain wide awake and, remaining awake, define themselves out of the human fold.

Waking Up

Awakening is described as the reintegration of the individual with his useful tasks. Miranda, having replenished the drained reservoir of her psychic strength after her father's protracted revelations, is prepared to encounter Ferdinand and to face the test of her maturity with which this meeting confronts her. Her father, guardian of her waking and her sleeping soul, recalls her to consciousness (I,2):

> Awake, dear heart, awake! thou hast slept well:
> Awake!

One may remember his earlier exhortations to Miranda to lend him an attentive ear: the young human being is in need of her mentor's repeated reminders to face the tasks of the day. It is a matter of sleeping soundly, waking energetically, listening diligently.

Gonzalo awakens the instant the plot against Alonso is about to be consummated. Antonio has given the signal, "then let us both be sudden"; and Gonzalo comes to life with his toast to the king's preservation. While Ariel has had a hand in Gonzalo's momentous awakening, the substance of this awakening consists of Gonzalo's spontaneous reactions, which are instantly directed toward life, his own and his king's.

Skipping over the better part of three acts, we find the mariners about to awaken. They come out of the deep slumber to which their mighty efforts have entitled them. Appropriately enough they are awakened by the noise of their own craft, the repair work which is being done on the ship by parties unknown (V,1):

> . . . We were dead of sleep
> And,—how we know not,—all clapp'd under hatches,
> Where, but even now, with strange and several noises
> Of roaring, shrieking, howling, jingling chains,
> And more diversity of sounds, all horrible
> We were awak'd . . .

The good boatswain, hero of the wreck, is delighted with the expert job on the boat. He reports to Prospero that no sooner were they awake than

. . . we, in all her trim, freshly beheld
Our royal, good and gallant ship; our master
Capering to eye her . . .

The ship is the first thing they notice: as soon as they return to consciousness, they integrate themselves into their
accustomed working situations, ready to take up the job
where they left off before falling asleep.

E. Sex and Eros

Raping and Breeding

In Shakespeare, sex does not connote the immersion or
relapse of the human species into an animal state; this
would be non-creative, passive behavior. On the contrary,
the closer man comes to the sexual, the more challenging is
the need to penetrate the outer shell of *natura naturata*
with the rays of reason. The anarchy of nature must be
transformed in the direction of felt and experienced harmony. In sex relations this task is most difficult because the
ubiquitous force of the sex instinct, with its propensity to
violence, makes greater demands on man's presence of mind
than perhaps any other activity. Thus in a man's sexual behavior may be found an ultimate revelation of his humanity,
precisely because of the challenge offered by the danger of
reduction to the animal state.

Gratification of the sexual instinct does not seem to require any specifically human processes. It is therefore precisely here that the presence of rationality, of freely chosen
and justifiable action, determines whether man is in control
of himself or whether he is mere natural material, blindly
surrendering to non-rational forces.

Here too, as always, behavior at the extreme poles is
revealing. Caliban, Sebastian, Antonio, and Stephano, all
of whom represent the lowest levels of human development,[6] display basically identical reactions. The slightest
provocation or opportunity is sufficient to call forth—either

in deed or phantasy—sexual desire; and it scarcely matters how or with whom their instincts are to be gratified. As Caliban describes Miranda's sexual attractiveness, Stephano lasciviously asks: "Is it so brave a lass?" Similarly, the only response Gonzalo's Utopian daydream evokes in Sebastian and Antonio is that of sexual promiscuity (II,1):

Sebastian: No marrying 'mong his subjects?
Antonio: None, man; all idle; whores and knaves.

Caliban at least wants offspring. Earlier, in his splenetic outburst against Prospero, when he is reminded of his attempt to rape Miranda in her father's cell, he says (I,2):

O ho! Oh ho!
Oh ho! Oh ho!—would it had been done!
Thou didst prevent me; I had peopled else
This isle with Calibans.

When he offers Miranda to Stephano he assumes the butler is thinking along the same lines (III,2):

She will bring thee forth brave brood.

Here Caliban's very language suggests the pre-human level. Again he stands out as prime exemplar of the anti-rationalist, anti-individualist, pre-sensible brute.

Love: The Birth of the Individual

Ferdinand and Miranda, on the other hand, embody the truly human aspects of love. The two of them, meeting under the most primitive conditions, are completely unaware of each other's backgrounds or stations. They reenact, in a secularized world, the meeting in the Garden of Eden: a man alone and a woman alone are face to face for the first time. That is to say, they are essentially alone; Prospero in fact hovers near them, but the young people are unconscious of his presence. Their very first words as they become aware of each other set the tone: Miranda sees the

young man as "a spirit . . . it carries a brave form"; for
Ferdinand the young girl is "the Goddess on whom these
airs tend" (I,2). There is no notion here of any reenact-
ment of original sin, but rather a transfiguration of it. The
substance of their relationship, germinally present before
they have said a word to each other, is that of specific human qualities, which, in this particular case, find confirma-
tion in their childlike delight at finding they speak the same
language. They are two charming young Platonists.

What follows now in quick succession are stages of increasing awareness of the self and of the other. Prospero
endeavors to impede the affair artificially; while he observes
that "at the first sight . . . they are both in either's
power," it still remains to be seen whether this is more than
fleeting passion. He appeals to Miranda's childhood recollection of the days before their exile. The intention is to
excite hostile emotions against the young prince from
Naples, whom he labels an usurper and a spy bent on wrest-
ing the island from him. Miranda listens to all this quite
unmoved [7]; the specific accusations Prospero makes she has
neither the experience nor the factual information to deny.
But she can scarcely believe that a young man of so noble
a bearing is capable of such intentions. We encounter here,
also, a platonic facet of Renaissance ideology; the conviction
that outer beauty and inner worth are intimately connected,
that the beautiful is a manifestation of the good and the
true:

> There's nothing ill can dwell in such a temple:
> If the ill spirit have so fair a house,
> Good things will strive to dwell with't.

Prospero, threatening absurd punishment for absurdly
trumped-up charges, orders Ferdinand to follow him to a
place of confinement. Ferdinand resists:

> No,
> I will resist such entertainment till
> Mine enemy has more power.

The young man whom Ariel reported as in a kind of stupor but a few moments ago

> . . . cooling of the air with sighs
> In an odd angle of the isle and sitting
> His arms in this sad knot . . .

is now a very much composed and resolute person; and his refusal is actuated not only by the code of honor of a prince, but even more immediately by his desire to remain in the presence of his beloved. This extremely individualized type of conduct is taken up at once by Miranda:

> Oh dear father
> Make not too rash a trial of him, for
> He's gentle, and not fearful.

These words have, for their time, almost the same revolutionary connotation on the individual level that the boatswain's (I,1) words addressed to the feudal parasites—"work you, then!"—have on the social level. What Miranda expresses is the essence of the emancipatory process of an individual: freely chosen relationships have come to supersede tradition. She has made the first decision of her life, and has thus severed the original, unreflecting relationship with her father. She now follows the voice of her inner conviction. Mustering this new strength, she goes even further and attempts to prevent her father from striking Ferdinand with a sword. Prospero rudely brushes her aside: "Hang not on my garments!" Even her plea for pity—her childish "I'll be his surety"—is dismissed with a brusque "Silence!"

Prospero resorts to yet another of his testing devices: he challenges Miranda's perception of Ferdinand as a superior being:

> Thou think'st there is no more such shapes as he,
> Having seen but him and Caliban. Foolish wench!
> To the most of men this is a Caliban
> And they to him are angels.

The description assumes the authority of unchallengeable experience since it appeals to Miranda's ignorance in the matter of men; after all, she has no way of judging and discriminating, never having laid eyes on a young man before. For all she knows there really are yet more handsome men in the world than Ferdinand. But she replies:

> My affections
> Are then most humble; I have no ambition
> To see a goodlier man.

Her words are decisive, for they codify the essentials that make for the unique character of the individual. By choosing freely, against odds, in the teeth of tradition and outward command, Miranda has acted as an autonomous individual; she has created a new reality for herself. Her confession of love adds a new particle of reason, of self-created reality, to the world around her.

As we have seen in Cervantes, love appears as the key phenomenon in the autonomous development of the modern individual: it becomes almost identical with individuality itself. The point can hardly be overstressed. Love, whatever else it may be, represents an inner decision. The giving and acceptance of love brings rationality into focus more clearly than anything else. True, one might say that the process of falling in love is completely accidental and arbitrary; there appears to be no firmly rational basis for an individual to make his choice among all possibilities. But it is for precisely this reason that romantic love becomes the strongest expression of individuality. While it may be initially irrational, love creates its own situation, which, from the seemingly absurd moment of its acknowledgment, becomes a productive basis for a new rationality. A new situation, however isolated and unique, is introduced into human history once a person has *decided* that he has "no ambition to see a goodlier man" or woman.

Bonds entered into voluntarily do not create bondage, as do tradition, privilege, and subjection to extra-human powers; they are, rather, the content of freedom. Ferdinand no longer resists Prospero's command to follow him to his place of arbitrary punishment, once he knows where he stands with respect to Miranda. In his love is his freedom; compared to it (I,2) :

> My father's loss, the weakness which I feel,
> The wrack of all my friends, or this man's threats
> To whom I am subdued, are but light to me . . .

The world of Ferdinand and Miranda begins with the experience that is their own and only their own:

> Might I but through my prison once a day
> Behold this maid: all corners else o' th' earth
> Let Liberty make use of; space enough
> Have I in such a prison.

With Ferdinand's speech we have retraced our steps to Don Quixote's scene with the Duchess. Man, Shakespeare tells us as Cervantes did, finds himself alone in a universe without moorings and without predictability; he has, nonetheless, the task of restoring sense to the chaos which the passing of the old order had left. And this sense, since it could no longer come from without, had to be achieved by individual acts of ordering and re-creation. Upon the individual devolved the burden of remaking his world. And his individuality was pressingly put to test when he was called upon to make intimate decisions concerning himself and those nearest him—those involving love.

3.
SECULARIZED HUMILITY

Inherent in the play is the Baconian idea that man develops his humanity by acquiring and applying knowledge; knowledge begets the power to control nature. Nature is both in and around us, and the sciences are divided accordingly. The science of man rests on introspection and empathy; turned to the past, it becomes History. Prospero's story about his past, however, is not only information but also leads to the practice of Education. And when methods and findings of introspection and empathy are generalized, we enter the realm of Ethics. Thus in *The Tempest*, behavior may be observed as a basis for prediction of moral propensities: Prospero studies the development of Ferdinand and Miranda, as Ariel studies the repentance of the lords.

What, finally, has emerged from the experiment on the island? In terms of the five themes we have selected for study each member of the small, isolated society has acted out the potentialities of his own nature. The question remains: how should individual variations in human nature ultimately be explained? Why is Prospero essentially good and Antonio, to say nothing of Caliban, essentially evil? Theories of human nature from the Renaissance to the late eighteenth century leave this question unanswered; whether man is considered intrinsically good or intrinsically evil, the basic postulates do not allow us to deduce why some should be more successful than others in overcoming their original destructive bents or in maintaining their original innocence. *The Tempest,* at several places, comes close to formulating this dilemma. Prospero describes to Caliban the pains he has taken to give him a decent education, to teach him "with human care" how to work, how to think. In the end, despite labor and kindness, he has failed. Caliban has betrayed his mentor and his own humanity by trying to rape Miranda and by using language mainly for cursing. The only explanation Prospero can find for his failure is to take recourse to the key concept of the Renaissance intellectual—that arcanum of all secularized knowledge as well as ignorance: nature. He says (I,2):

> . . . I endowed thy purposes
> With words that made them known: but thy vile race,
> Though thou did'st learn, had that in 't which good nature
> Could not abide with.

Similarly, Prospero can only account for his brother's behavior by concluding that Antonio's "ambition expell'd remorse and nature." A few lines later he calls Antonio "unnatural though thou art." (V,1)

The image of man which we get from *The Tempest* is that of a free agent, whose possibilities lie in several directions. If it does not say why some should choose one direction and others another, the play at least demonstrates the consequences of a variety of choices. Implicit is the belief that no formal and arbitrary code exists for self-discovery and that, in fact, the very process of self-discovery may lead to breaking certain rules otherwise taken for granted.

The Irrational Deviant: Caliban

In several instances in *The Tempest* people behave in a way that appears inconsistent with the portrayal of their characters. They do not behave as they might be expected to on the basis of what we know about their prior behavior and attitudes. Whereas in Cervantes deviations from the norm were discovered in figures marginal to the society at large, in *The Tempest* deviations occur by a reversal of previous patterns within the individual.

Again, two basically different types of reactions are displayed in inconsistent behavior, as they were in "normal" behavior. Caliban, the prototype farthest removed from self-control and creativity at one point seems to overcome his sullen, dumb, and blunted personality. To Stephano, who has initiated him into the delights of liquor, he voluntarily offers all the services that Prospero forces him to perform. He goes even further and volunteers to do many extra services (II,2):

> I'll show thee the best springs; I'll pluck thee berries;
> I'll fish for thee, and get thee wood enough.

Or:

> I prithee, let me bring thee where crabs grow;
> And I with my long nails will dig thee pig-nuts;

Show thee a jay's nest and instruct thee how
To snare the nimble marmoset; I'll bring thee
To clust'ring filberts, and sometimes I'll get thee
Young scamels from the rock.

Twice he asks Stephano for the privilege to "kiss thy feet." Twice the former specialist in cursing becomes inventive in similes, as if to emphasize the high respect in which he holds the person for whom he is willing to work. He implores to be permitted to "follow thee" and not only calls him a "wondrous man," but asks him to "be my God"; he introduces his speeches with a polite "I prithee." He follows up his dedication to Stephano by a grotesque rejection of Prospero:

A plague upon the tyrant that I serve!
I'll bear him no more sticks, but follow thee,
Thou wondrous man.

Caliban presents himself suddenly as a superworker for whom no strain and exertion seems too much. But again his behavior is that of a pre-rational human being fixated in an infantile stage of development. He adapts himself to whatever seems to offer immediate satisfaction of bodily needs and desires, completely uninterested in consequences, like a baby or an animal grabbing a toy or a morsel of food. His words describe a Utopia in reverse—he voluntarily subjects himself to perpetual servitude and to an uninhibited exploitation of nature. He reminds us of the contemporary uprooted adolescent on the loose, in search of a leader and in need of compensating for his submission to authority by committing, under its protection, senseless acts of cruelty. Miranda as well as nature's flora and fauna are for Caliban nothing but opportunity for rape and violence. While in the humanistic Utopia of Gonzalo the exploitation of nature is limited to the irreducible minimum of providing for survival, the sadistic wish-dreams of Caliban are filled with senseless anticipations of cruel acts. He rejects Prospero's rational solutions for his plight—in fact, he experiences them only as threats. He now wants to eliminate the source of those solutions entirely, by bludgeoning the brain that devised them. The terror he feels as a result of his subjection to an overpowering leader, he can project and act out by an attack on the weak and defenseless.

The misery of Caliban—who is unable to comprehend that he is in the service of a decent master, and who equates liberation with humiliation and with alienation from humanity—reveals the possibilities for regression which the breakdown of feudalism had bared. His whole life is circumscribed by the necessity to follow commands, the rationality of which he is neither willing nor able to grasp. His sole motivation is mutiny against rationally functioning institutions of civilization.

Individual Fulfillment: Ferdinand, Miranda, and Gonzalo

At the other extreme, Miranda, Ferdinand, and Gonzalo seem to display deviations from their own standard of morality: they refuse to follow orders, or they break the word they have given. All three deviate, in their various ways, from the unconditional performance of duties they had originally accepted.

When Antonio, Prospero's brother, and his co-conspirators had set about to send Prospero and Miranda to certain death on "a rotten carcass of a boat," Gonzalo had been chosen to execute the plan. In violation of the usurper's orders, he had provided the rightful duke and his daughter with means of livelihood sufficient for them to survive Antonio's attempt to murder them.

Miranda, for her part, performs a whole series of acts that are in clear violation of her father's instructions and at variance with her heretofore child-like dependence upon him. She asks Ferdinand to loaf when her father is not present (III,1):

> . . . My father
> Is hard at study; pray now, rest yourself:
> He's safe for these three hours.

Furthermore Prospero has expressly forbidden her to tell Ferdinand her name, but when he asks it, she answers without hesitation:

> Miranda.—Oh, my father!
> I have broke your hest to say so.

Finally, as do many of Shakespeare's women in love, she reverses the mores of male-female relationships by offering herself in marriage and not waiting for the young man to ask the question.

> . . . Hence, bashful cunning!
> And prompt me, plain and holy innocence!
> I am your wife, if you will marry me;
> If not, I'll die your maid: to be your fellow
> You may deny me; but I'll be your servant,
> Whether you will or no.

To this we should add an inconsistency of Ferdinand, who obviously cheats in chess with Miranda (V,1):

> *Miranda:* Sweet lord, you play me false.
> *Ferdinand:* No, my dearest love,
> I would not for the world.
> *Miranda:* Yes, for a score of kingdoms you should wrangle,
> And I would call it fair play.

All three—Gonzalo, Miranda, and Ferdinand—deliberately engage, then, in actions which on first sight deviate from their general mode of conduct. Each case represents a decision in a direction that not only is unsolicited by other people, but is in violation of instructions or rules. At the same time, all three would have violated their own natures, the substance of their rationality and morality, if they had not committed these rebellious acts.

Gonzalo, in betraying his employers, acts, as Prospero formulates it, "out of charity." The preservation of human life is for him a higher value than obedience to an order that implies its destruction. It is not far-fetched to interpret Gonzalo's act as resistance against the arbitrariness of tyranny; he avails himself of the right of disobeying the sovereign if the sovereign violates the natural rights of men. He is here closely related to Don Quixote who, in his perspicacious craziness, detects such violations at every turn. In defying his masters, Gonzalo acknowledges a higher duty and realizes a higher truth.

Miranda's three acts of disobedience to her father display the development of an autonomous and free individual. For her, it is romantic love that is the touchstone of free and rational development. When she gives Ferdinand her name, she lives up to the implications of nominalist philosophy; her name denotes her individuality. Then, it is incompatible with reason that Ferdinand should slave to expiate a crime he never committed. Her bodily frailty is transformed by her moral strength when she endeavors to alleviate his forced labor. Finally, to hide her love would be a lie. No price is too high for the truth, even the violation of a parental order.

Ferdinand's setting aside of the rules is, of course, harmless, but it has its importance. When he obviously forfeits the advantage of chess moves which his less experienced opponent has made possible and which, in strict obedience to the rules, he ought to execute, he forfeits the supposed male superiority in intelligence within the charming context of a game. Miranda's awareness of his tricks and her understanding of his voluntary mistakes shows her, in fact, to be his equal in intelligence. The ideal relation between man and woman, in the imagery of the Elizabethan Renaissance, does not consist in the biological, naturalistic satisfaction of instincts, but in the recognition of one individual's reason by another, tempered by consideration of human limitations and by ensuing acts of indulgence.

The selection of chess as a motif in the love of Ferdinand and Miranda is an artful figure. No other game so completely shuts out the element of chance as does chess; called the game of kings and philosophers, and symbolizing the peak of humanly attainable reason, it is an appropriate token of ideal human behavior in a situation of leisure. The lovers who have found in each other a congenial spirit engage in the pleasures of reason even when alone and at play, and thus show an exemplary discipline under tempting conditions by playing the most intellectual of games.

Pity

Pity is for Shakespeare the one foundation for morality. Within a theological context, to be sure, pity had its rewards; man was credited for its exercise in the offices of heavenly bookkeeping, and his fate depended upon the entries. But such post-mortal expediency became weaker during the Renaissance, and the very decline in theological certainties created a challenge to the individual, forcing him to redefine his relation to others. Man now viewed pity as the outcome of self-awareness and of accepting personal responsibility for one's own and mankind's fate: pity—as it was now postulated—consists of insight into the limitations of finite reason and finite life, and compels acts of mercy. The exercise of mercy was the final maxim Don Quixote passed on to Sancho Panza in teaching him the rules of wisdom for statesmanship and judgment.

In *The Tempest*, pity is a dominant and recurrent element. Gonzalo pities Prospero and Miranda at the time he executes the brutal exile order; Prospero takes pity on Caliban and tries to teach him some of the techniques of civilization; Miranda pities Ferdinand when she sees him burdened with heavy work; Gonzalo takes pity on his mourning king; in a very delicate way Ferdinand pities Miranda for her shortcomings in chess; Ariel has pity on all the lordly passengers of the ship, including the criminals; and Prospero, listening to the voice of his conscience, realizes that wisdom should make him "kindlier moved" even than Ariel. In practically every major theme we have analyzed, pity is present: in work as demonstrated by Miranda, in learning as demonstrated by Prospero, in language as demonstrated by Gonzalo, and even in sleep, if we remember the careful way in which the tired seamen are put to rest.

The expression of pity as a consequence of the recognition of human frailty reaches two peaks as the play nears its end. When Prospero, at the beginning of the fifth act, finds in himself the strength of pity, he divests himself of his magic (V,1):

> . . . But this rough magic
> I here abjure; and, when I have requir'd
> Some heavenly music,—which even now I do,—
> To work mine end upon their senses that
> This airy charm is for, I'll break my staff,
> Bury it certain fathoms in the earth,
> And deeper than did ever plummet sound
> I'll drown my book.

Now, without benefit of superhuman powers, he twice tells his brother that he forgives him. Thus, in a gesture of the kind we are familiar with in Gonzalo, he applies insight and theoretical knowledge to practice: having himself experienced the blessings of humanistic pity, he applies it now even to those who deserve it least.

A final expression of human sympathy is reached at the end of the play, when Prospero speaks an epilogue to the audience:

> Now my charms are all o'erthrown,
> And what strength I have's mine own;
> Which is most faint: now, 'tis true,
> I must be here confin'd by you,
> Or sent to Naples. Let me not,
> Since I have my dukedom got
> And pardon'd the deceiver, dwell

In this bare island by your spell;
But release from my bands
With the help of your good hands.
Gentle breath of yours my sails
Must fill, or else my project fails,
Which was to please. Now I want
Spirits to enforce, art to enchant,
And my ending is despair,
Unless I be reliev'd by prayer,
Which pierces so that it assaults
Mercy itself and frees all faults.
As you from crimes would pardon'd be,
Let your indulgence set me free.

In its most obvious reading, the speech is a conventional appeal by the chief actor of the play for applause. But the nature of its references to the play suggests another meaning, one that can sum up for us the situation of the individual at an early stage of modern history.

It reminds us of Don Quixote's speech about Dulcinea; the borderline between reality and illusion is fluid, and so are the status and location of the individual. There are no objective criteria for deciding whether it is Prospero, or an actor, or the poet himself, who is speaking; we do not know whether these words are still an integral part of the play or whether, as in *Don Quixote,* the poet views his creation as a part of himself about which he then reflects. The image is that of man removed from a specific setting and set of relationships, other than those he can create for himself. Divested of the tools of learning and technology, his magic "charms all o'erthrown," deserted even by his fellow actors, man appears as the modern individual in all his aloneness: "what strength I have is my own." In acknowledging individual existence he realizes, at the same time, the limitations of individual power, "which is most faint."

This, then, is the image of Elizabethan man, living in a world in which he develops his responsibilities to himself and his pity for others, anticipating that the future will fulfill his hopes. But in one important respect, the image of man will now change radically: with the advent of tighter social controls, the individual will never again feel himself so completely his own master.

Chapter IV: THE CLASSICAL
FRENCH DRAMA

So far, the emphasis of our study has been on the individual. In Cervantes and Shakespeare, organized society is present only as a conditioning background; the human being who emerges sees himself as the responsible creator, willingly or unwillingly, of important segments of his own reality. He seeks to overcome the vacuum left by the disappearance of the feudal order not so much by relating himself to the new society as by searching his own nature. Society as an experience is an almost accidental meeting with other individuals, and the literature records the successes and failures of these meetings. Man is limited, of course, by his experiences and contacts with others, but these do not jell for him into an image of society.

The relation of the individual to the world at large began to take on a new character. The seventeenth century in Europe saw the gradual emergence of a struggle of a new type. The victory over feudalism became final, and the new middle class started on its path of conquest with the spread of industry and trade and the growth of new urban cultural institutions. The political framework in which this class appeared, however, was still that of an absolute monarchy which continued to surround itself with an aristocratic coterie.

Against this background of politico-economic stabilization and struggle a new social consciousness arose. We find that the tensions displayed in literature are no longer merely those within the person; they are increasingly those of the self-conscious relation of man to his society. The long process of middle-class socialization had begun. The French theater in the seventeenth century admirably illustrates the various facets of this process. In Corneille's drama, man adapts himself by subordinating his personal desires and claims to the exigencies of the state; the subordination resolves his tensions and conflicts and becomes the true path of his self-realization. Racine's drama portrays, on the other hand, an irreconcilable conflict between the individual and the power apparatus, and his characters find no home in the absolute state. In Molière work, the middle class emerges as a force in its own right; his characters feel their way into the new institutions and learn, although with reservations, to conform to the shared modes and values of middle-class life.

The theatre of Corneille is an exercise in political behavior accepting conditions of absolute monarchy. The tragedies of Racine are an exercise in middle-class behavior expressing intellectual and emotional resistance to the same social institution—the monarchy. The comedies of Molière are an exercise in behavior under conditions that demand conformity to a new social order. In Corneille the individual finds self-realization only after having adjusted to the state; in Racine, he finds it in resistance to the state; in Molière, he is again adjusted, this time into a pattern of conformism to the values of an emergent bourgeoisie. These characterizations are simplified and stand in need of qualification, but they can serve here to emphasize briefly three divergent approaches of European man to his social situation in the period of the rise of the middle class and before its final political victory.

In his studies of the final decades of the seventeenth century, Paul Hazard declared that "never was there a greater contrast, never a more sudden transition" than that from what people "held dear" in the seventeenth to what they believed in the eighteenth century.[1] This statement is largely true for philosophy, religious beliefs and political theory. If, however, we examine closely the great trio of French dramatists, we shall find this period of transition reflected in a decidedly less sudden way. We see not only the progressive shift of psychological views but also the gradual broadening of the social space within which the dramatic action takes place. In Corneille, the upper class is by itself, in Racine it is joined by the intellectuals—the professionals and educators—and in Molière we are faced for the first time with an almost homogeneous middle-class world.

I.

CORNEILLE (1606-1684)

"If he were alive once more, I would make him a prince." With these words Napoleon made Corneille a contemporary of a period when the political, legal, and economic institutions of middle-class society had achieved a definitive character. The words attest to basic social traits that had persisted over a time span of almost two hundred years. In both Corneille's and Napoleon's time, central government had to combat well-organized resistance. Strictly speaking, the similarity ends here; the government of Louis XIII set out to destroy the traditional prerogatives of the old nobility, whereas the Directory and Empire of Napoleon, by dissolving the Committee of Public Safety, wrote *finis* to the tendencies toward political and economic radicalism of the French Revolution. However, while the historical situations differ, they harbor sociological similarities. When Corneille wrote *Cinna,* a play dealing with the suppression of a political conspiracy against Augustus, he was rewarded, if not with the post-hoc generosity of Napoleon, at least with Richelieu's permission to marry a titled lady. It thus would appear that ruling groups more than 150 years apart identified Corneille with something more than mere poetical whims; the question of the social relevance of his work has been answered by persons of far-reaching influence. And if Richelieu and Napoleon did not find that the *dramatis personae* of Corneille realistically typified the actions of their contemporaries, they at least wished this were the case.

Public Power and the Individual

At first sight the major works of Corneille appear to contain motivations and conflicts similar to those found in Shakespeare. The story of *Horace* reminds us of *Romeo and Juliet;* the story of *Cinna* is thematically and even chronologically very close to *Julius Caesar;* in *The Cid,* lovers whose fathers compete for honors from the crown remind us of *The Tempest*'s Ferdinand and Miranda, whose fathers also were engaged in a struggle for political supremacy. However, all these similarities are more apparent than real. Shakespeare's people stand or fall with the development of their own essential being. It is not by chance that the monologue is an indispensable dramatic vehicle in almost all his plays; the actions of his characters are the outer manifestation of internal processes. Tragic endings neither condemn nor justify the social agencies that shatter the lives of Anthony or Romeo, but are the result of individually applied creative reason or its opposite: Verona stands for the foolishness of a Montague and a Capulet; Rome for the enlightened intellectuality and morality of Octavius Caesar. Even the dramatic histories of British kings make events contingent upon the individualities of the rulers, whose interactions with other individualities seem almost accidentally to create the social world. Unity, cohesion, or disorder in society proves to be nothing but unity, cohesion, or disorder in individuals, turned outward. Every event, every institution in Shakespearean drama is translatable into a psychic process of a particular individual.

But if in Shakespeare's work society reflects the individual, in Corneille's it is the individual who reflects society. The dynamic processes are reversed. Corneille's figures achieve stature only in institutional roles. The state gives them distinguishable contours and provides them with principles for organizing and structuring otherwise chaotic modes of reaction and behavior. Individuation is experienced—as it will tend to be in literature from now on—as socialization.

In Corneille's time, middle-class life had gained tremendous momentum, mainly as a result of the state's mercantilist policy supporting the development of industry and trade. For despite its aristocratic look, the prosperity of the absolute state depended upon the very economic gains which were bringing the middle class with its way of life and its ethos to the fore. Prior to Corneille, the problem facing the individual had been survival within an environment disrupted by the disintegration of the old order as well as by the appearance of the new. Now the problem changed radically; it was no longer one of self-orientation midway between a twilight of chaos and a dawning reconstruction, but of accommodation in one way or another to a flourishing absolute state with its rind of regal pomp and core of stable industriousness. Corneille's dramas are full of special pleading and rhetorical persuasions designed to demonstrate that acceptance of public power is both expedient and moral.

The unity and harmony of individual existence now emanates from social agencies. The process may be described in this way: the social agencies, specifically the state, force the individual to subordinate self-interest to public interest, and this public interest is ultimately experienced by him as eminently suited to his self-interest. The subtitle to *Cinna* is *The Mercy of Augustus*. The mercy of God transplanted into the psyche—an extreme consequence of Renaissance secularization—is now replanted into the state, for there is no doubt that in the play Augustus represents the state. Mercy is taken from the sphere of individual frailty and given to a trans-individual social agency with executive strength. The *raison d'état* begets its own acts of mercy whenever they serve its purpose; the individual is thus the recipient but not the source of mercy. He must learn how to internalize and reenforce these acts of the state, but the possibility of his initiating them is removed.

The State and Interpersonal Relations

Love—like mercy—is no longer in itself an ultimate creative act. Only insofar as it is compatible with and subordinate to the claims of the state, can love be a legitimate expression of the individual. The *raison d'état* must determine the consummation, or even the destruction, of intimate relationships; personal catastrophes or satisfactions amount to little as compared to the necessities of state. Thus in *Horace,* brothers, sisters, husbands, and wives, forfeit their happiness, and even life, when the state demands it. Corneille has Horace declaim:

> To die for the Fatherland is such a pleasant fate, that everyone
> yearns for it;
> But to sacrifice what one loves for the state, to enter into lists
> against one's other self,
> To fight the brother of one's wife, the betrothed of one's sister,
> To arm oneself for the fatherland against one for whose blood
> I'd give my life,
> That is a fate worthy of a Roman.[2]

At the end of the wars between the Albans and Romans, the only surviving protagonist is Horace, who has killed not only his brothers-in-law but also his wife; still the play does not become a tragedy of aloneness. On the contrary, he receives from the head of state these instructions:

> Live, Horace, live, great-hearted warrior.
> Your virtue will pale your fame about your deed.
> Your high-spirited ardor caused your monstrous crime.
> With so beautiful a cause one must take whatever result follows.
> Live to love your state.[3]

Don Roderick, the Cid, who has slain the father of his beloved Chimène, will be united in marriage with her after the bereaved daughter has observed a suitable period of

mourning. While waiting, he will engage in patriotic deeds.
The king addresses first Chimène and then Roderick:

(*To Chimène:*)
Take, if you will, a year to dry your tears.
Meanwhile, let Roderick win new victories.
(*To the Cid:*)
You have destroyed the Moors upon our shores,
Shattered their hopes, repulsed their wild assaults,
Go now and bear the war to their own land,
Command my army, pillage their domain.
At the very name of Cid they quake with fear;
They call you lord and they would make you king.
But through all mighty deeds keep faith with her:
Return if possible more worthy of her;
And make yourself so prized for your exploits
That pride will join with love to make her yours.[4]

There is no conflict, in the end, between duty to the state
and one's own private happiness; the latter will be im-
mensely increased, guaranteed and glorified if one behaves
as a noble soldier.

The same system of values is displayed in *Cinna*.
Augustus forgives Cinna, offers the former conspirator a
responsible position and reunites him with his beloved
Amelia—all for reasons of state. Amelia had forsworn
her passion for Cinna because of his leaving the conspiracy
of which she was a part; now when Augustus proposes to
make Cinna her husband at the same time he nominates
Cinna as Consul, Amelia responds to the offer and thus to
the system of social values in these words:

My hate is dying, that I believed immortal;
Is dead, and in its place, a loyal heart.
Henceforward, in stark horror of this hate,
Ardor of service shall replace its fury.[5]

Her hatred had been directed against Augustus for
exiling her father as a political enemy; it had also included
Cinna when he withdrew from the anti-Augustan conspiracy. Prior to the denouement, Amelia is torn between
loyalty to her father and love. Shakespeare's Miranda,

finding herself in a similar situation, resolves her conflict through her own unique and unaided decision; there is no reference to any other moving force. Corneille's Amelia has her problem solved for her by the head of the state; her decision is simply to accept the imperial decree. By her submission, the general or social rationality represented by the decree brings order and meaning into her inconsistent and mutually exclusive desires. The superior *raison d'état* becomes her *raison d'être;* she "finds herself" by obedient identification with the political system, not by self-identification.

Prospero educates Miranda in order to make his educational efforts dispensable, and to help her achieve personal autonomy. The educational impact of organized society makes Amelia its pawn forever.

Honor and the State

The Renaissance image of mankind as a community of discrete individualities has given way to the concept of a social structure that is more than the sum total of individuals within it. The reality of the state replaces the individual dream. In Corneille's drama, the acceptance of governmental coercion is internalized and becomes a voluntary act which is glorified by the name "honor." However, it would be a sociological mistake to confuse Corneille's concept of honor with that of Calderon. For the Spanish dramatist, honor is the expression of the rigid value system of feudalism, of a society that has become obsolete; Calderon would dignify an outworn pattern as a defense against the present, but the France of Corneille is a progressive nation and his work reflects the distinction quite clearly. He is thus much closer to Calderon's predecessor Lope; both were poets of the new nationalism. But Corneille places the dynamics of secular power within the individual. Its acceptance becomes a purposive act through voluntary identification of the self with the state. His

idea of honor points to the need for man to adopt the
morality of the state. This becomes clear in the words of
Augustus to Cinna:

> My favor makes your glory, out of that
> Your power grows; that only raised you up,
> And held you there, 'tis that the Romans honor,
> Not yourself. You have no rank or power
> Except I give it you, and for your fall
> There needs but the withdrawal of my hand,
> Which is your sole support.[6]

The words are echoed by Cinna to whom they are directed:

> Let but my duty, reborn in my heart,
> Pledge you a faith already basely broken,
> But now so firm, so far from wavering,
> The very fall of heaven could not shake it.[7]

The Cid is a particularly good example of the conflict
between the new concept of honor and the old, offering a
portrayal of the process of socialization called for by the
absolutistic state. The first significant action of the play
is a jealous outburst between the Cid's father, to whom the
education of the crown prince is entrusted, and Chimène's
father, who feels that he himself should have been given
this distinguished task. The result is a duel between the
Cid and Chimène's father; the latter is killed. The Cid
has avenged his father's honor but has also embittered
Chimène who now feels obliged to avenge the honor of her
house. Honor at this stage reverts to the old feudal forms.
It commands Chimène to avenge her father's death even
in the choice of a husband, and the Cid to alienate the
woman he loves. For three acts the Cid suffers this condition until he finally breaks out and declares to his father:

> Let me at last give voice to my despair;
> Which has too long been stifled by your words.
> I feel no mean regret for having served you;
> But give me back the joy this blow has cost me.
> My arm for you was raised against my love
> And by that stroke I lost my heart's desire.

Tell me no more; I have lost all for you;
That which I owed you, I have paid too well.[8]

Whereupon the father retorts:

We have one honor only. Mistresses
Are plentiful! Love is a pleasant toy,
But honor is a master to be served.[9]

An impasse has been reached: Chimène cannot marry her
beloved, the killer of her father; the son has to subordinate
his personal wishes to the honor code of the feudal gentleman, and the father takes no interest whatsoever in the
personal desires of his son. In the end, however, the play
arrives at a complete reconciliation. When the principals
are faced with the symbols, tasks and proclamations of the
state represented by the king, a scaling down of personal
interests satisfactory to all is achieved. Love, honor, and
personal initiative are acceptable values—if subordinated
to the state and "your king." These are the closing words
of the play, directed to the Cid:

King: Rest hope upon your courage and my word,
    And since already you possess her heart,
    To still that honor which cries out against you
    Leave all to time, your valor, and your king.[10]

The State as the Ego

Corneille's moral beliefs might be likened to Cartesian
metaphysics. For Descartes, the process of reason meant a
cognitive progress by the individual toward ever more clear
and distinct perceptions of himself; for Corneille, it meant
the ever more clear and distinct perceptions by the individual of the state. *The Cid,* for example, starts with a
confused semi-private, semi-official situation arising from
the necessity to find a tutor for the crown prince; it ends
with the problems of foreign politics and military might.
So long as the *raison d'état* is perceived only in terms of
private interests, rationality will fail and individuals will

behave erratically in their official as well as in their private undertakings; once the superiority of the state is fully acknowledged, individuals and state act in unison, and reason triumphs. It is not without significance that the initial dramatic motif of *The Cid* is the education of a future ruler.

The location of Corneille's dramatic themes in the past, particularly in Roman antiquity, also reflects a Cartesian-like concern for safety, security, and reliability. When the data of history have been sifted again and again, the residuum assumes the qualities of unquestioned fact. Past events have become established knowledge: everyone is familiar with the early Roman wars, the conspiracy of Cinna and the fights of the Spaniards against the Moors. In addition, Roman and early Spanish history contain well-known examples of governmental practice; Corneille's models were safe and acceptable for presenting exemplary lessons on the socialization of the individual in a powerful state. Everything is accessible and articulate; nothing remains doubtful.

Thus while in Shakespeare there remains an eternal doubt as to whether Utopia will ever come about or even whether Prospero, once he has returned to Milan, will put his lessons into practice, the issue in Corneille is settled once and for all. We do not know whether the next generation of Montagues and Capulets will be more enlightened or be as big fools as their fathers, but we are certain that the Cid and Chimène will pass on to their offspring what they have learned and that the conflict of the play will be forever resolved. To the extent that Corneille's individual reconciles his private life with his social duties, he has fulfilled his potentialities; the rest is not silence, as in *Hamlet,* but articulate business in the service of an hierarchized "we" that endows the "I" with meaning.

Corneille's formula for a static harmony of the individual and society is, in its way, perfect. If the actualities of the state lived up to his idealization, all would be well, and we should no doubt have arrived at the end of drama. The individual, however, came to experience his position in the absolute monarchy as a kind of moral and social restraint that could not be resolved in the abstractions of pride and honor. Corneille's solutions came to exist only for a moment in time; history added the question mark he tried so hard to eradicate from his ideal representation on the stage.

2.

RACINE (1639-1699)

Racine, too, wrote 'classical' plays. They are worlds apart, however, from those of Corneille. If one changed the costumes of Corneille's characters to the contemporary garb of his time, most of them would be indistinguishable from French royalty and high military and civilian officials. Racine, too, wrote about kings and high persons, but they had no counterparts in the France of his day. There are no similarities between Louis XIV and the Nero of *Britannicus,* the Theseus of *Phaedra* or the Pyrrhus of *Andromache.*

A most significant change Racine effected in the *dramatis personae* is the introduction of a new type of man, the tutor; he is the unofficial intellectual, a person Corneille would not have tolerated. There are other differences. Although Racine, like Corneille, goes to antiquity for his themes, he avoids imperial Rome in favor of Greek times, and the legends he draws upon do not celebrate state power but individual passion. In addition, the titles of Racine's plays are significant, being almost invariably the names of women; and women certainly did not serve as spokesmen in the male-dominated society of seventeenth-century France. Each of these differences serves to stake out the broad gulf between the two French dramatists. Racine's plays do not point to the state as the *raison d'être* of human existence. Kings rule over states that are close to unrest, sometimes even to chaos; educators moralize from a position detached from the state machinery; women, who have no political power, become the major spokesmen for ethical viewpoints; and the locales underline the individualistic focus of the themes.

The State and Individual Self-Expression

In Corneille's drama the relations of the individual to society are shown as a successful reciprocity in a secularized world. In Racine, the relation breaks down; the state loses its sacred quality and becomes merely a worldly power. Moreover, it is often an obstacle to the self-realization of the individual who no longer accepts the state's hierarchy of values, and who can no longer reconcile his personal aspirations with those of the preordained system.

Both Corneille and Racine show us persons who rise in stature as a result of heightened self-awareness. In Corneille, however, the criterion for this awareness consists of deeds in the service of the state; his heroes become administrators or military leaders. In Racine, the touchstone is language. The heroes and heroines are encouraged by their tutors to speak out, to say what they feel. The tutors are spokesmen for freedom of expression. Social implications become apparent once the individual realizes that such free self-expression runs counter to the demands of the prevailing institutions. Racine's heroes and heroines do not live according to a superimposed morality—personal aspirations are acknowledged, and there is no ready solution to the conflict between individual and society. Phaedra, for example (as Racine himself says in a preface to the play), is neither entirely guilty nor entirely innocent, and individual passion is not *per se* a sin against God or man. In short, Racine's characters appear more sinned against by the social and political order, than sinning.

The Tutor as Intermediary

The role of the tutor serves a specific function in this re-emergence of individual claims. Rarely do any of Racine's *dramatis personae* make such long speeches as does Burrus,

Nero's tutor, or Theramenes, the tutor of Hippolytus, and what they have to say are not contributions to individual introspection as in the case of Shakespeare's Gonzalo. They are, directly or indirectly, bitter attacks on a social order that permits a ruler to destroy personal happiness.

Although political stratification at Racine's time closely resembles that at the time of Corneille, the moral perspective has shifted radically. This shift has the effect of revealing the instability of the social pyramid: the tutors (to whom we may add Phaedra's nurse, Oenone) help their wards to become aware of the moral inadequacy of the state and teach them to look to themselves for their true fulfillment.

The function of the tutors is not to try to impose their own values and motives upon those they advise, but to help them break their inner silence and put their wishes into words. (Leo Spitzer has aptly characterized them as "humanistic historiographers." [11]) When Phaedra tries to hide from herself her infatuation for Hippolytus, her nurse, Oenone, warns her:

> If you must blush,
> Blush at the silence that inflames your grief.[12]

Similarly, when Hippolytus tries to ignore his deep affection for Aricia, the royal prisoner of his father, his tutor Theramenes encourages him to speak his real feelings:

> What good to act a pride you do not feel?
> If you are changed, confess it! [13]

The numerous confessions that appear in Racine's plays reveal an important change in the image of the self from the images in Cervantes and Shakespeare. Racine's people find out for themselves that they are tremendously complicated and that a person cannot be adequately described merely in terms of reason or the lack of it. If the Renaissance (to use Jacob Burckhardt's formulation) is the age of discovery of the individual, the seventeenth century in France witnessed the birth of his psychology. Racine's people begin to learn that the individual's encounters with his environment may activate the development of terrifying inner conflicts, but that the outer world will not in turn offer any solution for such tensions. The serene value system that posits a rational individual, whether he is autonomous as in Shakespeare or an obedient citizen as in Corneille, is now breaking down under the impact of heightened social pressures. This process leads to a great increase in knowledge of the self. The noblest of all men in Racine's dramas, the guiltless and loyal Hippolytus, pronounces the breakdown of an optimistic image of the rational individual when he confesses his love to Aricia. He tries to "find himself," as Shakespeare would have said, by introspection into his own nature, but the result is a negative one:

> The fruit
> Of all my sighs is only that I cannot
> Find my own self again.[14]

He can no longer find the naive calmness on which he relied before Theramenes helped him to be true to himself, and he rejects his once optimistic belief that

> Reason did approve
> What Nature planted in me.[15]

Secularization and Love

Many writers have already dealt with the influence of Jansenism and Calvinism on Racine. They have pointed out that his people are, ultimately, helpless; the heroes and heroines are exposed to sinful passions and, presumably, dependent on divine grace. These critics may be correct in their estimate of the religious undercurrents in Racine's work, although it remains open to what extent his late biblical dramas were an intentional concession to the hostility of the clergy. Our interest here, however, lies in the extent to which the roots of Racine's drama emerge from the subsoil of the society of his time. From this standpoint, his characters are truly individuals who are unable or unwilling to control their passions through reason, but who nevertheless are precise observers of their inner states. Whatever the validity of religious interpretations of Racine's work, it remains possible to examine these self-observations against the social background in which they take place. The process of self-articulation becomes the basic content of the drama. The characters look in vain for a way of life that would free them from their misery, and during the genesis and the interplay of the symptoms of their condition they become increasingly aware of their inner conflicts.

Love is the most important theme in Racine's drama. It appears as the great libidinal motor force of the human being, and its range extends from mere instinctual infatuation to steadfast dedication beyond death. *Andromache* could almost stand as a textbook on the subject, including the intertwinement of love and hate. Racine uses the Greek legend to display the psychological effects of a series of unrequited loves. Orestes is in love with Hermione, daughter of the beautiful Helen of Troy. Hermione, however, is engaged to and in love with Pyrrhus, the king of Epirus, who is in love with Andromache, a prisoner from the late Trojan war and the widow of Hector. Orestes is being sent by the Greek states to Pyrrhus to ask for Andromache and her young son, who are the prisoners of Pyrrhus, in order to make sure that the survivors of the Trojan royal house will not become the core of a new Troy and therefore a danger to Greece. Before the journey, Orestes thought that his "passion had been turned to hatred" [16] but discovers when he sees Hermione that he had "never ceased to love her." [17] Pyrrhus, who loves Andromache but is spurned by her, says of his condition:

> I tell you that the heart that can no longer
> Love passionately, must with fury hate. [18]

Hermione, in her love for Pyrrhus, goes through a similar experience. When the nurse Cleone asks her:

Have you not told me that you hated him?

Hermione answers:

Hate him, Cleone? Could my pride do less,
When he neglects my favor, given freely?
The heart I learned to love was treacherous.
He was too dear not to be hated now.[19]

Orestes, bent on winning Hermione, is even willing to
accept hate as a messenger of love. When he berates
Hermione for wasting her affection on Pyrrhus, she answers
that there is no "need" to "envy him," "unless you crave
that I should hate you." But Orestes replies:

Yes,—
For love might spring from such a strange beginning.
I whom you wish to love,—I cannot please you,
But if you wished to hate me, only love
Would be obeyed, and I should have your heart.[20]

Hermione interprets him, correctly, as meaning that her
hate for Pyrrhus is prompted by her love. Her concentra-
tion on this theme through five acts of the play finally brings
her to the psychological state of the *crime passionel* that
culminates in the words:

I will find
Some way to bring me close beside my foe,
To stab the heart I could not reach with love.[21]

The sentiment is remarkably similar to that of Phaedra
when she is thwarted in her passion for Hippolytus:

My hands are ripe for murder,
To spill the guiltless blood of innocence.[22]

Pyrrhus, Orestes, Hermione (and Phaedra) are all in
love with those who do not love them and experience the
counterforce of hate which the situation awakens in them.
The only unambivalent lover is Andromache who is lost in
the memory of Hector, a dead man.

Racine's people are aware of the relaxing of rational con-

trol that passion brings about. The tutor of Britannicus
comments: "Love never waits for reason";[23] Orestes says
at one point: "The voice of reason only wearies me";[24] and
Phaedra declares: "Now you must serve my madness, not
my reason." [25] Such examples—and they could be multi-
plied—do not represent a revival of the old Stoic view of
the opposition of reason and passion; these qualities, rather
than adding up to a formula, give rise to personal insight:
psychic conflicts are raised to the level of awareness.
Racine's people are shown making the kinds of discoveries
about themselves which become increasingly typical in middle-class literature. When Phaedra is reminded by Hippolytus, who has spurned her love for him,

> That Theseus is my father and your husband, . . .

she answers:

> Why should you fancy I have lost remembrance
> And that I am regardless of my honor?

then adds almost immediately:

> I am not half so hateful to your sight
> As to myself.

The same self-awareness is as true for guilt as for love.
Phaedra tells Hippolytus that he should not think:

> That in those moments when I love you most
> I do not feel my guilt.[26]

Later she reasserts, "I know my madness well," [27] in
much the same way as Aricia experiences her affection for
Hippolytus, her political enemy, as "the maddening draught
of love." [28] The very fact that madness and guilt become
almost synonymous signifies the ascension of personal insight over a schematized system of absolute values. (Corneille would have had a neat solution to the love of
Hippolytus for Aricia.) Theramenes, Hippolytus' tutor,
asks him "Why should you fear a guiltless passion?" [29] and
Hippolytus himself reflects that "surely innocence need

never fear," [30] and that "the gods are just." [31] But, in the
end, his mental turmoil gives the lie to these comforting and
reasonable words.

In his character portrayals Racine emerges as a depth
psychologist. Besides the hate-love involvement, he shows
us a number of more subtle effects which sadism and cruelty
may have on love relationships. Nero, who is in love with
Junia, the bride of his enemy Britannicus, makes her a
prisoner in order to separate her from her lover and be
close to her himself. He finds he loves

> The very tears that I had caused to flow.
> And sometimes, yet too late, I asked forgiveness,
> And often found my sighs would end in threats.
> And thus I have been nursing this new passion.[32]

Nero takes pleasure in observing the suffering Britannicus
and tells his old tutor:

> I know quite well my rival has her heart.
> I'll have my joy in making him despair!
> How pleasant is his anguish to my fancy,—
> And I have seen him doubting if she loves him!
> I'll follow her. My rival waits for you,
> And he will vent his fury. Go, torment him
> With new suspicions. Make him pay most dearly
> For boons that he despises. I will witness
> The tears she sheds for him! [33]

Theramenes helps Hippolytus to understand that his love
for Aricia is prodded by the very fact of his father's hate
for the young princess. The tutor says to his master:

> His hatred kindles you to burn, rebellious,
> And only lends his enemy new charms.[34]

In *Britannicus* again, Racine, in another surprisingly
modern touch, notes the extremes of ambivalence in the
mother-son relationship when Nero's mother anticipates his
latent murderous intent:

> Deep in your secret heart I know you hate me.
> You would be free from gratitude's hard yoke.[35]

Poet of Personal Rebellion

Racine is the poet of personal rebellion. His people begin to question the relationship between the *raison d'état* and their own legitimate concerns. The mood of their resistance to their social world is not such a far cry from the revolutionary temper of the eighteenth century as might at first appear. Even the theology, of the secular plays at least, is mainly negative. In passage after passage the gods are cursed; without them and their human counterparts in the state apparatus the individual might, we are made to feel, have a chance. While seventeenth-century man is of course not yet aware of a potential revolutionary situation, Racine's people herald this awareness in their efforts to arrive at a new understanding of themselves.

Public affairs mean little to Racine's characters. Pyrrhus is primarily interested in his own passion; his responsibility for the security of the state or toward his allies in Greece is comparatively irrelevant. He threatens to kill Andromache's son unless she reciprocates his love; if she yields, he will allow the boy, who is also the son of the old archenemy Hector, to live. Similarly, when Phaedra is made to believe that her husband has died and that the Athenians want her to reign in the name of her infant son, she uses this political event for personal ends, as a lure to win the love of Hippolytus (who had also been a candidate for the succession). She instructs Oenone:

> Go, and on my behalf, touch his ambition,—
> Dazzle his eyes with prospects of the crown. . . .
> He shall control both son and mother;—try him,—
> Try every means to move him, for your words
> Should meet more favor than my own could find.
> Urge him with groans and tears,—say Phaedra's dying,
> Nor blush to speak in pleading terms with him.
> My last hope is in you,—do what you will,
> I'll sanction it,—the issue is my fate! [36]

All psychological tactics and all political means are permissible to reach a goal dictated by personal passion. Pyrrhus and Phaedra are extreme examples, but it seems equally clear that the goal for Britannicus is not Rome but Junia, for Hippolytus not Athens but Aricia, and for Orestes it is not the peace of Greek citizens but Hermione. Orestes, when he tries to forget his love for Hermione by taking on political missions, tells his friend Pylades:

> I hoped to find
> Freedom from other cares, in this new work,
> I hoped that, if my strength came back to me
> My heart would lose remembrance of its love.

But this act of submission to the state does no good, and he adds:

> But soon enough
> I found my lovely persecutor taking
> Her old place in my heart.[37]

In Corneille's dramas, when political responsibility falls on the shoulders of one of the heroes he rises to the occasion and eventually frees himself from his individual desires. But in Racine the morality of the state has ceased to be internalized. Phaedra says:

> I reign?—And shall I hold the rod of empire,
> When reason can no longer reign in me?
> When I have lost control of mine own senses? [38]

Another woman, Junia, in *Britannicus*, pronounces the estrangement of the state from genuine human morality in these words:

> Perhaps my frankness may not be discreet,
> But never have my lips belied my heart.
> Since I was not at courts, I had not thought
> That I had need to learn dissimulation! [39]

Speaking to Britannicus she proclaims the need for finding a human home—a home for lovers outside the society that has come to be:

Judge not his heart by yours, for you and he
Pursue two different courses. I have known
Nero and his court but one short day,
Yet I have learned, if I dare speak of it,
How different are their words from what they think;
How little mouth and heart agree in them;
How lightly they betray their promises.
How strange a dwelling, this, for me and you.[40]

The Concept of Fate and the Indictment of the Gods

In the beginning of *Andromache,* Orestes, coming unex-
pectedly upon his friend Pylades, thanks his "fortune" for
this good turn; but, soon after, he asks himself, "Who
knows what fate is guiding me?" [41] Later he says, "I can
never know what fate has ordered." [42] And, again, when
giving a report of his adventures since he returned from
Troy, he speaks of his "persecuting fates." [43] When
Pyrrhus confesses his love to Andromache, he says of her
and Hermione: "Fate brought you both alike into
Epirus." [44] This idea of fate is quite different from that in
Shakespeare, where fate dissolves into the actions of people
and becomes human history. For Shakespeare the world is
man's home, sometimes his hell, but "fate" is always a
consequence of individual actions, moral or immoral, rational or irrational.

Racine's introduction of the idea of fate is not just a
relapse into mythology, but reflects a comparatively open
society in which people meet by chance and are brought
into unpredictable situations by political, social, and economic mobility. Usually, fate appears in a context of governmental affairs; state business is full of traps that can
spring on the individual; even the leaders sometimes become
victims of these traps or at least react ambivalently to a
social order that appears to impose insensible restraints.
The person can only see himself as a victim of the blind
chances of a system he did not create. When Pyrrhus, a

ruling king, explains to Hermione his love for Andromache,
he, paradoxically, becomes the spokesman for the individual
caught between his own needs and the demands of the state:

> My heart accuses me. Its voice is strong.
> I cannot make a plea I know is false.
> I wed a Trojan woman. Yes, I own
> The faith I promise her was given you.
> I could remind you that our fathers made
> These ties at Troy; that we were never asked,
> Nor were we ever bound by any choice
> Or love, that was our own. But I submitted.
> It is enough for me. . . .
>   . . . Until this day
> I thought my oath would hold in place of love.
> Yet love has won, and by a fatal turn,
> Andromache has gained a heart she hates.[45]

The gods as well as the exigencies of the state are blamed
for such conflicts. When Phaedra reveals her love to
Hippolytus she says:

>   . . . The gods will bear me witness,—
> They who have lit this fire within my veins,—
> The gods who take their barbarous delight
> In leading some poor mortal heart astray! [46]

When Theseus finds that both his wife and son have killed
themselves, he cries out:

> The gods are ruthless. They have served me well,
> And I am left to live a life of anguish
> And of great remorse.[47]

The dying words of Hippolytus to his tutor are: "The gods
have robbed me of a guiltless life." [48] Similarly, Phaedra
tells her husband with her last breath:

> The gods had lit a baleful fire in me,
> And vile Oenone's cunning did the rest.[49]

These unhappy people, having lived all their lives within
what seemed to be a well-ordered external and spiritual

world, are finally driven to realize that this world and its deities are not reliable. The cursing of the gods is, to be sure, ambiguous and does not differentiate between a rejection of social forces and the incapacity to solve one's own internal difficulties. This ambiguity suggests the intimate struggles of Racine and other intellectuals of his time, beset as they were by doubts about the stability of both their inner and outer worlds. This doubt is patently present when the gods are blamed for one's own passions, and it emerges unequivocally when they are held accountable not only for personal tragedy but for a bad state of society as such. In a most telling passage, Orestes sums up the state of the world in these words:

> When have the gods been so perverse before,
> Hunting the guiltless down, with crime unpunished?
> I turn my eyes, and everywhere I see
> Troubles and sorrows that condemn their justice.[50]

Corneille's positive theology of the state has given way to Racine's negation of theology by the individual. In the future man must look for other and newer forms of society. If the struggle of Racine's protagonists against power lacks the rationale of a planned campaign, it is nonetheless a declaration of war. Who remains alive when the drama comes to an end? Lonely kings whose wives, fiancées and children have died, and lonely innocent youths near insanity; on the one hand, the brutal Nero, the duped Theseus, the frustrated Pyrrhus—on the other, the heartbroken Aricia and Orestes. The glory of Corneille's empire does not find continuation in Racine, and only broken idols remain to take its place. The sadness of this dramatic configuration is the sadness of separation; historically it sets the tone of the prologue to the drama of emotional emancipation from an aging political structure. Racine gives us our first insight into the dynamics of the men who are about to write those enlightened treatises of the eighteenth century which will denounce the value system of the absolutistic monarchy.

3.

MOLIÈRE (1622-1673)

Dominant Motifs and Philosophical Assumptions

"Experience teaches me," Molière has one of his protagonists say with pride in *L'Avare*,[51] and we soon discover that the familiar adage has a very precise meaning. It is the advice often given to the young man to learn to adapt to the world for his own good; it is as well the motto of the tradesman learning how to get along with his customers. "Experience," we find, definitely means the outside world and particularly the social world; we are taught only by closely observing it, by keeping a watchful eye on its mores and demands. Inner experience appears to be excluded. In fact, Molière intends this exclusion; one who listens too well to his own reason or his own passion is precisely one who does not learn from "experience." The statement also implies a special definition of the world itself. The world one learns about from experience is an evolving structure; it is no longer a ready-made idea as in Corneille, and we can find out about it only by attending to its changing qualities. The expression, we begin to see, sums up an entire morality and way of life: in three words it gives us the rationale of conformism.

Earlier we related Corneille's moral beliefs to the rationalism of Descartes by equating the state with the Cartesian ego. According to Corneille, the individual proceeds step by step to a position of secure knowledge by overcoming any uncertainties he may harbor about the rational essence of an absolutist society; the self-evidence of the rationality of the state is in effect a social extension of the self-evident rationality of Descartes' individual. For the philosophical counterpart of Molière we should have to look to empiricism, to a philosophy that found its ultimate certainty, not in innate ideas, but in sensation or the perception of discrete qualities, which have no guaranteed organization. The progress from Corneille to Molière indeed parallels closely the progress from rationalist metaphysics to empiricism then taking place. Corneille's protagonists take the state and the traditions of absolute monarchy for granted; a society thus grounded assumes an *a priori* and secure rationality. Molière's people, on the other hand, take nothing for granted but what they can observe and test. Experience is the teacher.

Molière for a time was a student of the philosopher Gassendi, an early forerunner of empiricism. In a famous philosophic exchange, Descartes sent to Gassendi, among others, his *Meditations* with a request for critical comments. Gassendi replied in a long letter that concludes with the following remarks:

> These, my good Sir, are the observations that occurred to me in connection with your *Meditations*. I repeat that you ought not to give yourself any thought about them, since my judgment is not of such moment as to deserve to have any weight with you. For as, when some food is pleasant to my palate, I do not defend my taste, which I see is offensive to others, as being more perfect than anyone else's; so, when my mind welcomes an opinion which does not please others, I am far from holding that I have hit upon the truer theory. I think that the truth is rather this— that each enjoys his own opinion; and I hold that it is almost as unjust to wish everyone to have the same belief, as to want all people to be alike in the sense of taste; I say so, in order that you may hold yourself free to dismiss everything that I have said as not worth a straw, and to omit it altogether. It will be enough if you acknowledge my strong affection for you, and do not esteem as nought my admiration for your personal worth. Perhaps some matter has been advanced somewhat inconsiderately, as is only too likely to happen when one is expressing dissent. Any such passage which may occur, I wholly disavow and sacrifice; pray blot it out, and be assured, that I have desired nothing more than to deserve well of you and to keep my friendship with you quite intact.[52]

The passage is quoted at length because it is in many ways a very remarkable document. The philosophic exchanges of the time tended toward extraordinary bitterness; among them this letter is an astounding and exceptional example of tolerance. No adherent of Descartes, Spinoza, or Leibnitz could have written it. The remarks anticipate the concepts of common sense and of compromise in the era of liberalism, and they highlight an attitude that Molière was to take up and develop in his plays.

In his ethics, Gassendi considered the end of human existence to be a state of beatitude that results from a maximum of pleasure and a minimum of misery. Virtue consists of moderation, the absence of extremes, and is fostered by prudence, temperance, fortitude, and justice. Anyone familiar with Molière's plays will feel that these doctrines sound like abstracts of his work. The plays announce no absolute truth. Except for the Misanthrope, no one fights to the bitter end for principles. The dynamics consist of efforts to arrive at an equilibrium in human affairs. The pervading atmosphere is one of optimism and the equilibrium is usually achieved; some people get what they want most, and those who do not (omitting outright scoundrels and the Misanthrope) still are not left in misery at the end of the fifth act.

The analysis of Molière meets with a peculiar difficulty. In the works previously analyzed, it was relatively simple to categorize the value systems of the persons portrayed. But rigid yardsticks are lacking in Molière's people, who are remarkably mundane and who regulate their lives in an experimental, almost pragmatic way. Their orientation shifts as the situation demands it, and they have a multiplicity of motives generic to a pluralist society. What we see is a small aspect of individual behavior—a glimpse of the reality of a highly mobile society—observed through the artist's eyes for the one or two hours the action of the play requires.

The Comedy of Social Tensions

With the exception of the Misanthrope, there is not a single person in Molière's plays who claims the right and the responsibility to create the world in the image of his reason as did the figures of Shakespeare and Cervantes. A completely new tone is evident. Except for a light touch of ritualized deference, no major figure in Molière feels in any way motivated by affairs and ideologies of the state, and except for the Misanthrope no person goes into mourning and despair as a result of alienation from the established mores of society. The characters refer to their concrete experience with the world as a justification for their actions; they even play games that create a laboratory for empirical observation for those who need it. There are no longer such coercive or violent forces as in the literature we have previously discussed. Middle-class society is entering a period of common sense and adjustment.

But the adjustment is not easy. The middle-class individual learns his lessons painfully. Molière's protagonists find themselves in far more difficult social situations than do the heroes and heroines of Shakespeare, Corneille, and Racine. Since they lack any final principle of justification in themselves, they must learn the lessons their society has to offer and for which they have little prior guidance. Tragedy, we begin to see, is only possible if there is at least a potential choice between the ways of the world and the self. If adaptation is shown as difficult but necessary—its manner of achievement perhaps unknown but at the same time the only possible solution—we are in the realm of comedy. We are also in the realm of anxiety, wherein even suicide, as in Racine's *Phaedra,* would be no resolvement and would most often be merely ridiculous. For Molière's people even a noble defeat is out of the question.

The Intermediaries

The tutors and other intermediary persons in Molière's plays differ radically from their counterparts in Racine. In the latter, they serve as spokesmen who mediate between the protagonists and their own inner natures; they have no importance in their own right. In Molière's plays, the intermediaries are themselves protagonists and are the friends or close relatives of the persons they advise. Chrysalde is the friend of Arnolphe;[53] Cléante is the brother-in-law and adviser of Orgon;[54] Philinte is the friend of Alceste.[55] The advisers are never simply catalysts as in Racine; they give outright information and even interfere by direct action where they believe it is needed.

The intermediaries all talk like disciples of Gassendi. They preach moderation and a measured degree of hedonism; they are spokesmen of a reasonably regulated middle-class life, giving duty and pleasure each its due. These advisers are on good terms both with social reality and with the individuals to whom they are close, and by their good offices they bring their friends to similarly good terms. If they reject absolutes of virtue or vice, it is not because they have anything against these positions *per se;* they reject them merely as impediments to good-natured understanding and to the harmonious conformity of the social group. The intermediary figures might well be looked on as model personalities for Molière's time and as prototypes of the era he anticipates. They symbolize the Middle Way, mediation, and compromise, and they pronounce and practice social adaptation and adjustment as the highest virtues.

These mediating figures are central to Molière's work, and the manner in which they are portrayed is of considerable importance. They are never mere colorless bystanders and their behavior is never immoral. Their key motif is the avoidance of any extreme action. They are, in short, *bourgeois* in more than one sense of the word. Cléante warns Orgon, who is victimized by Tartuffe almost to the point of complete ruin:

> You exaggerate again! You never preserve moderation in anything. You never keep within reason's bounds; and always rush from one extreme to another! [56]

Chrysalde warns the aging Arnolphe, who is making a fool of himself by trying to wed a young girl:

> To behave well under these difficulties, as in all else, a man must shun extremes.[57]

Philinte, the friend of the Misanthrope, tries to impress upon him that:

> Good sense avoids all extremes, and requires us to be soberly rational.[58]

These interventions sound, of course, like philistine righteousness, but to interpret their function as humourous would be to misconstrue the dramatic intent; it is not the interveners but the people they are trying to help who become objects of ridicule.

Individual Possibilities and Social Limitations

Molière's protagonists illustrate very specifically the social change that has taken place—the transition from a tradition-bound to an open society which does not prevent its members from engaging in the relatively free development of their idiosyncrasies. True, Molière's highly eccentric types emerge as caricatures and are ridiculed; nevertheless, these extreme cases of behavior are not suppressed by an absolute and universally accepted moral code. If he wants to make an interest in his own health the center of his life, no social agency prevents the Malade Imaginaire from doing so. The Miser can if he wishes focus his whole life on the accumulation of money. The Bourgeois Gentilhomme can spend his money aping the aristocratic style of life without interference from any authority. Finally, Tartuffe, the materialist hypocrite who cloaks his appetites with ascetic virtue, and Alceste, the obsessional moralist who tries to force his precepts on everyone in his environment, are headed for opposite poles of the individualist franchise.

But such apparent liberty is deceptive: if there is less institutionalized coercion, there is certainly no less social pressure. If these people are odd, it is because society sees them as odd or because they fail to understand social reality, and not because there is any individual principle that may be worthy or entirely natural in its own right. Alceste is a Don Quixote who tends to become ridiculous. Man is no longer alone; at the very moment he challenges the reality and reasonableness of the world around him, he condemns himself to passivity, to comic ineffectuality. The more the protagonists maximize their individuality and the farther they remove themselves from the common sense represented by the intermediaries, the farther removed they find themselves from the productive center of human affairs. The intermediaries, on the other hand, accept the normal vicissitudes of social life as the boundaries of a space within which they can develop themselves and fulfill their desires. The pseudoindividualists (since they are caricatures, it is hard to think of them as true individuals) do not meet with heroic failure, which was the fate of Don Quixote and which almost befell Prospero; they are not destroyed but are ignominiously cast aside, left to their own absurdities. Molière's "radicals" are not tragic heroes whose memory is kept alive as a symbol of an ideal or a never-ending task; they are simply consigned to oblivion while the main stream of society goes on about its business. (The Misanthrope remains the special case.)

Moral Experimentalism

Certain basic trends in the relations of the individual to society remain constant: the world is not something given as in the Middle Ages but requires from man an act of continual production; the way in which man should behave is not prescribed by a set of inherited traditions but must be tried out by men themselves. However, these acts of creation and experiment are no longer conceived as the prerogative and responsibility of an unique individual, but as the efforts of socialized persons who act within a framework of consensus and whose behavior is intimately geared to the mechanism of social approval or disapproval.

When Molière uses the word *decorous* he is not referring simply to politeness and good manners; what he has in mind is, broadly, the individual's capacity for right conduct within the sphere of collective conduct. The decorous individual conforms sympathetically and successfully within the social pattern. This is not to say that the display of good form is not in itself of importance as the outward flourish of culture and breeding; but, more essentially, *décor* may be interpreted as the symptom and symbol for a new order in human affairs conceived of as the result of continuous consensus in behavior.

The world has become social practice. Orgon, the victim of Tartuffe, stops being his victim once he has decided to "judge by appearances." [59] True, as he speaks these words he is mistaken, since he believes his son and not Tartuffe to be the real villain; but, when his family helps him to witness a considerably larger piece of reality in observing his own wife's attempted seduction by Tartuffe, he is cured. We see the would-be gentleman of *Le Bourgeois Gentilhomme* being cheated by the worthless nobleman; if he were in the position of the audience to see it (or could be made to), he would be cured of his folly. There are no inner turmoils; everything is clear as day. We the audience have the answers the people on the stage would have if they knew as much as we, or if they looked at what was happening as realistically as we do. Molière gives *us* the reality, and whenever the protagonists appear ridiculous it is because they do not or cannot see it.

If they cannot see it for themselves, they are often made to see it in experimental situations. There is a considerable

difference between the experiments of Shakespeare and
Molière. In Shakespeare they are an arrangement for
proving the individual and his responsibility to himself;
interaction with others does not deny or weaken this autonomy. The truly important phenomena reside in the inner
life, and outer events serve only to confirm them.

In Molière, experiment has a radically different connotation. As the reality of middle-class society is acted out in
his plays, the experiments force this reality to the attention
of his deluded protagonists. The world is seen as consisting
of a rapid series of happenings that are as empirical as the
middle-class world is in its daily practice, and the quick give-
and-take of his people have made his comedies a pleasure
for three hundred years. The extremist protagonists ob-
trude themselves from this background by their lack of
ambience, and the experiments serve to show them their
place. Perhaps rather than "experiments" one should say
"tricks," since they are in the nature of jokes with, however,
the serious purpose of helping the extremists to gain insight
into the median reality of things. (The tricks are, in fact,
often arranged by the intermediaries, who see more of the
real from their central vantage point than the off-center,
half-blinded protagonist can.) In every case, the trick tells
us that if there is no absolute truth, there is always some
pragmatic truth that can be found out empirically.

In *The High Brow Ladies* socially ambitious girls swoon
at lackeys when the latter are dressed as aristocrats. Orgon
is made to hide under the table and watch the scoundrel
Tartuffe flirt with his wife. The faked theft of the
Miser's cashbox proves that Harpagon is only too glad
to trade the pleasures of love for the rewards of monetary
possessions. All the tricks demonstrate that moral reality
is pragmatic and observable and that the values of men are
realized truly and exclusively by their actions. At the same
time, the tricks have a very specific societal connotation:
they are the result of joint decisions. In none of them do
we find a Prospero or a Don Quixote who keep to themselves or find in themselves the reasons for their experimen-

tation. In *The Miser* it is a plot of the children-in-law and their lovers; in *Tartuffe* the trick is the combined effort of Orgon's brother-in-law, the children, the wife, and the maid; in *The High-Brow Ladies* there is an agreement between the two lovers, with La Grange expressing the moral thus:

> We will play them such a trick as shall show them their folly and teach them to distinguish a little better the people they have to deal with.[60]

While the individual seems now to have a multitude of possible ways of behaving, society restrains and limits these possibilities. Molière's plays define these limits by asserting the virtues of discrimination, self-restraint, moderation, and common sense within a social structure that does not impose, so to speak, built-in limitations of its own. In marriage, for example, all combinations of persons seem to be possible. In *The Miser,* Harpagon, the tightwad, wants to marry Mariane who is in love with Cléante, Harpagon's son; Valère's father Anselme wants to marry Elise, the daughter of Harpagon, who is in love with Valère. Similar combinations occur in *Tartuffe* and to an almost absurd degree in *The Misanthrope.* But the resolution always sharply delimits these ambitions and is never absurd. The extremists are shown up as unrealists, the young people are united, and the intermediaries emerge as the true heroes who sometimes, as in *The Misanthrope,* gain personal advantage from their common sense.

The ability to adopt different social roles is also shown to be considerable; the people are able to change roles with astounding ease. The scoundrel Tartuffe appears as a preaching moralist; the upper-class Valère poses as a steward; the woodcutter Sganarelle in *The Physician in Spite of Himself* (*Le Médecin Malgré Lui*) pretends to be a physician; the bourgeois merchant Jourdan trains to become a gentleman of parts. Yet in the end everyone finds himself limited to the role which is appropriate for him in the context of social reality.

The King and the Bourgeois at Home

The comedies obviously presuppose an urban society. Role-playing, trick-playing, a diversity of social contacts, the interplay of the various strata of society—all these characteristics are possible only in cities. The miser, the hypochondriac, the hypocrite would have no field of action if it were not for the wide possibility of anonymous contacts. Scapin, in *Les Fourberies de Scapin,* can only hope to escape from the consequences of his frauds by fleeing to an anonymous crowd. The very possibility of translating the Misanthrope's moral programs into social action ends at the moment Alceste turns his back on the city and retires to the country.

The comedies show very specifically the exigencies of life in an open and mobile society. The aristocrats who come on the scene are shown in a realistic setting, and have hardly any social intercourse with the middle classes. The middle classes furnish the bulk of the protagonists and it is always their ethos that is by far the most influential. The servants, who are accepted partners in the tricks and games, display an astounding amount of middle-class knowledge. While the servants have no real life of their own, they bolster up the atmosphere of the plays and form part of the urban collectivity.

In none of the comedies does the monarch enter the scene. By and large, the people are left to their own affairs. Only when some business seems to get completely out of hand, as in *Tartuffe,* does a representative of high authority appear, but his intervention has no political meaning: Tartuffe turns out to be a criminal and it can be assumed that any high tribunal in France would have prevented his actually carrying out his fraud—while an executive act solves the dilemma of the play, still the king himself remains invisible. The absolute power of the state is no longer the dispenser of moral values as in Corneille, nor the stumbling

block to individual development as in Racine. In Molière
the image of the state is reduced to a mere means of keeping the affairs of men in manageable shape. In his comedies
the bourgeois individual lives, emotionally if not institution-
ally, under a political order whose prime articles are the
virtues of human interaction and the necessity of a middle
course. The greatest praise the King's officer can bestow
on the monarch is to endow him with middle-class qualities:

> Blessed with great discernment, his lofty soul looks clearly at
> things; it is never betrayed by exaggeration, and his sound rea-
> son falls into no excess.[61]

Molière's plays do not exalt the virtues of family life as
the sermonizing novels of eighteenth-century England will
in a succeeding generation, but they nonetheless contain the
family morality in essence. There are many instances of
marital upsets in the plays: Elmire has trouble with Orgon
when he seems to be forsaking his family for Tartuffe; the
wife of the would-be gentleman who is eager to acquire a
titled mistress does not have an easy time of it; and, on a
lower level, Sganarelle, the woodcutter, has spats with his
wife Martine, and Jacqueline, the nurse, has trouble with
her husband Lucas, the servant. But husband and wife are
never locked in a tragic struggle, and the defects that do
arise in marriages are remedied before the plays end. In
fact, the last act usually brings the young couples together
as the final happy solution to the troubles that have been
depicted—in short, the happy ending, modern middle-class
style, according to which the consummation of marriage
leads to unqualified bliss.

Middle-Class Optimism

In the framework of Molière's comedies, death has no
place. Such a solution, when it is ventured at all, becomes
material only for a joke. As Mariane threatens suicide
after her father announces his intention to force her into

marriage with Tartuffe, her maid Dorine answers ironically:

> Very well. That is a resource I did not think of; you have only
> to die to get out of trouble. The remedy is doubtless admirable.
> It drives me mad to hear this sort of talk.[62]

The fool Orgon, in his devotion to Tartuffe, engages in such
absurdities as saying to his brother-in-law:

> I could see brother, children, mother, and wife die, without
> troubling myself in the least about it.[63]

Not even the Misanthrope seriously considers suicide even
though he is the only figure in all the plays who could come
to a tragic end without appearing absurd.

We are at the height of middle-class optimism. Two
hundred years later, an audience will feel self-conscious at
the depiction of the sacrifices an individual must make on
the altar of conformity, and will force Ibsen to change the
ending of *A Doll's House* that had Nora close the door on
her conformist husband. In the age of Molière, the Misanthrope's friends felt they should go after him and bring him
back to his senses, bring him back from his "savage,"
"philosophical spleen" into the life of "ordinary customs"
where we "torment ourselves a little less about the vices of
our age" and are "a little more lenient to human nature." [64]

But even this attitude of optimism is not without its implications of difficulty and instability. The values of conformity contain their own limitations and are precariously
dependent upon the social climate. Only in *The Misanthrope* did Molière come close to an explicit rendering of
the less optimistic side of the relation of his individuals to
the society around them. The issue of Alceste's struggle
must have been pitifully ambiguous for Molière. At bottom, Alceste is made to appear quite right in laying bare
social hypocrisy; on the other hand, he shows himself as
something of a fool for trying so hard. To his creator as
well as to the spectator, Alceste is the comic underdog who
awakens sympathy. Molière seems to express the concern

of the intellectual that as society tends toward the stabilization of its mores and institutions, it becomes increasingly difficult for the creative individual to express himself and defend his individual claims. Molière's problem can easily become, and without much shifting of the terms, one not of adaptation but of alienation.

It may seem odd that Molière should emerge as the poet of middle-class life when, after all, he was part of a flourishing absolutistic state. French monarchy had perhaps never seemed so secure, and European aristocracy still had a long history of political and social privileges ahead of it. Nonetheless the assumption that underlies the plays is the desirability of an integrated society of the middle-class type; more than that, Molière takes for granted that the value system of such a society is already an achieved reality. He takes us beneath the surface facts of political history and shows us the everyday ethos of his time, a reality that is not just an official pronouncement or an extraordinary event. Long before the middle class could think of asking for political power, it had laid a firm hold on the everyday reality of life. It might even be said that this class could more thoroughly go about the business of making everyday reality its own by not worrying about political power. Molière was the reporter of this time of "settling in." He stands at a social crossroad: he sprang from a past of Renaissance individualism; he saw this individualism sharply curtailed in his own time by new social controls; and he sounded a note of prediction for the time when the middle class was to make the world its own on all socially relevant levels.

Chapter V: FROM *WERTHER* TO *WILHELM MEISTER*

With Molière we have reached the threshold of contemporary history: from now on every authentic writer will face the problem of the integration of the individual into society. The keynote of this problem has already been sounded by Alceste; conformity, we see, involves severe limitation. We have come a long way from Cervantes and his Knight, to whom the very notion of conformity was alien as an ideal and as a norm of behavior. Molière's individual operates more or less unwittingly within a middle-class frame of reference and avails himself of middle-class metaphors; in short, what we looked for and found expressed in Molière was the manner in which he manages to codify man's relationship to modern civilization.

I.

INDIVIDUALISM AND THE MIDDLE CLASS

Molière to Goethe

Goethe admired Molière extravagantly and consistently. "I have known and loved Molière from my youth and have learned from him during my whole life," he told Eckermann. "I never fail to read some of his plays every year that I may keep up a constant intercourse with what is excellent."[1]

As late as 1828, as he approached his eightieth birthday, he commented once again on *Tartuffe* and *The Misanthrope* (a play which never ceased to astonish him) in two important book reviews.[2] His particular delight as a dramatist was the *Malade Imaginaire*.[3]

Goethe's own answer to the problem of man's socialization was not nearly so uniform as Molière's, if only because his career as a man of letters in a way served as a
summation of all the social characteristics and tendencies
which had waxed and waned in Europe since the end of
the feudal period. Endowed with the urge to see himself as
the "representative" of the world about him, he expressed
this analogy between his own career and the growth of his
country in a striking phrase: "I am glad," he once told his
ubiquitous interlocutor, "when I was eighteen, Germany
was in its teens also, and something could be done." However he added a sad comment on the increasing social
pressures: "But now an incredible deal is demanded, and
every avenue is barred."[4]

Goethe's position with respect to the individual's place
in the social framework is more optimistic and more pessimistic than Molière's, depending on the stage at which
he is writing. If again Molière's attitude is more consistent than Goethe's, it is only because Molière moved in
a comparatively more settled society than the constantly
changing, eventful social scene in the Germany between
1750 and 1830. Whereas Molière's reactions, for example
his ambivalence, remain steady and predictable, Goethe
spans the whole gamut of conflict with society.

Goethe agrees with Molière in one fundamental respect;
he recognizes the existence of the middle class and its value
system as a *fait accompli*. The nobility which snubs
Werther is a nobility in the final stages of decay. For
Goethe to have said, "I accept the middle class" would
have been rather like Margaret Fuller's "I accept the
universe," to which Carlyle remarked that "she had damn
well better." Goethe no more than Molière could ignore
the conflicting claims of individual development on the one
hand, and collective benefit and decorum, on the other. He
inherited Molière's questions: What price individualism?
What price conformity?

Goethe as a poet conceived of his artistic creation as
"fragments of a great confession"; it was impossible for

him to maintain the position of a calm, observant moderator which characterizes most of Molière's plays. In the various stages of his development, Goethe comes up with different solutions to the problem of the individual's relation to society. He tried ultimately to arrive at a synthesis which would take into account the kinds of social cooperation and integration which occupied Molière, while keeping in mind—as Molière did not always do—the claims of the individual. As a result, he not only recapitulates the history of the individual since the Renaissance; he preserves it.

Goethe: The Political Background

Goethe represents the culminating point in the long tradition which Cervantes began. His position in what was both a backward and a rapidly developing nation gave him a superior vantage point from which to view and connect past and present. If we think in terms of social development, the Germany of Goethe's youth antedated Molière's France; but in his eighty-three years he lived to witness a stage of society far more modern than that which Molière could have envisioned. By the time the middle class came to political power in Germany, the price of adaptation by the individual had become very high. To the end of his life, Goethe hoped for a reconciliation of an optimum growth of the individual and the optimum good of society as a whole, but he became increasingly aware of the dangers threatening such a reconciliation—dangers which later would provide the core of Ibsen's social drama.

It was in Goethe's lifetime, and particularly in the sixty-five years of his maturity (1767 to 1832) that German territories became once again—after almost two centuries of internal division and impotence—partners of some consequence in international political affairs. It was during his lifetime, too, that industrialization in Germany developed rapidly. Roughly in mid-century—with Kant,

Lessing, Wieland, Klopstock—German philosophers and writers entered the mainstream of European intellectual activity; only a decade or two later the German theatre became an important force in the national life. As the middle class extended its sway, Goethe witnessed the rise (as well as its temporary fall in the reactionary era of Metternich) of constitutional government in a number of the petty monarchies. He was cognizant in his work of the several stages of the political development of Germany; at the same time he lived and wrote within a highly sophisticated European civilization. In the end he was able to claim for Germany honorable entrance into "world literature."

Only one significant post-Renaissance development was absent in Goethe's Germany. There is no trace of Corneilleian rationalism and patriotism in Goethe. In France, the national state represented by the Crown had brought a final end to the remnants of feudalism. To the French mind, the monarchy meant unification, peace, and internal progress. To the middle class specifically it meant at least the possibility for expansion, if not for control. The trivial despotism of the many miniscule German states tended, on the contrary, to create an atmosphere of continual revolt, resistance, and depression. By the time the nation was finally unified, there was no longer any need for a symbol of centralization to combat a disorganized feudal structure. The middle classes by then already possessed real, if not nominal, power, and the monarch became increasingly an ally of their control.

Goethe belonged to the eighteenth-century German intellectuals who had little use for the kind of political obstructionism which was prevalent before the middle class gained control. He was no revolutionary on any level; and he certainly was the very opposite of a patriot. But this outspoken lack of national allegiance in him is not really quite all of a piece. When, in *Werther,* he attacks the nominal ruling groups, he is being the young intellectual radical, very intimately in touch with the intellectual currents and sensibilities of his generation. When, in his old age, he grumbles sardonically about "our dear Germans," he is speaking rather more as Nietzsche was to speak fifty years later, from the viewpoint of the good European who is appalled by the perpetual provincialism of what is already a major power-state. The second, far more than the first, is the expression of an artist who feels himself increasingly isolated from his public.

2.

WERTHER: THE DISLOCATED INDIVIDUAL

The Novels Compared

This chapter will be based on a brief examination of *Werther* and both of the *Wilhelm Meister* novels. Goethe's first novel was a product of his early manhood; the second, of his early middle age; the last, of his full artistic ripeness. The novel had by now become the specific art-form of the middle classes; it is no accident that it reached its highest development in the century of the middle class, the nineteenth. As an artistic medium for concerted social thought, the novel will eventually surpass all other genres.

Each of Goethe's novels[5] bears witness to its author's endorsement of the full participation of the individual in society; but the situations by which he enforces this thesis change radically between *Werther* and *Wilhelm Meister*. The first postulates a society which precludes intelligent participation; the second, a society which invites it. In the first, an unenlightened segment compounded of petty despots and antiquated snobs is held up to angry ridicule for its refusal to embrace a sensitive and potentially energetic human being. The tone here is hostile, rebellious, even splenetic; it is very much the work of a young man with an axe to grind. In the second novel, the individual is counselled to give to society the very best his talents have to offer and to abide by its mores.

Significantly, the society Goethe condemns in *Werther* is an outmoded group of small-time aristocrats; the society he celebrates in *Wilhelm Meister's Apprentice Years,* that pedagogic novel *par excellence,*[6] is the society of an increasingly democratized middle class. Hence it is that young Werther, even at his most passive, is always clearly the hero and sounding board of his tale, while *Wilhelm Meister* very strongly conveys the impression that Wilhelm, even at his most active and outspoken, is really less the novel's moving force than is the society which finally absorbs him. While Werther's personality influences and often actually dictates every incident in which he participates—whereby he becomes a prototype of his generation—Wilhelm Meister serves as a kind of blank sheet upon which the various educative forces to which he is exposed leave their impress. Werther acts as an agent while Wilhelm is reagent. Whereas *Werther* is rather narrowly autobiographical, *Wilhelm Meister* is broadly panoramic, cutting across all stratifications of labor and leisure. The difference between the middle class of *Werther* and the middle class treated in *Wilhelm Meister* is the difference between a class whose thoughts and feelings are accessible to the artist without its yet having attained political status and a class which has gained or is well on the way to gaining practical control of the state.

In *Wilhelm Meister's Travels,* the novel of Goethe's old age, sympathies are no longer with the individual in revolt, but with the society to which he is expected to submit. *Werther* argues the case of the dislocated human being; *The Apprentice Years* preaches individual exertion within the existing framework; the *Travels* counsels the subordination of individual claims, whereever these claims are in conflict with the pretensions of society at large (it will be recalled that the latter bears the subtitle *The Renunciants*).

But *The Renunciants* is not really Goethe's final answer, either; it seems more sensible to recognize it as merely another one of several possible solutions, as transitory an answer, in a way, as the answer given in *Werther*. In the long run, "renunciation" is only a relatively more admissible solution than rebellion. Goethe is reported to have said somewhere that "in the end the only thing that counts is progress," and his constant obsession with evolutionary theories, the continual onward-and-upward endeavors of Faust, and the critico-philosophical concept of "heightening" (*Steigerung*) all tend to reinforce the notion that to look for anything like an absolute answer is, to Goethe's way of thinking, to chase a will-o'-the wisp. It is all very well for the individual to "renounce" for the sake of the common good; but in the meantime society-at-large, the community, goes on making mistakes. The middle classes, once having achieved their triumphs, sit back to enjoy them, smoking their pipes and reading their newspapers, addictions which Goethe thoroughly abhorred. In time, they become complacent and frivolous, willing to accept frivolous entertainment complacently; and such a state of affairs threatens stagnation both to the artist and to his audience. Toward the end of his life, Goethe's utterances more and more come to reflect two (not necessarily incompatible) attitudes toward middle-class conformism: an affirmative and a critical one. The latter will be discussed briefly in a final section of the chapter, which touches upon the conflict between the serious artist and mass entertainment.

Let us look first at Werther.

Death of Werther

The Sorrows[7] of Young Werther all but closes with the notation that after the hero's suicide, it was discovered that Lessing's drama *Emilia Galotti* "lay open on his desk." [8] Goethe has frequently been berated for the "psychological" blunder involved in this: no young suicide, runs the argument, is likely to read himself to death with a stern bourgeois tragedy along austere English lines, when there are a thousand sentimental novels to be had for the asking. But Goethe's sociological instinct may have been a good deal sounder than the acumen of his literary interpreters. Werther is engaged in an act of identification: he recognizes in Emilia's catastrophe very much his own situation; both are the victims of an outdated and anachronistic group, the playthings of a decadent despotism. Lessing's play, refining upon his earlier *Miss Sara Sampson* and taking up where Lillo's *London Merchant* left off, provides us with an important clue for an understanding of Werther's motives and responses.

In contrast to the tradition of the French drama, which cloaked contemporary motives in ancient or exotic costumes (Greek in Racine, Roman in Corneille, Oriental in Voltaire), Lessing, in making use of a Roman story, put his characters in modern garb. The fable he adapted was the well-known and often-treated "Virginia" motif, the story of the girl whose father slays her in preference to surrendering her to the dishonorable schemes of a young tyrant. In Lessing's version the petty prince of a petty Italian principality tries to gain the favors of a middle-class patrician's daughter by having her abducted and her fiance murdered. In the end, father and daughter agree that death is her only way out of a life which is shameful and repugnant.

At first sight there seems to be little enough connection between Lessing's play and Goethe's novel. After all, Werther is in love with a decent middle-class girl who, having commitments elsewhere, simply rejects him. There is nothing of seduction or outraged honor here; Werther and Lotte gaze out the window together, watch the raindrops, and sympathetically invoke the name of their favorite poet. The situation is almost the reverse of the situation in *Emilia Galotti*. We have already suggested, in our remarks about Calderon's *Mayor of Zalamea*, that

Lessing's theatre audience and readers were aware of the social implications of *Emilia Galotti;* it was the tyrant who by rights should have felt the dagger's thrust, and though Lessing chose the device of translating his setting from Germany to Italy, it was generally understood that he did so on the grounds of personal security (the same grounds which compelled Schiller to remove the scene of the yet more controversial *Robbers* from his native Wuertemberg a few years later). Emilia consents to her death because the arbitrary and cruel actions of the prince have destroyed all chances for personal happiness. Werther, on the other hand, ends his life because his beloved has become the wife of a solid middle-class citizen. Lessing's tragedy seems to be rooted in the violation of the respected social institution of marriage, while the tragedy of Goethe's hero springs from the maintenance of that very institution.

Since a well-read young man such as Werther could have chosen any number of fashionable fictions to epitomize his action, is the selection of Lessing's drama merely an arbitrary gesture on Goethe's part? We think not. In his introductory remarks to the novel, Werther's friend, writing in the *persona* of editor and literary executor, tells the reader:

> And you, good soul, who are laboring under the same distress as he, draw consolation from his sufferings and, if you should be prevented by fate or your own fault from finding one more intimate, let this little book be your friend.[9]

"By fate or your own fault." The words bring back the problem of Racine: the twofold pressures on the individual stemming from situations over which he has no control and from passions which he is unable to master. The individual's reason is overcome by the turmoil of his psychic life, and harsh social conditions offer no means of reconciling the inner combat. Under such circumstances man is prevented from integrating his capacities and putting them to the service of society. Racine's heroes and heroines must waste their richness and imaginativeness in self-destructive and introverted outbursts, because their social world precludes applying these potentialities to useful and personally gratifying tasks. If such antagonism between political absolutism and the individual can be detected in the restrained language of Racine's characters, hidden behind the garments of the myths he chose, how much more apparent is it in Goethe's stormy novel, which underlines the immediacy of the problem. The conflict between private and public concerns are as inextricably interwoven in *Werther* as they were in Racine. Goethe's device of having Werther read *Emilia Galotti* at the final moment of his life may not have been intended to guide the reader to the innermost meaning of the novel; but it serves to make clear that Werther is more than a pathological specimen of the rejected suitor, while it underscores as well certain societal aspects of the novel.

Werther's Sufferings: Dislocation and Rebellion

When Werther discovers his love for Charlotte (he knows already that she is pledged to another man), he quits her neighborhood to take a job in the service of a high-ranking official, an ambassador. But since the position becomes an impossible one, Werther returns to the region where Charlotte has settled with the man who is now her husband. There Werther lapses into the state of depression which ends with his suicide. During the period in which he is absent from his beloved, a good deal has happened to him; in fact, many of the elements which seem to be involved in his depressed state have nothing to do with Charlotte and are introduced while he is separated from her.

To begin with, Werther profoundly resents the boredom of working for the pedant the ambassador turns out to be. Further, he feels himself hopelessly circumscribed by the snobbery of the aristocratic circles in which he is forced to move. The feelings of anger and frustration at the "odious social conditions" which fetter him reach some kind of climax when, at a party given by a count (himself friendly and approachable), he finds himself snubbed, even insulted, by the "aristocratic company of ladies and gentlemen"[10] who join the party after Werther's private dinner with the host. That Werther chose to remain after dinner was a *faux pas* and one which led to his undoing. In the course of the evening he finds himself pleasantly chatting with a young titled lady. This agreeable moment is interrupted by the girl's spinster aunt, about whom Werther remarks that she has "neither a respectable fortune nor qualities of the mind" and who, in short, "has no support in her old age other than her ancestral tree."[11]

It becomes embarrassingly evident as the evening progresses that he is not accepted or wanted here; finally the host, as tactfully as possible under the circumstances, asks him to leave. The incident rankles; the slight assumes increasing intensity the more he broods on it. What especially aggravates the situation is his recognition, the following day, that he has become a target for gossip among the good middle-class people of the town. He writes:

> And now when I am pitied wherever I go, when I hear those who are jealous of me exclaiming triumphantly that one could see what happened to arrogant fellows who boasted of their modicum of intellect and thought it gave them a right to set themselves above all conventions, and that sort of twaddle—it is enough to make a man stick a knife in his heart.[12]

When again, a day later, he has a chance to talk to the young lady with the dessicated aunt, the girl expresses her sympathies with him and expatiates upon the idiotic customs of her class; she also makes the mistake of apprising him of the malicious gossip about him which is making the rounds among the nobility as well. Werther, in despair, writes now to his friend:

> To hear all this from her lips, Wilhelm, in a tone of sincerest sympathy—I was overcome, and am still raging inwardly. I

wish someone would dare to cast it in my teeth, that I might
thrust his sword through his body! If I were to see blood I
should feel much better.

Oh! I have taken up a knife a hundred times to let air into my
suffocating heart. It is related of a noble species of horses that,
when they are frightfully heated and at their last gasp, they in-
stincively bite open a vein to help them to breathe. I often feel
like that. I would like to open a vein and achieve eternal freedom.[13]

And it is this very same state of mind which the fictitious
editor reports near the end of the book:

He could not forget the rebuff at the embassy. He rarely men-
tioned it, but one could feel imperceptibly that he considered
his honor irretrievably outraged, and that the episode had inspired
him with a dislike for a profession or political activity. He therefore resigned himself totally to the odd emotional and mental
idiosyncracies with which we are acquainted from his letters, and
to a bottomless passion which was bound to cause the eventual
extinction of all his vital energies.[14]

Thus we see that the idea of suicide does not occur to
Werther for the first time toward the end of the novel,
nor is it inspired exclusively by motives of romantic frustration. On the contrary, his first impulse in that direction is
explicitly linked to the rebuff at the embassy. The personal tragedy is rooted in a social tragedy no less than
Emilia Galotti: the tragedy of a young and spontaneous
individual kept from identifying himself productively with
those social instincts and social institutions to which he
might apply his "stormy spirit."[15] In his frustrations
Werther stands as an example of a whole class, the young
German intellectuals and professionals who would like to
work in the political order, but are prevented from doing
so by its obsolete structure. If Werther were really a
precursor of the latter-day bohemian (as literary historians
and critics have often interpreted him), the chances are
that he would never even have got to the point where it
becomes possible for him to be inspired "with a dislike

for a profession of political activity"; he would never to begin with have considered a profession of political activity in the sense of a broadly useful administrative job.

An interpretation of *Werther* as an early species of *épater le bourgeois* has been favored largely by Goethe's somewhat caustic treatment of Werther's successful rival-in-love. In point of fact, the society which Werther castigates at every turn is not the middle-class society of Charlotte and her fiance, for which Werther is actually full of sympathy, but rather the one at whose hands he suffers continual humiliation. His venom is expended on the pedantry and uselessness of his official position and on the shameful slights to which he is exposed when in the company of silly dowager-aristocrats. His letters report in detail the means by which the nobility manage to keep his potential social usefulness and social freedom in check. Werther's problem is not one of having been born maladjusted but of having maladjustment thrust upon him. He is forced by his profession into the company of the nobility; he is rejected by them as an undesirable. At the same time, the middle classes sneer at him for being a careerist (and not a successful one at that). He finds no milieu in which he can assert himself productively. In a later period Balzac's Rastignac might have enjoyed such a milieu; but in Werther's time, social action and social decor are still determined by the nobility.

As a consequence of social rejection, Werther is thrown back onto an institution with which he should not have come into conflict, the family. In fact, Werther is profoundly and instinctively drawn to family mores and ideals. Whenever Goethe shows him to us within the tableau of family life, the picture is of the utmost charm (and incidentally, Goethe was an enthusiastic admirer of Goldsmith's *The Vicar of Wakefield* [16]). Any number of passages in the novel attest to Werther's dedication to the family ideal; he is full of admiration for its structure and for the substance which it lends to the lives of both sexes and of various generations. To him the family is the backbone of middle-class life; it

supports and provides a refuge for the individual when all
else has failed.

If Werther had not been rejected by an antiquated social
group filled with clannish prejudices and invoking senseless
privileges, and if the state bureaucracy had not made it impossible for him to put his abilities to constructive use,
there would have been no tragedy in the first place. Werther's suicide articulates the same protest which the death
of Emilia Galotti articulates—in each case a decidedly social one: a protest against the mores and nostrums of a
tyrannical, petty, useless, and superseded society.

3.

WILHELM MEISTER: THE INTEGRATED INDIVIDUAL

Germany's Theatrical Mission

That Goethe's hero in his final moments reads a play
(rather than some other literary form) is probably more
than accidental. For the drama was the one available public
platform for the German middle class in the eighteenth century. Unlike England with her highly developed industrial
and commercial economy and her copious literary outlets,
and unlike France whose progressive aristocratic and middle-class intellectuals tended to make common cause to their
mutual benefit, Germany permitted her middle class virtually no voice in either practical or intellectual matters. The
theatre provided the conspicuous exception. One could almost write a social history of the eighteenth-century German middle classes by tracing their various attempts to
create permanent theatrical organizations (Lessing's early
effort to make the Hamburg theatre a national institution is perhaps the most notable of these efforts).

The theatre provides an excellent medium for the display
of interacting social forces. By definition a drama presents

a pluralistic world; it is hardly ever limited to a single person and seldom to a single institution, and usually ranges over many individualities and the social meanings of which they are the bearers. Further, the final act with its aura of human continuity lacks the inflexible finality and definition which the ending of an epic poem or a novel tends to convey. The play, by its very nature an imitative representation of life, can more easily be connected with reality itself; there is, in short, more "carry-over." Great dramatists from Corneille and Racine to Lessing and Goethe were well aware of this. They agreed that the moral message of drama may be continued in the life process of the audience, whose catharsis results from the re-enactment of conflicts between the individual and society. The dramas of the Storm-and-Stress period—which so often portrayed a character broken but not destroyed, bloody but unbowed, in a hostile political and social climate—were eloquent statements on behalf of the individual's interest; and in reading *Emilia Galotti,* Werther speaks symbolically for a generation of Werthers.

Wilhelm's Apprenticeship: Integration and Assent

The first volume of *Wilhelm Meister,* the novel on which Goethe began work after completing *Werther,* bore in its original version the title *Wilhelm Meister's Theatrical Mission.* The version which found its way into print was published as *Wilhelm Meister's Apprenticeship,* and it is centered in the theatre both as an institution and as a way of life. The book is largely concerned with extensive interpretations of plays, above all those of Shakespeare, especially *Hamlet.* Werther merely reads a play preparatory to dying; Wilhelm is educated in the theatre, helps to produce plays, stage them, act in them, elucidate them. Wilhelm Meister's apprenticeship to the theatre is his apprenticeship to life.

The literary artist deals with the individual's development of his inner capacities. In the Germany of the 1780's, one solution to the problem of self-realization was to act out, in the theatrical meaning of the term, one's personality. In our time, psychologists have often helped disturbed persons by having them act out, mainly in the form of playlets, their anxieties and concerns; the result has frequently been a vast increase in self-awareness, even self-confidence. We might say that the German theatre of 150 years ago was the psychodrama of the healthy middle class, who resorted to this means of awakening to the decay of their political and social environment, which had become as obsolete as the seventeenth-century Spanish monarchy had been in its time. In *Wilhelm Meister's Apprenticeship,* Goethe describes this experience in a variety of ways. Particularly interesting are the double aspects which the experience tends to assume. On the one hand, the individual uses the theatre as refuge from obsolete political and social tyranny; on the other, the theatre portrays a burgeoning civilization that cannot be prevented from coming to full fruition.

At one point in the *Apprenticeship,* Goethe describes the staging of a play in which a peasant and a miner argue the comparative merits of their respective occupations, and the necessity for their productive cooperation is portrayed. After the performance, Wilhelm (himself the son of a well-to-do businessman with widely ramified commercial interests) and his friends (most of them professional actors) discuss the play, and Wilhelm suggests that responsible government officials as well as the population-at-large might well look upon the theatre as an experimental situation of instruction.

Referring to the discussion between the miner and the peasant, Wilhelm asserts:

In this little dialogue we have a lively proof how useful the theatre might be to all ranks; what advantage even the state might procure from it, if the occupations, trades, and undertakings of men were brought upon the stage, and presented on their praiseworthy side, in that point of view in which the state itself should honor and protect them. As matters stand, we exhibit only the ridiculous side of men: the comic poet is, as it were, but a spiteful tax-gatherer, who keeps a watchful eye over the errors of his fellow-subjects, and seems gratified when he can fix any charge upon them. Might it not be a worthy and pleasing task for a statesman to survey the natural and reciprocal influence of all classes on each other, and to guide some poet, gifted with sufficient humor, in such labors as these? In this way, I am persuaded, many very entertaining, both agreeable and useful, pieces might be executed.[17]

Wilhelm Meister stands on the borderline between conformity and individual protest; it is this medial position which makes the novel a particularly important document for us. Despite the bustle of artistic and theatrical activities, one senses both the urge and the capacity to turn to the serious business of the real world. Goethe is constantly reminding us that the theatre is all very well, very useful, a handy reflector of larger issues, but that the issues themselves lie elsewhere, in the real activities of men, in society itself.

That is one side of the ledger. The other is expressed by Wilhelm himself. His friend Werner has just complimented him by letter on his increasing understanding of how to handle the affairs of the world side by side with his growing acquisition of statistical, technological, and rural knowledge. Wilhelm protests. As a true member of modern society, he recognizes only one goal: the perfection of his individuality. The rest are trappings, embellishment, ways of filling out the "well-rounded personality."

> To speak it in a word, the cultivation of my individual self, here as I am, has from my youth upwards been constantly though dimly my wish and my purpose. The same intention I still cherish, but the means of realizing it are now grown somewhat clearer.[18]

To a degree not hitherto encountered in our studies, the artist-hero self-consciously interprets his dilemma in terms of social conditions. What Werther blurted out in a highly emotional manner is now formulated by Wilhelm as a dignified and discriminating credo:

Being a simple burgher, I must take a path of my own; and I fear it may be difficult to make thee understand me. I know not how it is in foreign countries, but in Germany, a universal, and, if I may say so, personal, cultivation is beyond the reach of anyone except a nobleman. A burgher may acquire merit; by excessive efforts he may even educate his mind; but his personal qualities (*Persoenlichkeit*) are lost, or worse than lost, let him struggle as he will.[19]

In Molière's plays the development of individuality is discussed solely in terms of the middle class, imitation of the aristocracy being shown as absurd (e.g., *Les Précieuses Ridicules, Le Bourgeois Gentilhomme*) and aristocratic characters tending to become conspicuously vapid; in this respect, Molière appears to represent a rather more advanced stage of society than does Goethe, if one is to judge by the foregoing words of Wilhelm. Later, Wilhelm goes on to explain:

Perhaps the reason of this difference [between burgher and nobleman] is not the usurpation of the nobles, and the submission of the burghers, but the constitution of society itself. Whether it will ever alter, and how, is to me of small importance: my present business is to meet my own case, as matters actually stand; to consider by what means I may save myself, and reach the object which I cannot live in peace without.[20]

As a modern individual trying to "find himself" he is not content with a statement of the facts involved but is oriented rather toward the specific ways open to him for overcoming the obstacles of his society. This assertion of his individuality is thus to him the very essence of middle-class existence:

This harmonious cultivation of my nature, which has been denied me by birth, is exactly what I most long for . . . My inclination to become a public person, and to please and influence in a larger circle, is daily growing more insuperable.[21]

Well, what is left for somebody who wants to be a "public person" and at the same time is interested in "poetry and all that is related to it"? The answer is a foregone conclu-

sion and is given by the very context in which the question
is put: it is the theatre. In the theatre alone a person may,
be able to find all the modes of expression which he craves
and which society otherwise prevents him from realizing:

> Thou seest well, that for me all this is nowhere to be met with
> except upon the stage; that in this element alone can I effect
> and cultivate myself according to my wishes. On the boards a
> polished man appears in his splendor with personal accomplish-
> ments, just as he does so in the upper class of society; body and
> spirit must advance with equal steps in all his studies; and there
> I shall have it in my power at once to be and seem as well as
> anywhere.[22]

Dependence on Society

All these protestations notwithstanding, Goethe's version
of individualism is a far cry from that espoused by the
Renaissance. In *Wilhelm Meister's Apprenticeship* it is apparent that the complaints of Goethe's people include a
heavy admixture of the urge to "belong." The theatre itself
is a collaborative enterprise, in which the individual can display his creative strength only by joining himself to other
people in idea and in practice. Goethe reiterates the basic
post-medieval theme which asserts the re-creation of the
world out of man's activity. One of the revered figures in
Goethe's novel serenely defines man's task as that of structuring and restructuring reality for himself:

> Life lies before us, as a huge quarry lies before the architect:
> he deserves not the name of architect, except when, out of this
> fortuitous mass, he can combine, with the greatest economy and
> fitness and durability, some form, the pattern of which originated
> in his spirit. All things without us, nay, I may add, all things on
> us, are mere elements; but deep within us lies the creative force,
> which out of these can produce what they were meant to be, and
> which leaves us neither sleep nor rest, till, in one way or another,
> without us or on us, that same have been produced.[23]

Elsewhere this statement is extended to show that the creative personality is constituted in and through the social task. Wilhelm is advised by another one of his preceptors:

> It is all men that make up mankind, all powers taken together that make up the world. These are frequently at variance; and, as they endeavor to destroy each other, Nature holds them together, and again produces them . . . Every gift is valuable, and ought to be unfolded. When one encourages the beautiful alone, and another encourages the useful alone, it takes them both to form a man.[24]

In the continuation of the *Apprenticeship* which Goethe wrote in his old age under the title *Wilhelm Meister's Travels,* it is made even more clear that the individual becomes worthy of the name only through useful production and successful integration into society. He must find his way by limiting his desires and adjusting them to the needs of society; and Goethe could not have given expression to this law more succinctly than he did in subtitling the novel *The Renunciants.* It is only at this point that Wilhelm ceases to be the *Lehrling* and becomes truly the *Meister* of reality.

In Goethe's time, the fulfillment of the individual by his reconciliation to society is the prevailing motif. It will take fifty more years for the less optimistic aspects of the individual's social integration to become fully apparent. A plot analysis would show that in every drama of Goethe (and of Schiller as well) the conflicts premised in the first act find in the final act a resolution within the greater whole of society, whether in a real or an idealized form. This is as true of *Faust,* in which the aging philosopher experiences his greatest happiness in cultivating fallow soil for the good of mankind, as it is of *Don Carlos,* in which the attempted assassination of the tyrant anticipates, in imagination, the idea of the people freed from the yoke of absolutistic arbitrariness. Behind all the sadness which pervades the drama of German classicism is hidden a deep confidence in commonly shared virtues and values. The Marquis Posa demands "freedom of thought"; Iphigenia wants "friendship," "friendliness";

and in their context these are both middle-class articulations, the one avowedly political, the other communal and humane.

4.

WORLD LITERATURE AND POPULAR CULTURE

Artistic Integrity

To a very considerable degree, the idea of "world literature" (the phrase is Goethe's) was for him and his fellow intellectuals an ideal of a community of creative minds. Goethe's intimate knowledge of Molière in particular helped him to arrive at a concept of intellectual and professional continuity. Such identification with past writers, and above all past dramatists, was facilitated by the theatre, which— as we have noted earlier—functioned as a particularly suitable intellectual middle-class institution in Germany.

Goethe was inclined to identify the personal circumstances of the literary artists of the past with his own as a professional man of letters. In an earlier period Cervantes experienced acute difficulties in trying to confer an appearance of respectability upon the role of the artist as a useful member of society, and Racine and Molière in their private life had considerable trouble with the Court and the Church. Goethe —ignoring the role of patronage by the Court and the nobility—thought of Molière primarily as a success in a commercialized economy. In a conversation with Eckermann he referred to both Shakespeare and Molière approvingly as professionals who by their literary activities had made a living. In this respect he was disposed to share Dr. Johnson's impatience with writers who condemned an interest in earning money as a slur upon their artistic integrity. Goethe went on to speak of Shakespeare and Molière as useful and successful members of a social order, and he referred to them as principal witnesses for his own social philosophy which he espoused in *Wilhelm Meister's Travels.* Speaking of the problem of patronage for the theatre, he commented:

> For if a theatre is not only to pay its expenses, but is besides to make and save money, everything about it must be excellent. It must have the best management at its head; the actors must be of the best; and good pieces must continually be performed, that the attractive power required to draw a full house every evening may never cease. . . . Even Shakespeare and Molière had no other view. Both of them wished, above all things, to make money by their theatres. In order to attain this, their principal aim, they strove that everything should be as good as possible, and that besides good old plays there should be some clever novelty to please and attract. The prohibition of *Tartuffe* was a thunderbolt to Molière; but not so much for the poet as for the director Molière, who had to consider the welfare of an important troupe and to find bread for himself and his actors.[25]

Goethe was particularly fond of Alceste, Molière's Misanthrope. In a book review written late in life he describes Alceste "as the genuine human being." [26] Not without significance, Goethe used almost the same expression to describe Molière: "a genuine man; that is the proper term." [27] In the same year in which his review of *The Misanthrope* appeared, he wrote to his friend Zelter:

> The French themselves are not quite clear about the Misanthrope; now Molière is said to have modeled him on a certain rough courtier; now to have described his own person. To be sure, he had to wrench all that out of his own bosom; he had to describe his own relations to the world; but what relations! The most general imaginable. I'll wager that you've caught yourself in the act in more than one place. And are you not playing the same role against your contemporaries?'[28]

As Molière had left it indefinite whether he personally championed the rebel Alceste or the level-headed conformist Philinte, Goethe, too, in taking up and explicitly developing Molière's formulation of the moral dilemma of the intellectual, left unanswered whether the cultivated individual could entirely "find himself" by becoming a useful contributor to society. At the same time Wilhelm Meister becomes a symbolic figure of responsibility on the model of the industrious burgher, he voices concern lest the individual's gifts be leveled off by the social threats of compromise. Alceste was for Goethe a symbol of this social tension which he had found in "world literature":

> Earnestly contemplate *The Misanthrope* and ask yourself whether a poet has ever represented his internal being more completely and gracefully. We would fain call the substance and treatment of the play tragic; such, at least, has been the impression it has ever left upon us; for what is here brought to our view and our intelligence is just what often drives us, like him, from the world.[29]

And again:

> Here is represented the genuine human being who, having attained to considerable education, has yet remained natural and would like nothing better than to remain as true to and thorough with himself as with others; we see him, however, in conflict with the social world, in which one cannot get along without dissimulation and superficiality. Compared with him, Timon is no more than a comic subject.[30]

It is no longer a Werther that Goethe is thinking about fifty years later, when writing still, as in his youth, about "the genuine human being . . . in conflict with the social world." The motivation has now been reversed: Werther was driven to despair because society was closed to him; in the oncoming expanding and expansive nineteenth century, society opened its doors to all energetic Werthers. In this situation the artist begins to recognize that the price of identification with society can be as high as that of resistance; in fact, it may constitute an even graver, because more subtly precarious, danger to his individuality. Against a rotten society or social class, the artist is free to inveigh with a clear conscience. But what about a society which works to all appearances for the benefit of all its members and yet manages, by subtle influences, to poison the artist's work, to pit against a fine craftsman its own criteria of excellence, and thus to compel his consent and his conformism, precisely because the social milieu seems favorable to artistic autonomy? Onto Molière's Alceste, Goethe projects these difficulties—the difficulties of the avant-garde artist—and his concept of Alceste anticipates the non-conformist of later generations whose moral, artistic, or political convictions remove him to the garret, the ivory tower, or the barricade.

Also, in the conversation with Eckermann, in which Goethe characterized Molière as "a genuine human being," he indicated that the time had come when the artist would no longer be listened to as the principal intellectual spokesman for his generation. His remarks point to a condition we have since learned to live with, the defensive position of the arts under the impact of marketable products of popular culture. Goethe speaks bitterly of "the weak, sentimental, gloomy character of modern productions"; more specifically he observes:

> There is nothing distorted about him [Molière]. He ruled the manners of his day; while, on the contrary, our Iffland and Kotzebue allowed themselves to be ruled by theirs, and were limited and confined in them. Molière chastised men by drawing them just as they were.[31]

The writers alluded to here were mass producers of sentimental tragedies which enjoyed a tremendous vogue among theatre-going audiences all over the country. In contrasting these facile fabricators of popular entertainment with Molière, Goethe nostalgically formulates a problem which is central to a sociology of literature. Mass production comes into being as an easy propitiation of mass taste. But only insofar as the literary artist "rules" the manners of his day—that is, only insofar as he expresses the legitimate concerns of the individual in his encounters with the world—will he remain a reliable source for the understanding of a period. The moment he allows himself to be ruled by the fashionable manners, the exemplary role of his art will be in constant danger of being relegated to the margins of society. Hereafter the alternatives are whittled down to the two extreme types: *l'art pour l'art* for the élite; railroad

literature (as John Ruskin would have called it) for the
rest.

Threats from Below: "The Prelude on the Stage"

The gravity with which Goethe viewed the problem raised
by encroaching mass entertainment is reflected in the super-
ficially amusing but essentially serious "Prelude on the
Stage" to *Faust*. The prelude deals with the question as to
whether and to what extent an artist might make concessions
to the taste of the populace and to its predilection for mere
entertainment and passive relaxation. The piece is presented
in the form of a dialogue between the theatre Manager, a
cynical and caustic fellow, and the Poet, a slightly sardonic,
though sympathetic, caricature of the eternal malcontent.
The issue is the character of the works to be presented to
the public. The Manager, who is interested only in box
office receipts, has some definite ideas about "art," as mana-
gers always have. For him the secret of success is quite
simple: "a hash, a stew—easy to invent" will do the trick.
The public, he observes with a cynical shrug of the shoul-
der, is quite stupid, and its favor is won easily enough by
the simple expedient of "sheer diffuseness":

> Only by mass you touch the mass; for any
> Will finally, himself, his bit select.

When the Poet objects that "such a trade debases," and
that to produce "botching work" is inconsistent with the
artist's pride and love of truth, the Manager invokes the
age-old principle that the end justifies the means, that form
and content must be adjusted to the audience:

> A man who some result intends
> Must use the tools that best are fitting.[32]

The poet is compelled to cater to popular taste, says
the Manager. People come to the theatre bored, exhausted,
or, worst of all, "fresh from reading the daily papers."
They come "as to a masquerade": their sole motive is curi-

osity, or, in the case of the ladies, to display their finery. He invites the Poet to take a look at his patrons' faces: "The half are coarse, the half are cold."

> Why should you rack, poor, foolish bards,
> For ends like these, the gracious Muses?
> I tell you, give but more—more, ever more . . .[33]

The dialogue reveals a deep-seated change from earlier discussions concerning the cleavage between art and entertainment—from the justification of the one in terms of the other, which had been the court of final appeal to every artist after Horace. To writers such as Montaigne and Pascal, for example, it was axiomatic that entertainment furnish a means of satisfying the need to escape from inner suffering —a need to be gratified (on a high artistic plane), according to Montaigne, or to be denied gratification in favor of spiritual pursuits, according to Pascal. Here in *Faust* we find the discussion divested of its moral and religious overtones, and new components are introduced: a consciousness of the manipulative factors inherent in entertainment; the role of the business intermediary between artist and public, whose criterion is success and whose goal is merely economic; and a sense of conflict between the needs of the true artist and the fickle wishes of a mass audience. The Manager as much as says that the audience can be made to swallow anything, so long as they get quantity and variety, and he attempts to convince the Poet that the audience is so much putty in his hands. At the same time, the Manager does not advise the Poet to give his audience variety on the grounds of a Montaigne—that it is psychologically wholesome— but because by providing something for everyone, variety insures financial success. Similarly, when the Poet resists the Manager's exhortations, he does not do so in the name of Pascalian, transcendental values, but in terms of the specific mission of an artist.

Goethe on His Audience

Goethe foreshadows modern criticism of organized entertainment when he complains of the restlessness, the continuous desire for change, novelty, and sensationalism which characterized his contemporary audience. "The theatre," he says, "like the world in general, is plagued by powerful fashions," and fashions (we would call them fads) consist in pursuing an object with abandon one minute, only to "ban it later forever." [34]

Not only the theatre, full of the plays of Iffland and Kotzebue, reflects this absurd restlessness; it is evident, too, in the newspaper craze for which Goethe reserves his special venom.

> We have newspapers for all hours of the day. A clever head could still add a few more. This way everything—whatever everybody does, wants, writes, even what he plans, is publicly exposed. One can only enjoy oneself, or suffer, for the entertainment of others, and in the greatest rush this news is communicated from house to house, from town to town, from empire to empire, and at last from continent to continent.[35]

This restless urge for novelty would not have disturbed Goethe so much if it did not effectively prevent the kind of ripening which is essential to the creative process; in the constant reading of newspapers, one "wastes the days and lives from hand to mouth, without creating anything." [36] The artist abhors distraction on principle; and the newspapers constitute a particularly vicious form of distraction, because the sheer number of trivia which the reader is asked to assimilate day after day spells death to the synthesizing and generalizing faculties of the mind. Goethe congratulates himself on lacking all curiosity concerning these literally fruitless and stagnant miscellanies; he reports somewhere that he has just glanced through a five-year-old volume of newspapers, and is struck again by the total essential vacuity inherent in so much idle plenitude. "I have time only for the most excellent," [37] he remarks in another place, to explain why he has stopped reading Sir Walter Scott.

Another trait which Goethe noticed in the modern audience was its complete passivity. The audience, as he put it, is "soft wood given for splitting." They want to be given their money's worth of pleasure, but as for the message of a play, they have no real interest in that at all. Instead, they "throng into the theatre unprepared, they demand what they can enjoy directly. They want to see something, to wonder at something, to laugh, to cry . . ." [38]

And finally Goethe objects to the degree of conformism which he notices everywhere. He hints at the conformist urge of the public in his ironical remarks on the fashion display of theatre-goers, and he anticipates Tocqueville and other social critics (Toennies in Germany, Ward and Cooley in America, and above all, Karl Kraus in Austria) in his comments on the role of the newspapers as promoters of social conformism, rather than as outlets for truth: the so-called free press, he remarks frequently, is in fact contemptuous of the public; everything is acceptable except dissenting opinion.

> Come let us print it all
> And be busy everywhere;
> But no one should stir
> Who does not think like we.[39]

The art which appealed to the public's appetite for distraction was for Goethe not generically different from esoteric art, but merely "botching work." His characterizations of such esthetically inferior products anticipate another of the many elements of the modern critic's description of the popular art produced for the mass media. Inferior art, he suggests, aims only at entertainment. Thus he makes a distinction not between types of art, but a distinction on the basis of audience effect. He wrote to Schiller:

> The public in a big city . . . lives in a perpetual turmoil of acquisition and consumption. . . . All pleasures, even the theatre,

are only supposed to distract, and the strong affinity of the reading public to periodicals and novels arises out of the very reason that the former always and the latter usually bring distraction into distraction.[40]

He was not unsympathetic with the desires of the audience to be entertained, but he condemned those who capitalized on such desires by offering cheap wares. Although "everyone who fools the public by swimming with the current can count on his success," [41] he felt nevertheless that the bad taste of the public was to some degree the producer's fault. Supplied only with shoddy art, or what passes for art, the public might finally be reduced to shoddy thought as well.

The several stages of the issue of individualism versus conformism are reflected in Goethe's writings. At the outset of his career as a man of letters, in his *Werther* period, we find Goethe looking backward to the petty despot who stifles the individual's creative energy; this is the Storm-and-Stress Goethe, holding up to his generation the creative individual kept in check by a ruling group for whom the German intellectuals never had much use to begin with. During his middle years, in *Wilhelm Meister's Apprenticeship,* Goethe, to be sure, straddles the fence; if the individual is no longer the rebel, the reasons are largely that the grounds for rebellion are waning. During his entire career Wilhelm Meister proves to be the very suitable paradigm of the middle classes by professing his chief ambition to be the "cultivation of my individual self"; he is indeed an appropriate spokesman of his social group during a period of transition in the acknowledgment that this cultivation "is nowhere to be met with except upon the stage," as long as other public platforms are not yet available. As Goethe grows old and as the political, social, and cultural predominance of the middle classes becomes clearly established, he grows more and more suspicious of all personal exertion which is not rooted in the desire to benefit the commonweal; wherever individual action threatens to be in conflict with social action, it is the individual's duty to renounce. It has been said that "renunciation" is Goethe's life-long theme, as "freedom" is Schiller's, but "renunciation" may, after all, take an infinite number of forms; and the renunciants of *Wilhelm Meister's Travels* specifically subdue their private desires to the public welfare.

Yet this adulation of the commonweal was not Goethe's final word. He felt more and more uneasy about the climate of complacency which had set in. What earlier had been productive energy and creative ability had become an incessant urge to be amused, distracted, titillated. And once more Goethe's voice is heard, this time against the prevailing disposition to conform—to conform with what by now threatened to become cheap and suspect, devoid of intellectual content. Now the laws of decorum have been tossed to the winds of fashionable doctrine; and every fresh production bears the impress of its own mortality. The Philistine had entered, and in his old age Goethe pointed the way to the critical position that was to become Matthew Arnold's: "Culture works differently." If he became increasingly humane, Goethe also became increasingly exasperated, and to the facile conformists of his day he might have flung back Alceste's haughty phrase:

> I like to be distinguished; and, to cut the matter short, the friend
> of all mankind is no friend of mine.[42]

Chapter VI: HENRIK IBSEN
(1828-1906)

In the latter half of the nineteenth century, the institutions as well as the mores of society have come completely under the control of the middle class, and its ethos is challenged only by a handful of European artists and intellectuals. English utilitarianism now states this ethos of unmitigated progress in the most optimistic form conceivable: the good of the individual is identical with the good of society.

Ibsen is a true liberal. Nonetheless he emerges as one of the most severe critics of his age. He followed Lessing's advice to make the theatre a moral testing ground, but while Lessing had used his esthetic precepts to advocate social conditions which would permit the freer development of the individual, Ibsen, a century later, used the same principles to question whether these conditions had been met. The stage becomes a tribunal in which society is defended by its ideology and prosecuted by its reality. The characters (dynamic often to the point of self-contradiction) try by every available means to achieve the success and happiness that liberalism has promised them. The outcome of the trial is unequivocal: the sentence is to be found in the social meanings of the defeats the protagonists suffer.

This indictment and trial was intentional. Ibsen wrote in one of his letters:

> . . . a man shares the responsibility and the guilt of the society to which he belongs . . . to *write* is to summon one's self, and play the judge's part.[1]

The concern of writers with the relation of the individual to society had for some time been deliberately invoked as a weapon—first of defense, and then of attack—against the aristocracy and reactionary monarchies which at least until

1848 remained a threat in Europe. But now this social consciousness is used to examine and judge the middle-class world itself.

I.

PRIVATE LIFE AND SOCIAL FORCES

Liberalism conceives of society as a more or less elastic system whose function is to make possible the individual's pursuit of happiness. Ibsen appears to share this attitude. He does not write "social drama." Specific social, political or economic questions are touched upon only occasionally, as in *An Enemy of the People,* or *Pillars of Society.* Hardly ever does a policeman, soldier or other public official appear. The state seems to be reduced to the role of a night watchman. Official institutions appear only in such incidental business as the report of the prison sentence of old Borkman in *John Gabriel Borkman,* or as the threats of Dr. Wangel to call in the authorities against the Stranger in *The Lady from the Sea.* The scenes of Ibsen's plays are usually laid in the home, and the dialogue tends to be limited to the problems of the private person.

Here, however, we find the key to Ibsen's social concepts. He indicts society in the area of its strongest claims by allowing the prevailing social philosophy every opportunity, especially in the field likely to be most conducive to a favorable judgment: in the sphere of private life where the individual can reveal himself freely. And this revelation shows man as the focal point for contradictions that originate in the society.

Public and private interests of the protagonists are portrayed as being inevitably irreconcilable. Energies available for use in public affairs deteriorate as soon as private needs and desires come into play. Solness, the Master Builder of churches and settlement houses, finds his only happiness in friendship with a young girl, whereupon he becomes completely lost in his dreams. The sculptor Rubek confesses to an emotional crisis when

> all the talk about the artist's vocation and the artist's mission and so forth began to strike me as being very empty, and hollow, and meaningless at bottom . . . Yes, is not life in sunshine and in beauty a hundred times better. . . ? [2]

Allmers (in *Little Eyolf*) abandons his book, his great calling, to dedicate himself to the education of his son, little Eyolf, in order to "perfect all the rich possibilities that are dawning in his childish soul." [3] These either-or attitudes are products of the isolation of the spheres of life. Not only does the pursuit of happiness in one realm require neglect of human obligations in every other, but even voluntary withdrawal from society cheats the individual of the happiness he seeks. The Master Builder never erects his dream castle but falls to his death from a real tower. The sculptor Rubek's (in *When We Dead Awaken*) original zest for life and art is lost in the tedium of a banal marriage. Eyolf's father is tortured by his unproductive existence, as well as by the jealousy of his wife and finally by the death of his child. Whether man turns to private or public life, as soon as he begins to develop his potentialities in one he runs into conflicts and frustrations in the other.

Ibsen's portrayals thus follow a pattern. A person starts out with the expectation of fulfillment. Then he finds himself involved in a series of conflicts and troubles which almost always bring ruin to him and force him to injure others. The result is solitude, death, or worse still, the announcement of social programs that have been thoroughly discredited by what has gone on before. Mankind is trapped in a cycle of unattainable hopes and real suffering.

Ibsen's dramas display a virtual catalogue of failure—in daily life, in the professions, in the arts, in marriage, in friendship, and in communication between the generations. Either the person cannot make an adjustment to these relationships, or he develops some of his powers at the expense of certain others or at the expense of his fellows. The discrepancy between the apparent wealth of potentialities and the narrow range of their fulfillment is a steadily recurrent motif.

The Competitive Personality

For Ibsen, Molière's advice—that the road to happiness lay in observation, adjustment, and moderation—would have been irrelevant, if not absurd. Goethe had foreseen that the individual would come to feel increasingly the limitations caused by adjustment to social conditions, but he had not anticipated the frustrations demonstrated by Ibsen. The individual can no longer merely renounce certain claims in order to preserve others. He must, to adjust, develop certain sides of his being to a point where the whole man ceases to exist. Competition has now entered a new field, private life. In *Pillars of Society,* Consul Bernick can conduct his financial transactions successfully only at the price of slandering his brother-in-law and suppressing his love for his future sister-in-law. The merchant Borkman sacrifices the love and happiness of two women to his ambition to expand his industrial enterprises. Solness pays for the success of his real-estate development with the inner peace of his wife and the lives of his children. Rubek drives a woman crazy in order to complete his masterpiece.

In claiming the right of individuality for themselves, the characters often justify the damage they cause to those near them by claiming that they have created happiness, instead, for the many.

Borkman: I have loved power . . . The power to create human happiness in wide, wide circles around me!

Mrs. Borkman: You had once the power to make me happy. Have you used it to that end?

Borkman: Some one must generally go down in a shipwreck.[4]

Solness: That I might build homes for others, I had to forego . . . the home that might have been my own. I mean home for a troop of children—and for father and mother, too . . . But her [Solness' wife's] vocation has had to be stunted, and crushed, and shattered—in order that mine might force its way to—to a sort of great victory.[5]

Competition turns out to be not only a struggle for social and economic success among various individuals; it is also an inner struggle in which the individual must drastically curtail certain sides of his own being, his personality, in order to realize his particular ambitions. There arises a sequence of guilt and retribution. Bernick's projects lead him to the verge of collapse; Borkman ends in economic and social ruin; the Master Builder's plans are surpassed by those of younger men; the sculptor's creative power is exhausted. The Consul Bernick's lies do not, however, save him from melancholia; Borkman pays for his ambition with bitter misanthropy; the Master Builder succumbs to his guilt; Rubek flounders in discontent bordering on despair.[6]

Ibsen formulates the predicament of the modern individual: he is fated to become an exaggerated, one-sided being no matter what he chooses to do. The very concept of adaptation has acquired a new meaning from the one Goethe implied—to say nothing of Molière. What once was a bearable degree of anxiety about fitting oneself to new conditions has become veritable anguish; life becomes a game that one hopes to win by achieving success, only to find that the specialization and exertion required for this success add up, after all, to failure.

Marriage and the Family

Failure manifests itself right in the very center of private life, in marriage. For the eighteenth-century novelists the home was a stabilizing force in a mobile world. For Molière, marriage was the happy end, whatever the conflict. It was the impossibility of marriage that occasioned the suicide of Werther. Ibsen's plays, however, do not stop at the threshold of family life; on the contrary, it is precisely there that they begin.

In almost every case, the characters or interests of the partners are at variance and bring marriage to defeat or frustration. Weak husbands such as Tesman, Alving, Hellmer, or Allmers fail their wives and drive them to distraction.[7] Ibsen is not partial to either of the sexes; weak wives like Aline Solness, Irene Rubek, or Gina Ekdal have a similar effect.[8] Marriages may be ruined by the love for a third person (*Hedda Gabler* and *Master Builder*), by an unbridgeable rift between parents and children (*John Gabriel Borkman*) or between the parents on account of the children (*Little Eyolf*), and by increasing boredom (in nearly every play).

Consul Bernick and Borkman marry women whom they do not love, and the insincerity of the relationships brings feelings of guilt to the husbands and of inadequacy to their wives. Rubek marries a woman inferior to him as a personality and pays with nervous restlessness; she in turn, to avenge herself, deserts him. Ellida, in *The Lady from the Sea,* seems fated to stagnate in a marriage she had contracted merely to escape from an unbearable environment. Nora, in *A Doll's House*, breaks off a relationship in which husband and wife could educate neither each other nor the children to live together equably. In *Little Eyolf* the husband conveys to his wife his decision to concentrate on the education of his son; the ensuing dialogue illustrates vividly the manner in which the law of competition operates within the intimacy of the family.

> *Rita:* Now you have given yourself up to something worse.
> *Allmers:* Worse! Do you call our child something worse?
> *Rita:* Yes, I do . . .
> *Allmers:* I am often almost afraid of you, Rita.
> *Rita:* I am often afraid of myself. And for that very reason you must not awake the evil in me.
> *Allmers:* Why, good heavens, do I do that?
> *Rita:* Yes, you do—when you tear to shreds the holiest bonds between us.

Allmers: . . . it is of no use demanding anything. Everything must be freely given . . . I must divide myself between Eyolf and you.

Rita: But if Eyolf had never been born? What then?

Allmers: Oh, that would be another matter. Then I should have only you to care for.

Rita: Then I wish he had never been born . . . I will live my life—together with you—wholly with you. I cannot go on being only Eyolf's mother . . . I will not, I tell you! I cannot! I will be all in all to you. To you, Alfred! [9]

The family does not live up to the function of being a sanctuary where the hurt suffered in public life can be healed. Even the relationship between the two generations is one of interference, not of help. The death of the Allmers' child terminates the father's interest in education, which from the beginning was not rooted in generic sympathy for the younger generation. This is, briefly, the life of the Allmers family: incompatibility between public and private life, neglect of the wife because of the husband's preoccupation with the child, dull pressure on the husband's life from lack of confidence in his productivity, general spiritual disorder.

The atmosphere in Consul Bernick's house is similarly unpleasant. Bernick tries to justify his social and personal machinations with the claim that he is seeking to provide his son with a life work.[10] His eventual self-reproach disavows his previous life and program which had brought about a hypocritical mentality in himself, an inner impoverishment of his wife, and a guilt-ridden relationship toward his son.

Ibsen's characters voice dubious educational doctrines which actually conceal antagonism and competition. When John Gabriel Borkman's proposal that he and his grown son should build a new life together is coldly rejected, he has earned the same fate as Bernick and for similar reasons. The aging Master Builder is bitter against the younger generation:

Some one or other will take it into his head to say: Give me a chance. And then all the rest will come clamouring after him,

and shake their fists at me and shout: Make room—make room
. . . presently the younger generation will come knocking at my
door . . . Then there's an end of Halvard Solness.[11]

It is left uncertain how heavily the death of Solness's children lay on his conscience. Ideally, the long experience and
the mature wisdom of an aging man should invest him with
a higher humanity, the benefits of which he could pass on to
the younger generation. Instead, the sheer biological difference in age becomes a source of hostility. Biology itself is
incorporated into a category of property, and the limitations
of old age appear as a loss of property, a loss that has no
compensations.

Social Nature of Personal Conflicts

Social relationships intimately permeate the personal dis-
asters Ibsen portrays. In all the plays someone stands in the
way of another's needs or the protagonist frustrates his own
needs by the nature of the activity he has selected. The characters themselves explain these conflicts on the grounds of
inner necessity: they cannot change their natures.[12] This
explanation, however, leaves out of account the social connections which are clearly established. Ellida, the Lady
from the Sea, finds life unbearable after she recognizes that
her marriage actually rests on a sales transaction, and the
tawdry yet expedient middle-class career marriages of Bernick, Tesman, Allmers, and Borkman signify that we are
concerned with something else than innate human nature.
In other instances human problems develop which seemingly
do not have any connection with material questions or
broader social relationships, yet they are described in almost
the same language as that which is used to describe instances
of business and professional competition.

> Oh, it all seems to me so foolish. . . . Not to be able to grasp
> at your own happiness—at your own life! Merely because some
> one you know happens to stand in the way! [13]

Indeed, this remark from Hilda, the Master Builder's friend, is close to the Master Builder's own language when he feels threatened by his competitors. The professional pattern in which the success of one means the failure of another has penetrated intimate relationships. The aggressiveness of the Master Builder is matched by that of Hedda Gabler. Rubek must use the same force and drive to succeed in the art world that Borkman or Solness uses in the world of business and industry.

Acclimatization and Specialization

Like Cervantes and Shakespeare, Ibsen often puts truths into the mouths of marginal figures. Ballested, jack-of-all-trades and master of none in *The Lady from the Sea,* declares that man can and must "acclimatize" himself, that he must adapt himself to the "facts."

The men in Ibsen always respect the facts of their world: eliminating competitors, cheating partners, playing ball with public authorities—these are realistic and profitable activities. If these people seem to be crushed by a blind fate, it is because they live their social roles in their private lives but fail to see them for what they are, namely, as the struggle to succeed, to obtain more, and to treat all things in an acquisitive manner. The protagonists may prefer one lover to another, one generation to another, or one side of their own nature to another, but in every case the choice is pursued with a restlessness and tenacity identical to that by which they forward their careers. As their social roles are extended to private relations, they almost inevitably miss happiness in the very act of energetically pursuing it. The schema of utilitarianism backfires.

An outstanding characteristic of almost all of Ibsen's persons is that they are, in one form or another, specialists. Only a few escape the isolation resulting from a high degree of specialization, and even those who do pay a heavy penalty. The good-for-nothing Ballested is a painter, actor, decora-

tor, hairdresser, dancing master, and music teacher all in
one; he is, of course, a failure. The identity of self-interest
and social interest proves to be a misstatement of reality.
Selective, self-centered activity is the requirement for effec-
tive social participation; the alternative is to become an
ineffectual jack-of-all-trades. It is true irony that advice
to conform should be put into the mouth of a man who fails
to conform.

The social trait of specialization afflicts Ibsen's people in
their private lives. The position of husband, wife, friend,
father, or mother is seen as a form of existence at odds with
the prerogatives of the individual himself as well as with
those of the other members of his family. Hedda, who has
managed for a while to assert her integrity in spite of a
banal environment, tells a friend about the disappointments
of her honeymoon, which have become the leitmotif of her
marriage. She says:

> Tesman is a specialist . . . and specialists are not at all amusing
> to travel with. Not in the long run, at any rate.[14]

When the friend asks, "not even the specialist one happens
to love?" she makes a bitter reply.[15] The episode is particularly significant because Tesman is not unattractive to
women and his profession (he is a scholar) is hardly repell-
ing. Far removed as he may seem from the average pattern
of commercial activity, he still remains caught by a web of
narrow specialization.

Gunhild Borkman's hatred of her husband is a reaction
to his view of life which centers its emphasis on the sound
business reputation of the family. Aline Solness's tolerance
of her husband and his friend Hilda is not born of a limitless
feminine capacity for love but only of the naive, dutiful desire to assist her husband's business and to maintain a conventional family life. The asceticism of Pastor Manders has
more to do with his own bigotry than with morality. Hellmer's ethical pretensions spring from his anxiety to retain
directorship of the bank rather than from conscience and
remorse.

Although Ibsen states in various forms the view of Dr. Stockmann that he who stands alone is most powerful, nevertheless his dramatic work illustrates again and again that the enforced self-dependence of man leads to solitude and loss of vitality. The pursuit of special self-interest spells ruin, and not fulfillment. Such is the fate not only of his less engaging characters, for instance the overbearing merchants Bernick and Borkman, but also of the likeable ones. The latter—like Helen Alving, Hedda Gabler, Rosmer, and Rubek—finally go to pieces in the complete isolation into which they have been driven; the pressure of outside interests pursues them even when they seek to withdraw into themselves.

2.

THE DILEMMA OF FREEDOM
AND NECESSITY

Love and Anxiety

Men face each other as strangers. When Ibsen's characters speak of love they often tremble—a phenomenon which proves on examination to be historical and social in its origins. The division of the individual into a professional self and a private self frightens the wife lest her beloved turn out to be someone vastly different from the man she knows; he may even be different from the man he thinks he is. The man who binds himself for life to a woman—to a member of the sex which, in Ibsen's day, society still confined to an existence within conventional marriage—may also expect disappointment. An order of life in which husbands and wives are specialized beings intensifies the anxiety that in any case goes with love.

When his wife asks him what his first sensation had been upon meeting her, Allmers replies quite frankly: "Dread." [16] Wangel admits that "the terrible" plays a dominant role in his relationship with his wife.[17] Madly in love with the childish Hilda, Solness sees his world full of devils: "If only you could always tell whether it is the light or dark ones that have got hold of you!" [18] Ellida indicates what is problematic in her love in these words:

> Oh, there are times, you may be sure, when I feel as though there would be safety and peace in clinging close to you, and trying to defy all the powers that frighten and fascinate me. But I cannot do it. No no,—I cannot do it! [19]

Personal relationships are more fearful than comforting. "She must bear it all alone." [20] Love cannot efface this insecurity, and Allmers, who has tried to break away from public life completely, finds no peace.

> *Allmers:* There is something horrible in being alone. The thought of it runs like ice through my blood—
> *Asta:* O, but Alfred, you are not alone.
> *Allmers:* There may be something horrible in that, too, Asta.[21]

Several of Ibsen's plays seem to suggest that he nonetheless believed in the possibility of realizing a genuine human relationship within and despite the prevailing social aura. But while there are glimmers here and there of such hope, by and large, where true love seems about to be realized, it is only at the point of death. Solness, Hedda Gabler, Rubek, and Irene die at the very moment overpowering emotion tears these people from their self-preoccupation. Solness, we are told, is too frightened to mount a scaffold, but he clambers to the top of a new house the first time he feels truly and warmly human, and jumps off. Accustomed to a soft life, Rubek climbs the most forbidding mountains when he meets the mate who stands beyond all conventional conceptions of life, whereupon an avalanche buries them both. Hedda Gabler, tied down by a wealthy marriage, exults in the suicide of her friend as an expression of freedom and the beauty of life, and she confesses that she feels alive for the first time just before she shoots herself. Death climaxes the will to life of all these people. It stands in somber contrast to the complacent self-confidence of Molière, for whom suicide was absurd and ridiculous. The disparity between Molière's and Ibsen's resolutions illustrates the decline of the curve of middle-class optimism.

The Imagination and Art

Ibsen is obsessed by the dilemma of how to maintain the integrity of the individual under the impact of the prevailing social atmosphere:

> The fault lies in that all mankind has failed. If a man claims to live and to develop in a human way, it is megalomania.[22]

> So to conduct one's life as to realize one's self—this seems to me the highest attainment possible to a human being. It is the task of one and all of us, but most of us bungle it.[23]

The sum total is mostly negative. Face to face with the injury he has done to himself and to others, Solness condemns his professional accomplishments:

> See, that is the upshot of the whole affair, however far back I look. Nothing really built . . . Nothing, nothing! The whole is nothing![24]

What remains is loneliness without hope.

Even individual phantasy and artistic imagination—which ordinarily we would think of as the last strongholds against the inroads of the world—do not transcend social reality but merely reflect it. Wishdreams, for example, without ever being translated into action, are consummated in events that injure and kill. Solness wants his old house to burn; when his wish comes true, the fire destroys his children. Rebecca West (in *Rosmersholm*) desires the love of the married pastor, only to feel eventually that her innermost wishes were responsible for the death of his wife. Rita Allmers confesses her jealousy of her child and would rather it had never been born than that it detract from her husband's love for herself; the child dies.

Art, too, is engulfed by this process. At the beginning

of the liberal era, music sang triumphantly of joy and solidarity; in Ibsen's work the tune has changed to one of suffering and isolation. Hedda Gabler plays the piano in a moment of supreme distress, and she draws out, according to stage direction, notes of despair. In *When We Dead Awaken* Ibsen introduces the plastic arts. A comparison with the Greek legend might help to point up the character of Rubek, the sculptor. The ancient story tells how Pygmalion fell in love with his statue of a young girl, how then a goddess endowed her with life, and how finally Pygmalion married the product of his own creation. In this tale, inanimate material is released for the development of a human being, but Ibsen's drama displays a reverse process: the artist sees in his wife only the model. The egoism of the artist, on a special plane to be sure, is as boundless as the egotism of the business and professional man. He transforms human relations and men themselves into objects to be used for his own purposes; they have value for for him only when they serve his ambitions.

Idealism Disenchanted

For the Wilhelm Meisters, the language in which idealism set forth its values—truth, freedom, responsibility, and duty—was a meaningful part of the emancipation of the middle classes. Now, however, when these same words are pronounced by a Rubek, who is imprisoned in his egoism, or by a Bernick, whose whole life has been based on the deception and repression of his fellow men, or by an Allmers, whose weak soul can escape conventional norms only at rare moments, they have ceased to provide a genuine motivation for creative acts.

Two parallel themes run throughout Ibsen's works: the one shows an effort to live up to established social values and ideals only to meet with defeat, and the other shows the defeat of those who reject these values and have nothing to put in their place. Ulrik Brendel, a vagabond and down-at-the-heel writer, is a spokesman for such pointless disillusionment. The first time he visits his former pupil, Rosmer, to arrange for lectures on human freedom, he begs for some cast-off clothes. The plan for the lectures is abandoned when he becomes aware of the apathy and cynicism in the town. He visits Rosmer once more before leaving, and this time begs for "one or two cast-off ideals."[25] He announces cynically that life can be mastered only by men like Mortensgard, an unscrupulous climber "capable of living his life without ideals." "And that," he adds, ". . . is just . . . the sum of the whole world's wisdom."[26] Again a marginal figure has formulated a basic feature of society. A world of ideals is invoked to dignify the relentless pursuit of material advantage, and they dissolve as soon as their consequences are considered; man's life runs its course between the pursuit of material goods and the worship of powerless ideas.

Of the values implicit in the categorical imperative, duty had struck a particularly militant note; the equal commitment of all men to duty aimed at the elimination of hereditary privilege. In Ibsen's drama, however, this concept becomes self-defeating. Pastor Manders' life is governed by wholesale acceptance of moral and sexual conventions, and his every action and world are confounded by the mirror of truth that Helen Alving holds up to him. Yet this man, wallowing in the comforts gained by submitting to conformity, preaches duty to Helen Alving when she confesses her unhappiness:

> What right have we human beings to happiness? We have simply to do our duty, Mrs. Alving! And your duty was to hold firmly to the man you had once chosen, and to whom you were bound by the holiest ties.[27]

He says to this woman whose life has been wretched and whom he had humiliated when she revealed her love for him:

> And what a blessing has it not proved to you, all the days of your life, that I induced you to resume the yoke of duty and obedience![28]

When the curtain has fallen and the audience strikes a balance, it is found that "duty" has brought Chamberlain Alving and his son to a terrible end, shattered the life of Mrs. Alving, brought about the degradation of her husband's illegitimate daughter, helped establish a sailor's brothel, and destroyed an orphanage. This is the reality. The pastor's sermon is an insipid moral recipe.

Aline Solness, too, is a victim of official morality. Ruled by a domineering and unreliable husband, robbed of her children by a terrible accident, restricted to a narrow circle of gossipy companions, she clings to the doctrine that all that matters is duty. All she gets for her faith in this moral dictum is mockery from her successful rival, the Master Builder's young friend:

> *Hilda:* She said that she would go out and buy something for me, because it was her duty. Oh I can't bear that ugly, horrid word!
>
> *Solness:* Why not?
>
> *Hilda:* It sounds so cold, and sharp, and stinging. Duty—duty—duty. Don't you think so, too? Doesn't it seem to sting you? [29]

Time and again Ibsen's people sacrifice themselves and do what they believe to be their duty, only to achieve negative results. Sacrifice of human lives becomes absurd, unless it is linked with a value that transcends those lives. It is a sheer perversion of the idea of self-sacrifice when sickly and childish Hedwig Ekdahl commits suicide to satisfy the pathological ideas of Gregor Werle and the inner instability of the man she believes to be her father. When Rebecca West joins Rosmer in death to satisfy the feeling of guilt he has projected upon her, the result is only the heaping of human destruction upon destruction. Even Nora's renunciation of her home has something of the sadness of a futile sacrifice.

The Role of Women

Ibsen once wrote to his friend Georg Brandes:

> What will be the outcome of this mortal combat between two
> epochs, I do not know; but anything rather than the existing
> state of affairs—so say I.[30]

The standards for a life superior to the "existing state"
are set by women in Ibsen's plays. Although for them it
is not hunger and other material privations that indict
society, their frustrations are allied nonetheless to the
present "epoch." Ibsen occasionally links the situation of
women in his time to that of the workers. He insists on
the nobility of character as superior to the privileges which
come with property, and adds:

> This nobility. . . . will come to us from two sources . . .
> from our women and from our workingmen.
> The reshaping of social conditions which is now under way
> out there in Europe is concerned chiefly with the future position
> of the workingman and of woman.
> That it is which I hope for and wait for; and it is that that I
> will work for, and shall work for my whole life so far as I am
> able.[31]

Ibsen again turns to a minor character for the formulation of an important problem. In *The Lady from the Sea*,
Boletta, an elderly, dry, prosy woman, asks the sculptor
Lyngstrad, who is declaiming that the wife must accom-
modate herself to her husband:

> Has it never occurred to you that perhaps a husband might be
> absorbed in the same way into his wife? Might come to resemble
> her, I mean. . . . But why not the one as well as the other? [32]

Women fare badly in a society where economic and
social functions are almost exclusively male prerogatives.
They represent, in a sense, incomplete men. They must not
only suffer from the pressures of society, they must also

serve and seek the approval of the men. Or, as Ibsen himself says:

A woman cannot be herself in the society of the present day, which is an exclusively masculine society, with laws framed by men and a judicial system that judges feminine conduct from a masculine point of view.[33]

"Modern society is not a human society; it is only a society of males." [34]

But the disenfranchisement of women has positive as well as negative results. Thanks to the fact that public life is ruled by men, women retain traces of another kind of existence; they are at least capable of expressing true human traits. Their greater distance from public life does not free them entirely from social pressures (the latter are, as we have seen, too omnipresent for that), but it does allow them at times to transcend these limitations.

Insofar as women have any business life in Ibsen's plays, they are helpless, faltering and perverse—with the exception of essentially innocuous characters like Gina Ekdahl, who do have some practical ability. Nora forges a note with almost touching clumsiness and carelessness. Helen Alving is persuaded by Pastor Manders' spurious arguments not to insure her orphanage. But this removal of women from men's work serves in the end to protect them from complete surrender to social and economic pressures.

The unique human quality women retain is the steadfastness with which they cling to the truth as an absolute value. It is man, ready to combat others for his own success, who preaches the ideals of progress, humanity, duty—the ideals that are undermined by the conduct of his life. Ibsen's male protagonists almost never live up to what they preach, and they never admit the one principle by which they in fact do live, the materialism of personal profit. Women are also materialistic, but their materialism is significantly different and outspoken. It is dramatic irony that egoists preach morality and moralists egoism; Ibsen's women often say that desire for personal happiness is their only true goal, but, in fact, they love to the point of self-sacrifice. Not once does Ibsen honor a man by allowing him to come forth as a witness to the humanly desirable. Only women such as Ellida, Hedda, Nora, Irene, Mrs. Rentheim, and Rita Almers defend that faith. Ibsen remarks of his own wife that she never succumbed to the temptation of inertia in the present society.[34a]

The clash between the self-seeking world of men, and love and humanity, represented by women, is crucial in Ibsen's drama. Rubek, perhaps the most talented character in Ibsen's works, abounds in creative ability, passion and a feeling for nuance. His wife, Irene, has neither the intellectual superiority of a Helen Alving, the zest of a Hedda Gabler nor the healthy directness of a Hilda. In this instance, the husband towers above the male average, while the wife fails to reach the level of several other women in Ibsen's dramas. It is in this relationship, however, that the mutually exclusive principles become most clear: adjustment to the "fact" on the one hand, and unconditional love on the other. Rubek, as the youthful sculptor, pursued the ideal of symbolizing, in the form of a young woman, the awakening of mankind from its present state. Later, having "learned worldly wisdom in the years that followed," he placed this single figure far in the background and transformed the central theme of the work into an allegory of life with "men and women with dimly-suggested animal faces." Irene tells him: "There you uttered your own doom."[35] The sculptor has betrayed the promise of his youth; he has achieved material success by turning out works that did not come sincerely from his own humanity; and because of his guilt he represents himself in his sculpture as a penitent who indeed has forfeited his life. On the other side, Irene's steadfast love for Rubek signifies a humanity which any number of shocks and depressions could not weaken; it holds out against every difficulty, disappointment and convention. For Hilda, no outside world—neither reputation nor family—exists when she wants to erect her castle with the Master Builder. Hedda Gabler goes to her death without giving up her faith in beauty as the only worthy aim of life.

In male idealism, truth becomes mere talk. In feminine egoism, on the other hand, there is an element of truth, for desires are consciously recognized and defended. Helen Alving opposes the sermonizing call to duty by men with the idea of "joy." She says to her son:

> A little while ago you spoke of the joy of life; and at that word a new light burst for me over my life and everything connected with it.[36]

In the same vein, Irene's love casts light on Rubek's confusion, just as Hilda's need of happiness exposes the Master Builder's disorganized existence. Hedda Gabler's contempt for the world of the specialist shows the abyss between the latter and a total human existence.

By their intransigence, Ibsen's women uncover the rationalizations of men: the architectural ambitions of Solness, the artist's egoism of Rubek, the conceited scholarship of Tesman, and the pomposity of Bernick and Borkman. In fact, the relation between men and women can be compared to that of the neurotic and the psychoanalyst. The men say everything that comes into their heads; they express guilt feelings, justifications and accusations. In contrast women represent the ego-ideal of a structured, realistically grounded existence. As in the analytic session, everything is restricted to the field of conversation and there is no lecturing. But the comparison ends here. True, Ibsen studies the psychological effects of society upon the individual, but his work does not proclaim that the mere understanding of psychological difficulties will cure the social ills which are at the bottom of personal misery.

Ibsen's women are not judged by specific "good" actions as opposed to "bad" ones, but rather, by the good faith they bring to their acts. Their attitude toward sex illuminates their struggle for happiness. The men generally declare sensual pleasure inferior to more ideal varieties. Those of the women who are endowed with the greatest critical clarity and energy are also the most sensual, and they admit it themselves. Against weaklings like Rosmer, or the vacillating Allmers, the colorless Tesman, or cowards like Manders, or the thoroughly beaten Rubek, all of whom flee from women in pursuit of their ideals, Ibsen opposes women who admit their demand for sexual happiness with the same candor as that with which they berate compromises demanded by the world. True, Rosmer, Rubek, and Allmers have traces of the rebel, but their ideals express dissatisfaction only with certain facets of prevailing society. Their female partners, however, say "no" to the claims and pressures of society as a whole, and hence to the weak principles of their men.

The Role of the Artist

The naturalistic school, of which Ibsen was a leading figure, expressed an increasing conviction that esthetic purism—art for art's sake—must give way to the artist's concern with the concrete problems of men. Ibsen's critique of the ideals of modern society did not derive from a philosophy of relativism but from a desire to relate these ideals to the social struggle. He expressed the idea that the subdivision and independent existence of different spheres of life—the seemingly unconnected separation into economics, politics, and culture—are transitory and once wrote:

> I believe that the time will soon come when political and social conceptions will cease to exist in their present forms . . . I believe that poetry, philosophy, and religion will be merged in a new category and become a new vital force.[37]

In challenging the purely esthetic approach, Ibsen tried to avoid specialization and isolation, which he had stigmatized in his dramas as a danger to human development. While traveling in Italy, he wrote to Björnson:

If I were asked to tell you at this moment what has been the chief result of my stay abroad, I should say that it consisted in my having driven out of myself the aestheticism which had a great power over me—an isolated aestheticism with a claim to independent existence. Aestheticism of this kind seems to me now as great a curse to poetry as theology to religion. . . . Is it not an inexpressibly great gift of fortune to be able to write? But it brings with it great responsibility; and I am now sufficiently serious to realize this and to be very severe with myself.[38]

Yet, much as he tried to throw off the limitations set upon him by his milieu—by sharing "the responsibility and the guilt of the society" to which he belonged—he nevertheless displayed traits characteristic of the society he criticized.[39] Although his female protagonists speak of freedom and joy as goals that are incompatible with prevailing conditions, still the manner in which they express their desires is often reminiscent in terms and tones of the austere language of the professed idealism of the male; it remains part and parcel of the value system they themselves protest.

Austerity lives closely with misanthropy and arrogance. Dr. Stockmann, the enemy of the people, rejects the world in a pronunciamento of truculent self-sufficiency. Rubek imperiously lashes the mob for its lack of appreciation. Rosmer prefers to take his program for nobility to the grave rather than make it public. Ibsen himself possessed traces of the misanthropy displayed by these characters. He wrote in a letter to Georg Brandes:

What I chiefly desire for you is a genuine, full-blooded egoism, which shall force you for a time to regard what concerns you yourself as the only thing of any consequence, and everything else as non-existent . . . I have never really had any very firm belief in solidarity; in fact, I have only accepted it as a kind of traditional dogma. If one had the courage to throw it overboard altogether, it is possible that one would be rid of the ballast which weighs down one's personality most heavily.[40]

Suggestions of pessimism also may be found in the use of dumbness in his plays. He could have said with Goethe:

"Silence befits the man who does not feel himself to be fully rounded. Silence also befits the lover who cannot hope to be happy." [41] In any case silence is the answer whenever men are giving up the confidence that they can lead their lives, as Wilhelm Meister had hoped for, in the direction of "a harmonious cultivation" of their nature. Silence comes over many of Ibsen's persons when they find they do not know how to break through the hard shell of their environment. Ellida, the Lady from the Sea, cannot communicate what she calls the "incomprehensible" in her life. Similarly, Hedda Gabler engages in an abruptly muted conversation:

> *Brack:* Why should you not, too, find some sort of vocation in life, Mrs. Hedda?
> *Hedda:* A vocation—that should attract me?
> *Brack:* If possible, of course.
> *Hedda:* Heaven knows what sort of vocation that could be. I often wonder whether—(breaking off). But that would never do either.[42]

Irene confesses that in her youth she had hated Rubek but loved his work, and had kept quiet on the subject. Silent hatred and silent love, the aging woman's recollection of her earlier dumbness, these are signs of actual human isolation.

In Ibsen's plays the societal concept of man reaches a climax: his inner life appears at once as a reaction to social forces and a reflection of them; social forces continue to live inside the individual, and thus to control him. In this context, nature as the symbol of freedom becomes a significant issue: many of his figures dream of natural space as a counter-image to society. Ellida longs for the great open sea, Rubek and Irene have faith in the redemptive power of the mountains, the parents of Little Eyolf turn to the peaks and the stars. Even Oswald Alving's longing for Paris ("light and sunshine and glorious air") and the ecstasy of Solness and Hilda over their air castles imply a renunciation of the possibility of human fulfillment in society, and a surrender to the demiurge of nature.

Such generous hope for the salvation of the individual's integrity is destroyed—as we shall try to show—by Hamsun's image of nature.

Chapter VII: KNUT HAMSUN
(1860-1952)

In the periods studied so far, literary artists expressed through their characters the conviction that the activities of the individual are rooted in universally binding values and that therefore these fictional life histories could serve as a parable or a stimulus to others. By the end of the nineteenth century, however, the artist ceases to reflect this ideal of the ethical unity of men.

At his best the modern writer, like all writers, keeps alive the hopes of the individual and the ideal of his self-realization in society; even the defeats he portrays are meaningful within this context. At his worst, however, he can fall victim to an irrational escape into the arms of authoritarianism. Knut Hamsun was this kind of writer. In the twenties and thirties his work not only enjoyed an excellent international literary reputation but also was regarded—even by liberals and socialists—as politically above reproach. However, in his act of joining Quisling's party during the Second World War, he expressed in practice the authoritarian themes and moods that had long been implicit in his novels: the pagan awe of unlimited and unintelligible forces of nature, the mystique of blood and race, hatred of the working class and of clerks, the blind submission to authority, the abrogation of individual responsibility, anti-intellectualism, and spiteful distrust of urban middle-class life in general.[1]

I.

NATURE

In Ibsen, the hymn to nature as a last gesture of hope comes at the end of his final play, *When We Dead Awaken*.

Man has found, in the social realm, not true freedom but only a mirage. By contrast with its pressures and restrictions, nature appears as a realm of freedom and a source of happiness and consolation. In enjoyment of the countryside, nothing seems to remain of the perpetual toil and responsibility, competition and even hostility. Communion with nature holds out a new image of man, one that will counter the image of himself as a victim.

The meaning of nature in almost every age is inseparable from social considerations. In the Renaissance, nature meant at once a scene of man's activities, a field for conquest, and an inspiration; it formed the *mise-en-scène* of men's lives. To be sure, even then there was an element of protest—the idyls of natural life in the works of Cervantes and Shakespeare implied a rejection of the contemporary "unnatural" society. Nevertheless the concept of nature as a counter-ideal to society strengthened the optimistic belief in progress, since it provided men with a yardstick against which shortcomings could be more clearly seen and evaluated. In the history of Western European drama from Shakespeare to Ibsen, and of poetry from Petrarch to Hölderlin, the path to nature was not a flight but a stroll toward liberation.

However, with the coming of doubt and even despair about personal fulfillment within society, the image of nature was no longer a basis for a new perspective, but became an alternative. Nature was increasingly envisaged as the ultimate surcease of social pressure. In this context, man could submit to nature and feel at peace—at least in phantasy. His soul, inviolable in ideology yet outraged in reality, could find solace in such a submission; frustrated in his attempt to participate autonomously in the societal world, he could join the world of nature. He could become a "thing," like the tree or the brook, and find more pleasure in this surrender than in a hopeless struggle against man-made forces. This is the most significant change in man's imagery of his environment to take place in the closing decades of the nineteenth century in Europe.

The novels of Knut Hamsun portray this antinomy of society and nature in an extreme form.

Sentimentalism and Brutality

The image of nature in Hamsun's novels has little in common with earlier conceptions of nature as a source of directives for human conduct. It lacks the critical element that made Rousseau's naturalism, for example, a progressive political and cultural force in the eighteenth century. Since the Renaissance man had seen himself able, at least potentially, to conquer some of nature's forces. This attitude reflected his faith in the unlimited potential of reason and, specifically, his hope for political and social reconstruction.

In Hamsun, submission to nature functions as an escape from the burden of social responsibility. This passive attitude in part explains why Hamsun's heroes are able to profess sentimental pity for the unsheltered animal, the tree in the wind, or for the withering foliage. In the fate of nature's children, they see a reflection of their own helplessness. To be a victim in the world of men is a threat to dignity. There is a certain solace, on the other hand, in being a victim of majestic natural forces for which man cannot be expected to be personally accountable.

Paradoxically, this new type of submission to nature is closely related to political submission. The yearning for surrender to nature as it appears in Hamsun's novels not only glorifies the awareness of individual weakness but at the same time exalts reverence for superior power in general. In our time we have seen in Europe's totalitarian movements the apotheosis of unshakable political authority —unshakable, in part, because one cannot fathom it. The timelessness and magnificence of nature reinforces the finality of the political power under which man lives. The yearning at once for stability and for glory is a trait of fascist ideologies (Hitler's "thousand years of history") that appears alongside this new type of nature worship.

The home, in the Victorian period particularly, was a refuge from the harshness of business and professional life. In Ibsen, we saw the idyl of the home devoured by the monster of competition, and nature appeared on the horizon as the Utopian realm of hope. In Hamsun, flight to nature as protest becomes flight to nature as idolatry, and communion with nature is transformed from sentiment into sentimentality, and then into brutality.

Implicit in this change is an element of anti-intellectualism. The use of reason, in whatever form, is indissolubly bound up with the responsibility of the thinker. Thus the flight to nature for the sake of abdication of human responsibility soon comes to be rationalized in thought that abhors thinking. This anti-intellectualism must be distinguished from vitalist and pragmatist philosophies earlier in this century. Bergson, Dilthey, and certain American philosophers rebelled against rationalist rigidity, to be sure, but their works were nonetheless responsible theoretical enterprises oriented toward the goal of higher individual development. Vitalism (*Lebensphilosophie*) as it was taken up by the ideological spokesmen of fascism looked rather to the submergence of the individual; reason was rejected in favor of overpowering mythical forces, blood and race.

This submergence of reason accompanied a glorification of the peasant, an integral part of anti-liberal undercurrents. The peasant is seen as not alienated from his work; unlike the industrial worker, he does not seem to violate nature but follows, so to speak, its true rhythm. Since his work is hard, healthy, meaningful, and in harmony with natural processes, it is set forth as the model of true manliness, dignified and silent. In the analysis that follows, an effort will be made to show that the sentimental conceptions of nature and peasant in Hamsun's novels anticipate an intrinsic part of those political ideologies that forge the concepts of leader, social coercion and soil into a tool of brutality.

Flight into Nature

At first sight, Hamsun does not seem qualified to represent the emergence of a typically modern European authoritarian ethos. (It is noteworthy, however, that it was in Germany that Hamsun obtained his greatest response from the very beginning.) Coming from a small country that, unlike the larger nations, has primary economic interests in agriculture and fishing, Hamsun might be expected to portray themes different from those of writers in highly industrialized nations. But, in fact, it is just this disparity between Norwegian conditions and the situation of the larger and industrially more advanced countries that makes Hamsun's picture of his society so reassuring at first glance and so foreboding upon closer analysis.[2]

Hamsun's first novel, *Hunger,* written in autobiographical form and published in 1890, states the themes that are almost endlessly repeated in the later novels: abandonment of any participation in public life, submission to the stream of incomprehensible and incalculable forces, distrust of the intellect, flight from the city and escape to nature.

The opening sentence of *Hunger* evokes the fate of the average city dweller:

> It was during the time I wandered about and starved in Christiania; Christiania, this singular city, from which no man departs without carrying away the traces of his sojourn there.[3]

The theme of the city is set at once. The fate of the hero is not comprehensible in terms of any conditions specific to him (he is, in this case, luckless and starving), but only in terms of the most general fact, the city. When he has finally had his fill and leaves as a newly hired sailor, the novel ends on the same note with which it began:

> Out in the fjord I dragged myself up once, wet with fever and exhaustion, and gazed landwards, and bade farewell for the

present to the town—to Christiania, where the windows gleamed so brightly in all the homes.[4]

One of Hamsun's figures once replied to an apologist for the city:

> You have your home in the city, it is true, and you have deco-
> rated it with trinkets and pictures and books; but you have a wife
> and a maid and hundreds of expenses. In waking and sleeping
> you must struggle with things, and you never have peace. I have
> peace. Keep your spiritual goods and the books and art and
> newspapers, keep your coffee houses and your whiskey which
> always makes me sick. Here I can roam about the woods,
> and I feel fine. If you put intellectual problems to me and try
> to drive me into a corner, I merely reply that God is the source,
> and that men are in truth only specks and threads in the uni-
> verse. Even you have gone no further.[5]

The motif of peace is rare in Hamsun's writing;[6] its use here as the key to the blessings of rustic life could perhaps be interpreted as a legitimate protest against urban conditions. When, however, a protest in the name of a seemingly higher idea becomes a wholesale condemnation of civilization, when it does not discriminate between marketplace manipulation and family life, between the newspaper and artistic creations, between anxious restlessness and emotional pleasure, between the futility of mere distraction and the earnestness of serious reading—all of which Hamsun spurns with equal rancor—then we are not dealing with alert social criticism, but with anti-intellectual resentment. Hamsun in the same breath ridicules the cheap pictures on the wall and jeers at the intellect. The final outcome of such impotent resentment is the surrender to brute power.

But first we must trace the steps of this process. What did Hamsun's heroes seek and what did they find in their flight to nature?

Solitude

When Hamsun speaks of man's solitude in nature, he seems at first glance merely to advocate liberation from the pressures of society:

> And there is another thing with which I am never finished, namely, retreating and sitting in the solitude of the woods, surrounded by beauty and darkness. That is the final joy.[7]

Nature appears to hold forth the promise of fulfilling the desire for relationships in which gratitude, joy, and rest can come to fruition:

> Thanks for the lonely night, for the hills, the rush of the darkness and the sea through my heart! Thanks for my life, for my breath, for the boon of being alive to-night; thanks from my heart for these! . . . By my immortal soul, I am full of thanks that it is I who am sitting here! [8]

But on closer inspection, it becomes clear that a new approach is in the making, according to which nature is more than a soothing balm:

> You must not believe that nothing happens here . . . I could send significant tales from here, but I don't do it. I have sought the woods for solitude and for the sake of my great irons. I have a few great irons within me, and they are getting red hot.[9]

These passages do not conjure up an idyllic and peaceful image of nature, but introduce a note of boastful resentment. A few pages later in the novel, the hero, thinking of the reindeer, ponders the secrets of his existence:

> I think all these things.
> And you? Have you compared your two newspapers, and do you know now what is the public opinion in Norway today about old age insurance? [10]

Hamsun anticipates his imagined antagonist's retort, and with considerable resentment:

Here you will certainly help yourself and make sport of me; you can say many droll things about the tree stump and me. But deep down you know that I am superior to you in this as in everything else, once I admit that I do not have as much city knowledge and that I was no student, ha ha. You can teach me nothing about wood and fields, for there I feel what no man has felt.[11]

The idea of a private kingdom to which man stubbornly clings (we have only to think of the dreams of fulfillment with which Ibsen endows his women) is transferred by Hamsun to the solitude of nature. This nature, however, is not merely an extra-human place where one can go and from which one can return; it is a substitute for human society. Nature is the seat of magical qualities of a new kind. In the old fairy tales, men learn to speak the language of animals; in order to be lords of all creation, they seek to overcome the barriers of nature by bringing the animal world into the human through the medium of speech. Hamsun's hero, however, seeks to draw from nature the meaning which he can no longer deduce from history. What he "overhears" (the tales he could tell but does not) is not meant to increase man's knowledge of his world and himself; if the tales were told, they would report only his own resentment and contempt.

Identity

The philosophy of liberalism did not encompass the idea that the whole world had come within man's power. Subject and object were opposed in the forms of active man and conquerable nature. Nature was raw material and man the unrealized potential; man realized himself in its conquest. Social relationships were implicit in this interaction; the knowledge of nature was won through communication of man with man, and nature was transformed by organized societal enterprise. The relationship toward which Hamsun's ideas tend is of a totally different kind. Nature is no longer looked upon as an object for scientific and practical control; instead Hamsun's hero consecrates his life in rapt surrender to nature and even in mystical identification:

> We are in the midst of an omnipresence. That is truly God.
> That is truly we ourselves as parts of the whole.[12]

To Hamsun, nature means peace, but a peace which has lost its spontaneity and its will to know and to control. It is a peace based on submission to every arbitrary power, a pantheism which offers an escape from the gloomy framework of history. Nature comes to mean the solace of the unchangeable and the all-pervasive:

> . . . he lost himself, was carried away and wrapt in the frenzy of sunshine . . . He was in a mysterious state, filled with psychic pleasure; every nerve in him was awake; he had music in his blood, felt akin to all nature, to the sun and the mountains and everything else, felt surrounded by a whisper of his own ego-sense from trees and tufts and blades of grass.[13]

The hero avoids asking any embarrassing questions about the rest of mankind. He shows concern only for his own fate. There is even a hint that nature is his private property and that his enjoyment of it is a kind of personal possession. Paragraph after paragraph of exalted description communicates neither observation nor knowledge, but only a desire for personal omnipotence and for pantheistic possession of the world by emotional immersion:

> The sky all open and clean; I stared into that clear sea, and it seemed as if I were lying face to face with the uttermost depth of the world; my heart beating tensely against it, and at home there.[14]

The timelessness of such pantheism gives the illusion of an immediate, complete possession of the entire world, a possession that at the same time cuts off historical progress. Gone is the optimistic dualism of liberalistic philosophy which always maintained close contact with history, considered the transitoriness of the human situation, and often gave birth to a conception of the future, Utopian to be sure, in which a final stasis of perfection might be reached.

Hamsun's identification with the whole of nature can be consummated with no exertion and with no fear of disillusionment. What the Utopians had envisioned as a potential unity of man and nature comes to be proclaimed as already realized: the meaning of man's life is to be found in natural factors such as blood and soil. When such a myth is consciously used in the interests of a power apparatus, as it was under fascism, men are told that their inevitable and irrevocable share of nature is their "race" and their nation.

Fury

The shift to an authoritarian concept of nature is apparent also in the changed imagery of the fury of the elements. Compare Hamsun's descriptions with similar ones in earlier literature. Hamsun writes:

> . . . lightning flashes, and soon thereafter the thunder rolls like an immense avalanche far beyond, between the mountains . . . Lightning again, and the thunder is closer at hand; it also begins to rain, a driving rain, the echo is very powerful, all nature is in an uproar, a chaos. I want to enfeeble the night by yelling at it, otherwise it will deprive me mysteriously of all my strength and will power. . . . More lightning and thunder and more driving rain, it is as if I were whipped by the echo nearby . . .[15]

Kant, too, once wrote about the power of nature:

> Bold, overhanging, and, as it were, threatening rocks, thunderclouds piled up to the vault of heaven, borne along with flashes and peals, volcanoes in all their violence of destruction, hurricanes leaving desolation in their track, the boundless ocean rising with rebellious force, the high waterfall of some mighty river . . .[16]

At first sight there appears to be no essential difference between the two passages. For Kant, however, the sublimity of nature and the experience of man's helplessness before it are counterbalanced by the concept of nature as subordinate in the face of humanity. It is man's own knowledge and imagination which creates the conception of the grandiosity in nature that dwarfs him. In the end, the rational faculties of man are of a higher order than the elemental force of nature, and they allow him to see it as sublime, instead of simply terrifying:

> . . . we readily call these objects sublime, because they raise the forces of the soul above the height of vulgar commonplace, and discover within us a power of resistance of quite another kind, which gives us courage to be able to measure ourselves against the seeming omnipotence of nature.[17]

Thus for Kant, nature is not to console man for frustrations, but to stimulate his moral and intellectual development.

In Hamsun, the relation of man to nature takes on an entirely different cast.

> I stood in the shelter of an overhanging rock, thinking many things; my soul was tense. Heaven knows, I thought to myself, what it is I am watching here, and why the sea should open before my eyes. Maybe I am seeing now the inner brain of earth, how things are at work there, boiling and foaming.[18]

The locus of knowledge has become nature itself, mysterious and beyond man's capacities to know. Hamsun's questions are framed so they cannot be answered; his tired individuals seek to silence themselves as quickly as possible. They really have nothing to say, and they welcome the storm that can roar loudly enough to drown out their own silence. The relationship of man to nature as seen by Kant is reversed; for Hamsun the storm serves as an occasion for increasing the individual's awareness of his own insignificance.

> When a moment of sadness and realization of my own nothingness in the face of all the surrounding powers comes over me, I lament and think: Which man am I now, or am I perhaps lost, am I perhaps no longer existent! And I speak aloud and call my name, in order to hear whether he is still present.[19]

Anxiety enters as a component of Hamsun's pantheism. Kant's pride in human autonomy is replaced by a sentimental uneasiness that is announced in every thunderstorm and that is subsequently ramified as a jumble of mawkish sympathies for both natural objects and spiritual difficulties.[20] Hamsun's nature world foreshadows the affinity of brutality and sentimentality, a well-known phenomenon in Nazi Germany.

Rhythm

When Hamsun speaks of nature, it is generally the forest and the sea. In the world of the forest, the law of rhythm, another significant element in Hamsun's imagery of nature, emerges:

> There is nothing more glorious than the soughing of the woods. It is like swinging, rocking—a madness: Uganda, Antananarivo, Honolulu, Atacama, Venezuela.[21]

The countries and cities have no concrete significance: what is essential is the sound of their names, which serves only to evoke and echo the order of natural motion. The rhythmic cycle of the seasons is also incessantly noted in the novels, where hypnotic prose again seems to imitate the phenomenon itself:

> Then came the autumn, then came the winter.[22]

> But the road leads on, summer follows spring in the world . . .[23]

> The days passed, time passed.[24]

Innumerable sentences of this kind sometimes take the form of a linguistic leitmotif, such as the ruthlessness of life, the procession of the seasons, the march of time, the men who go over the field or walk along the road, the measured steps of life, and so forth.[25] Elsewhere we find the seasonal and the daily rhythms unified:

It is the autumn season now, a silence in the woods all round; the hills are there, the sun is there, and at evening the moon and the stars will come; all regular and certain, full of kindliness, an embrace.[26]

The rhythmic principle can also take on a normative character. What is wrong with certain people is that

they won't keep pace with life . . . but there's none should rage against life.[27]

Even man's sexual relationships are oriented to the regularity of nature. The shepherdess will walk past the hunter's cabin in the autumn just as infallibly as she comes to him in the spring:

The autumn, the winter, had laid hold of her too; her senses drowsed.[28]

Uniformity of rhythm and tempo is sought in both the natural and human spheres; the passage of time brings recurrence, and not change. Nature's timetable replaces the timetable of history. This tendency displays the same simplification that is found in Hamsun's selection of landscapes. Whoever senses and accepts these rhythmic patterns as fundamental has full knowledge immediately and without rational effort. At the same time, the endless reproduction of natural phenomena, the cyclic order of nature, as opposed to the apparent disorder and happenstance of all individual and historical facts, testifies to the powerlessness of man. It is the extreme opposite of human self-assurance before nature. In this new ideology, which seeks to transfigure helplessness and subjection, the individual in seemingly free volition lays down his arms before a mythical power. Once, nature was held to be "autonomous" only insofar as it was not yet recreated as the product of human activity. Now, however, man must expect a life without meaning unless he obediently accepts as his own what may be called the law of nature. And the social counterpart to the law of natural rhythm is blind discipline.

2.

HERO-WORSHIP

When Hamsun speaks of the forces of nature to which man should subject himself, it is, as we have noted, mostly of the woods and the sea. But when he speaks of man himself, as he should be, he leaves these unspoiled provinces behind and speaks foremost of farming. Hamsun's emphasis is not upon the social conditions of the farm; rather, he is again involved in constructing the myth which demands the necessity of man's submission to nature. The peasant tunes himself to forces stronger than himself, and that is supposed to be the lesson he can teach us. In addition vigorous youth and women are portrayed as truly obedient to nature's forces. Hamsun gives us, in fact, a gallery of unheroic heroes, whose qualities are primarily those of subjection and discipline.

The Peasant

Hamsun's peasants are not individuals; they are aspects of nature, and his apparent admiration of them is not a love of man, but a reverence for the domination of nature over its inhabitants.

> His [the peasant's] life was spent in this work and that, according to the season; from the fields to the woods, and back to the fields again.[29]

This sentence is typical. The peasant himself is not characterized; he is presented only as a natural phenomenon that comes and goes like the blossoming and withering of the leaves in the forest. That is precisely the identity which Hamsun seeks, an identity established by nature, not by man:

. . . looking up at blue peaks every day of your lives; no new-
fangled inventions about that, but fjeld and rocky peaks, rooted
deep in the past—but you've them for companionship. There you
are, living in touch with heaven and earth, one with them, one
with all these wide, deep-rooted things.[30]

The course of history is reversed: "Man and nature don't
bombard each other." [31] In Hamsun, nature has no place
for the individual as such; his irrelevancy is not only described but glorified in the person of the peasant who is
reduced to a biological speck in the rhythm of life.

'Tis you that maintain life. Generation to generation, breeding
ever anew; and when you die, the new stock goes on. That's
the meaning of eternal life.[32]

Daniel is the name of this peasant, but any other peasant
could serve as well. "Daniel was the same today as yester-
day . . ." [33] And the elements in nature with which the
peasant deals are always the same, too.

Wherever there was a tiny patch of fertile ground, there hay
or potatoes or barley grew; in summer the cattle were out in the
pasture, in winter they stood in their stalls—it was all so eternal
and so changeless.[34]

In the course of the flight to nature, Hamsun's individual
is stripped of his singular human qualities and subjected to
"eternal" naturalness. " 'Tis the land I'm here for." [35]
Service to nature is the real law of peasant life, and happiness means only that he has fulfilled his naturalistic destiny.
Only submission to the laws of nature that dictate, for example, the cultivation of grain makes man an admirable
figure:

Growth of the soil was something different, a thing to be
procured at any cost; the only source, the origin of all.[36]

For generations back, into forgotten time, his fathers before
him had sowed corn; solemnly on a still, calm evening . . .
Corn was nothing less than bread; corn or no corn meant life
or death.[37]

The products of cities are devaluated or totally ignored, in a kind of travesty of the theories of the physiocrats:

> "There isn't a human being anywhere in the world who can live on banks and industries. Not a single human being in the world."
> "Ho! What do they live on, then?"
> "On three things and nothing else," replies Ezra. "On the grain of the fields, the fish of the sea and the birds and beasts of the forest. On those three things. I've thought it all out."
> "There's quite a few that live on their money—"
> "No," said Ezra. "Not a single soul!" [38]

As contrasted with the emptiness of urban existence, the concreteness of the peasant's world seems to comprise the meaning of life itself:

> He did not feel poor and forlorn, as he really was; why, all the stones he had cleared looked just like a crowd of people around him, he was personally related to every stone, they were acquaintances every one, he had conquered them and got them out of the ground. [39]

The authoritarian state did not have to invent the idea of man's roots as being in blood and soil, nor devise the manipulation of this slogan as a solace for want. "We will not be any happier if we eat more bacon," says Hamsun's peasant in defending life on Norwegian soil against a life outside that might mean greater material success; the worst fate is

> . . . to be torn up by the roots from our own barren soil and transplanted into richer . . . [40]

If we accept this belief, we do not scorn the hardest labor,[41] for we know "where we really do belong." [42]

> It is a good thing to belong to one's class, otherwise one becomes an upstart and gets one's originality frittered away. [43]

A good thing if you are a peasant, that is. Hamsun's eulogy of the peasant, apparently undertaken in the spirit of social critique, ends up as a sermon on temperance, humility, privation. The message is to keep one's roots where they are, even though the soil may be very poor indeed.

As we might expect, Hamsun combines his cult of the hero and that of natural forces with praise for the vigor of youth *per se*. In comparison with this vigor, the restrained wisdom of maturity counts for little; the demand of youth for power is natural obedience to the "law of life."

> Old age should not be revered for its own sake, for it merely restricts and hinders the progress of mankind. Even primitive peoples despise old age,[44] and they emancipate themselves from it and its hindrances without further ado.[45]

He applies to human beings the lessons of biology—more precisely, of botany—thus:

> And what have you learned from the woods? But what did I learn in the woods? That there are young trees there.
> Now the young stand behind me, ridiculed shamelessly and barbarously by every fool, simply because they are young.[46]

This resentful yet sentimental sermon is tied to an attack on leaders who are old enough to have learned from experience.

> One should not rely too much on the leaders; the country's youth should be our hope. No; a leader is apt to prove a broken reed. It is an old law that whenever a leader reaches a certain age he pauses—yes, he even turns right about face and pushes the other way. Then it is up to the young to march on, to drive him ahead or trample him down.[47]

Hamsun's heroes do not often speak with such harsh frankness. He lends exultation to the rough tone of the young male in order to glorify manliness in general. He is happy that the peasant, reverent and serene as he is, knows how to bring his wife to her senses: "To think that a man's hard grip could work such wonders!" [48] The myth of manliness is created out of "natural" qualities of superior force.

The Vagabond

Along with the peasant, the vagabond receives affectionate treatment in every period of Hamsun's career. August, his favorite, longs "to shoot the knife out of the hand of a man who was trying to make off with his wallet" because that would be a thrill for the "children of the age" in their dreary existence.[49] As a matter of fact, Hamsun seems fascinated by such brutal mischief:

> And steal a bag of gold and silver plate from the market, and hide it in the mountains, so that a blue flame can float over the spot on autumn evenings. But don't come to me with three pairs of mittens and a side of bacon.[50]

In this pseudo-romantic flirting with a nuisance crime, he ridicules the "unheroic" spirit of urban efficiency ("no thunderbolt ever falls");[51] he cries for "gigantic demi-gods" and blunders into a political program of violence:

> The great terrorist is greatest, the dimension, the immense lever which can raise worlds.[52]

The peasant with his roots in the soil and the bohemian vagabond with no ties to anything may seem mutually exclusive idols. Still, Hamsun's ability to sympathize with such apparently opposite types has a certain logic; their common denominator is the rejection of organized urban culture, in favor of the application of raw, unmediated "natural" force. Incidentally, it was the socially uprooted literati (the "armed bohemians," as they have been called) who performed the spadework of German fascism, playing up the cult of the hero and the maintenance of one's roots in the soil.

In Hamsun, the function of such marginal figures as the vagabond is emphatically different from that in the literature thus far discussed. From Cervantes through Ibsen, marginal characters have stood outside society and criticized it in the name of freedom and self-determination. In

Hamsun, however, such figures serve as coquettish expression of his veneration of brutality and power.

The Relation of the Sexes

The endorsement of violence and mischief seems to be a far cry from the theme of passive surrender to nature. But the connection between violence and passivity becomes unequivocal in Hamsun's treatment of the relation between the sexes. In his novels there is a conspicuous absence of genuine yearning for love. When one of his characters is seized by a strong passion, it is quickly transformed into sado-masochistic torment of himself or of the partner. This is as true of the desperate ecstasy of the hero in *Hunger,* or of the literally speechless and unexpressed affair between the main characters in *Victoria,* as of the mutual hatred of the partners in *Pan.* The hero of *Mysteries* enjoys telling his beloved the most frightening and brutal stories;[53] the hero of *Pan* shoots his dog and sends the corpse as a farewell gift to the beloved from whom he has become estranged.[54] What passes for love is closer to hostility:

> Does she then love a dead man to the point of hatred and cruelty and is she still trying to hurt him? Or is Glahn still alive and does she want to continue her torture? [55]

In general, however, sadism is much less developed than masochism. People seem to find happiness only when subjected to strength, power, and authority. On occasion one can readily observe the shift from sadism to masochism:

> Eva answers: "It was cruel of her to laugh at you."
> "No, it was not cruel of her," I cry . . . "it was only right that she should laugh at me. Be quiet, devil take you, and leave me in peace—do you hear?"
> And Eva, terrified, leaves me in peace. I look at her, and repent my harsh words at once; I fall down before her; wringing my hands. "Go home, Eva. It is you I love most. . . . It was only a jest; it is you I love." [56]

In one of his earliest novels as well as in one of his last, a lover asks for harsh treatment:

> Only you torture me too much with your forbearance; how can you put up with my having more than one eye? You ought to take the other, you ought to take both; you shouldn't allow me to walk along the street in peace and have a roof over my head.[57]

> Hurt me in return! Do you hear! Otherwise you'll go off and believe I've been ruined by some one, but that isn't true.[58]

Satisfaction in love seems possible only in the sexual sphere, and even then it is not because sensual pleasure signifies any feelings of affection and identification, but on the contrary springs from malice and disdain, particularly for women:

> "Come and show where there's cloudberries," said Gustaf . . . And how could a woman say no? Inger ran into her little room and was both earnest and religious for several minutes; but there was Gustaf standing waiting outside, the world was at her heels, and all she did was to tidy her hair, look at herself carefully in the glass, and out again. And what if she did? Who would not have done the same? Oh, woman cannot tell one man from another; not always—not often.[59]

This spiteful eulogy of lust brings Hamsun back to his point of departure: the definition of man as mere nature. In an early novel promiscuity seems to thrive in gaiety and freedom:

> "Iselin, I saw what you did," he says again; "I saw you."
> And then her rich, glad laughter rings through the wood, and she goes off with him, full of rejoicing from top to toe. And whither does she go? To the next mortal man; to a huntsman in the woods.[60]

But even this cavalier concession to pleasure and satisfaction describes only another form of isolation, for there is complete lack of interest in the happiness of one's partner. Sexual relations are ruled by the laws of nature which men and women instinctively obey.

> There she goes, a human being like the rest of us, a wanderer in the earth, a little girl, ah me! a life gone astray, a flying seed. She was fairly undejected in her walk . . . She had the packet of papers under her arm, she knew what awaited her at the barn, and there she went. Some call it free will.[61]

> . . . he broke through all rules of propriety and was very friendly, picked the hay from her bosom, brushed it from her knees, stroked, patted, threw his arms around her. Some call it free will . . .[62]

Whatever is distinctly human and spiritual is forgotten. Love, which for Cervantes and Shakespeare appeared as the key phenomenon in the autonomous development of modern man, becomes reduced in Hamsun to a bawdy jeer at free will.

Women

Hamsun belittles Ibsen's women, and thumbs his nose at Ibsen himself for his description of Nora (in *A Doll's House*):

> I know a sage, and he wrote of woman. Wrote of woman, in thirty volumes of uniform theatre poetry: I counted the volumes once in a big bookcase. And at last he wrote of the woman who left her own children to go in search of—the wonderful! But what, then, were the children? Oh, it was comical: a wanderer laughs at anything so comical.[63]

Woman attains fulfillment of her destiny when she limits her functions to those of a housewife and a mother. This enshrinement of biological function leads Hamsun to bitter hatred for any emancipation, intellectuality, or political reforms that women might desire[64] and finally, in an attack on actresses, to utter contempt for the "modern woman":

> You ladies pretend to look down on domestic life, pretend to be indifferent to the scanty personal respect you enjoy; you are either not mothers at all, or very bad ones, either incapable of bringing up children or pitifully incompetent at it—every day

of your lives you sink into deeper shame on account of this
impotence. That is the truth.[65]

The ideal peasant woman, wife of the ideal peasant in
Growth of the Soil, unpleasant in appearance and not always faithful, has a meaningful existence as a housewife
and mother: A "good nature, a clever nature," [66]

> . . . the Margravine . . . is indoors preparing the meal. Tall
> and stately, as she moves about her house, a Vestal tending the
> fire of a kitchen stove. Inger has made her stormy voyage, 'tis
> true, has lived in a city a while, but now she is home.[67]

This theme is constantly reiterated: woman receives her
true consecration as a mother. Of the tragic ruin of a
woman who sought to run away from an unsatisfying marriage only this is said:

> She had no occupation, but had three maidservants to her house;
> she had no children, but she had a piano. But she had no
> children.[68]

It is another woman, a paragon of mediocrity, who receives
the accolade:

> A mother many times, realizing life—it was worthy of a great
> reward.[69]

In such idealization of fertility, biology takes precedence
over the conventions of middle-class morality; as in the case
of Inger, sexual vicissitudes are blinked—indeed are con-
doned—provided the end or denouement is that of produc-
ing children. This was also a stock in trade of the Nazi
ideology, which reduced womanhood to a biological function. Hamsun's language becomes almost epic when he
speaks of woman as the bearer of progeny: she becomes a
fertility-heroine:

> A real girl shall marry, shall become the wife of a man, shall
> become a mother, shall become a blessing to herself.[70]

3.

URBAN SOCIETY

The idolatry of nature is set up against "a world where cheating goes on in the dark." [71] The composition of this rejected world is quite apparent. It is, in brief, an inventory of modern urban society that Hamsun condemns—industry,[72] public officials,[73] the natural sciences,[74] the teaching profession,[75] the coffee house,[76] the corporation,[77] and countries under liberal governments—as well as the city, the intellectuals, the workers and platforms of social reform; these are all surveyed in the novels and dismissed as hateful. Significant, for example, are his contemptuous remarks on Gladstone,[78] and his rejection of "the modern type, a man of our time," who believes "all the Jew and the Yankee have taught him." [79] He has warm words of praise for Sweden because she is oriented toward Germany, not toward Switzerland,[80] and he tells the English that they "will someday be whipped to death by the healthy destiny of Germany." [81]

Numerous are his attacks on Switzerland—not just coincidentally the model of democratic experimentation. In one of his novels, a man plans to build a comfortable home for his family in the "Swiss fashion." He is taken to task by Hamsun for believing he can learn something

. . . from a miserable little people up in the Alps, a people that throughout its history has never been or done anything worth speaking of.[82]

These attacks are typical of a romanticizing primitivism anticipating in literature the sneering propaganda of the middle-European authoritarian parties against "effeminacy" and the "morass" of the big cities. When Hamsun assumes the posture of social critic, he focuses his attention only on superficial, secondary aspects of industrial society. Everything the inquiring mind finds of interest and of crucial importance—including consideration for mutual help—is flattened out, or swept away with an imperious gesture. Not accidentally, a chief butt of his ridicule are the manufacturers of consumer goods, whom he epitomizes in those who seem most readily to lend themselves to caricature, such as producers of canned goods, candies and herring-meal.[83] "Butter?" he asks:

> One did not churn butter any more—one went to the store and bought margarine. Storehouse and shed full of meat, pork and fish? One would have died of laughter at anybody who kept salt meat . . . wasn't there food to be had in tins—tinned food? It was ready cooked, it was chewed too, it was ready to put into a cloth to make a child's sucker of for all mankind . . . What did mouths want with teeth anymore? Weren't there false teeth hanging on a string in the toothmaker's shop? And as for the tinned foods . . . it dealt gently with people who had already got stomach-trouble from eating it.[84]

Middle Class

For Hamsun, intellectuals and public officials exemplify middle-class triviality. The work of the journalist, the teacher and the historian find no favor in his eyes.[85] Scientists are represented as having wrought a permanent injury against man; science is an empty mechanism, an incomprehensible hodge-podge of data.[86]

The brunt of the attack is on civil servants[87] and clerks in general:

> . . . officials—believe me, they are a miserable tribe . . . Nothing but mediocre abilities and stunted energies; the triumph of the commonplace.[88]

In the midst of a hymn to nature ("I am never done with grass and stones"), Hamsun plunges into an attack on the "sons of clerks," the "official residence," and the "garden of the commonplace" where everything is decided "on account of age, length of service, and school learning." [89]

. . . with such useless hands as theirs, which they could turn to no manual labor, they could only sit in an office writing . . . such servile work as writing the letters of the alphabet . . . The most that can befall them is to fail in an examination . . . I pity them . . . bent over a table so long that they are round-shouldered; they are helpless with their hands; they generally wear glasses—a sign that as learning poured into their brains, it sucked the sight from their eyes . . .[90]

Now—as we see the clerk, the bureaucrat, the intellectual portrayed as sickly, decadent, impotent—there emerges by implication the counter-image of the self-assured, vigorous, tough Nordic hero. Those who do not display these virtues are summarily disqualified.

Working Class

Contempt for factory workers and for workers' movements permeates Hamsun's novels. It first appears in the disguise of his romanticizing naturalism:

What was more, I liked to be among field and forest, not with lumbermen and proletariat.[91]

But soon in the same novel the disguise falls away and resentment comes to the fore:

These gentlemen of the proletariat think a good deal of themselves; they look down on farm workers, and will have nothing to do with them . . . Then, too, they are more popular among the girls. It is the same with men working on roads or railways, with all factory hands . . .[92]

This contemptuous sarcasm remains a key motif. In one of his last novels we read:

The moment that Alex had found himself with a job and with money in his pocket, food in his belly and clothes on his back, he had crawled to his feet and begun stalking around like a man, had even applied for membership in the trade union, to which he pointed with considerable pride.[93]

The competitive interwovenness of urban lower strata appears as a threat to the "heroic" *status quo*—life on the soil.

> The others, the workingmen, businessmen, the day-laborers, go about showing their teeth at one another and fighting. That is life. They are really fighting over the old landowner, they are fighting over his possessions.[94]

For Hamsun the struggle for an increase in material welfare is merely vulgar. Whatever rational justifications such claims may have is no concern of his. He engages in a variety of attacks on "the proletariat's strong and blind craving for food," [95] on "the roar of the masses," who unfortunately have learned from "mechanical reading and writing" how beautiful it is to "live by others' labor." [96] But worst of all are the destructive tendencies that are bound up with the workingman's "worldly greed."

> They [the masses] want to roar and turn things upside down, and when it comes to a pinch even their own leaders can't hold them in. The whole thing's crashing, let it crash! [97]

Here indeed we are face to face with the nihilistic furor of the authoritarian mentality.

4.

NIHILISM

Anti-Intellectualism

At the peak of liberalist optimism, popular manifestations of confidence in scientific progress made the coffee houses and beer halls the layman's university, with natural science, medicine, and politics the favorite subjects in the curriculum. True, these flourishing ideas were without influence, not only in the groves of Academe, but in society at large; still, the constant critical concern with the affairs of science and public life served to perpetuate a confidence in the efficacy of each member of society.

The incomprehensibility and inexorability of the social process has increasingly given rise to pseudo-philosophies and pseudo-sociologies which claim to possess superior wisdom, keys to the mystery of human relationships, recipes for the best and quickest possible solution to man's dilemmas. The attraction, in recent decades, of innumerable panaceas for curing the ills of the world through programs which promise to discover the meaning of life in nature illustrates this trend. Nudism, astrology, dietary and breathing fads are cases in point. Man seeks to draw from nature the meaning he cannot find in society.

At the same time, the results of science and education are often not experienced by broad strata of the population as aids to progress. What was actually to be gained from the work of the natural scientists, from the apparatus of schools and other cultural institutions?—so people asked. To the extent that these activities seemed unrelated to universal improvement in material welfare, an impression grew that learning was an empty program, busywork, or pointless pastime. Anti-intellectualism is intimately linked with disillusionment in the credo of progress among broad social strata in Europe. To them, the intellect appeared either as an instrument of domination or as an abstract conglomeration of phrases and slogans having no reference to their own concerns.

This loss of faith by Europeans in their rationalistic daydreams, wherein their power had seemed to grow without bonds, was given respectability by the anti-liberal literati's devaluation of reason. Hamsun's anti-intellectualism soon became apparent in his attacks on earlier nineteenth-century writers. One of his heroes calls Maupassant "crude and soulless," [98] Tolstoi "a fool in philosophy" who talks "twaddle," [99] and Ibsen a "little writing oddity" [100] who has brought shame upon his country, a land which has engendered nothing but "peace conferences, the skiing spirit, and

Ibsen so far." [101] In 1892, Hamsun already contributed to the authoritarian *Führer* cult—which jeers at the moral anxieties and compulsions of the intellectual, while arrogantly exalting the morally insensate body-beautiful ideal of the racial hero—when he joined his contempt for one of Ibsen's more remarkable sayings with an alleged physical weakness of the playwright:

> The great poet produces a pursed-lips expression, braces his chicken breast to the utmost, and delivers himself of the following words: "To make poetry is to summon oneself to the Day of Judgment." [102]

Philosophy of Life

Hamsun's heroes are querulous in posing the problem of their destiny. The hungry one asks:

> Was the hand of the Lord turned against me? But why just against me? Why, for that matter, not just as well against a man in South America? [103]

The journalist Lynge never finds an answer to his question:

> Why could not everything be good, and why could not men be happy in life? [104]

A lover poses the problem:

> The other he loved as a slave, as a madman and a beggar. Why? Ask the dust of the road and the leaves that fall, ask the mysterious God of life, for there is no other that knows such things.[105]

When August, the vagabond, meets with misfortune, the question is raised:

> Possibly somewhere away out in the universe there was a great eye which was watching him, a power which in some way or another had learned of his labours in the desperate service of nothing at all.[106]

In the end, the answer to all these questions of suffering humanity is invariably surrender—surrender to a sphere of power existing before and beyond all individual existence. Man is not capable of changing it in any way, nor is he entitled to do so. "What is life's? All! But what is yours?" [107] And the answer demonstrates once more the worthlessness of the individual. "Life could afford to waste her, to throw her away." [108] That is true of every floundering human being—and every human being is going under. "Life is a loan . . . I know no one who has not fared as badly as myself . . ." [109] Hamsun again and again gives expression to the passivity and obedience which such inexorability of life requires. While life itself "has thrust me away into something hostile to myself," there is no court which must answer the question, "why should Life do that?" [110] There is only one law here: "Life can afford to waste." [111]

Hamsun's philosophy of life has a twofold social function. On the one hand, it offers the socially less successful the consolation that their insignificant role in the economic process can be compensated for by the acceptance of the greater, metaphysical context of the omnipotence of life:

> And so it is: the mere grace that we are given life at all is generous payment in advance for all the miseries of life—for every one of them. No, do not think we have the right to more sweetmeats than we get. [112]

The individual is to become reconciled to his condition in society by perceiving himself as a necessary sacrifice to a natural process, a sacrifice not merely mechanical but full of meaning.

On the other hand, this mythology offers no tangible expectations for alleviating deprivation and disillusionment. The consolation turns against those consoled. They must accept life as it is, and that means the existing relations of domination and subordination, of command and serve.

The Image of Man

Hamsun's mythology throws new light on his misan-thropic contempt. His exalted picture of life stands side by side with the image of crawling and creeping man, in the same way that authoritarian propaganda later combined os-tensibly lofty notions with expressions of vulgar misan-thropy. A metaphysics of the miserableness of man is mo-bilized against the idea of human progress. Every desire for a more rational organization of society becomes incon-gruous.

It is significant that Hamsun uses the analogy of the ant hill, so popular in liberal reformist literature as a model of constructive social order, as an image of planlessness:

> . . . but that made no difference to the town, the town re-mained the little crawling ant-hill it was, and this in itself must have been a proof that life itself went its way in spite of all theories . . .[113]

> Oh, that little anthill! All its inhabitants are occupied with their own affairs, they cross each other's paths, push each other aside, sometimes they trample each other under foot. It cannot be otherwise, sometimes they trample each other under foot.[114]

We have returned with the ants to the starting point, the myth of nature. Every recollection of historical existence has now been obliterated. We are left with an apotheosis of the merely natural—of force without reason. The exo-dus from social reality is complete.

Behind Hamsun's bitter responses to contemporary civi-lization lies the cold and nihilistic negation of the very image of man on the road to freedom. His characters are not truly individuals but irrelevant particles in an ahuman process forever beyond their control. Both as an artist and as a political partisan, he was unequal to the challenge of the great heritage of libertarian thought in the West. Cervantes and Shakespeare, Racine and Molière, Goethe and Ibsen, had this in common: all embraced the struggle of the individual with his social and natural environment; all refused to place limits on human imagination and achievement; all, with fervor and tenderness, served human liberty.

Appendix

Shakespeare's *The Tempest,* Act I, Scene 1

The storm and shipwreck that introduce *The Tempest* deserve intensive analysis. In this brief scene, Shakespeare confronts us with persons from widely separated social classes and places them in an extreme situation which enables him to study their essential characters. The analysis of the scene is presented both as a sample of close textual criticism and as background material helpful to an understanding of sociological implications in the rest of the play.

What may have appeared to Shakespeare's people as a matter-of-fact set of relationships is for us problematic. In interpreting them at all, there is the risk, of course, of making Shakespeare appear unduly aware sociologically. The purpose here, however, differs from textual literary criticism; the intent is not to burden Shakespeare's words with many meanings on different levels, but simply to listen carefully to the evidence implicit in the lines of the scene. In a sense, it is the evidence of that which was taken for granted in Shakespeare's day that is the objective of our search. Such an approach need not distort or overburden his meanings—at worst, it examines his characters, their roles, and their relationships, in the light of a larger picture of social change than he himself could possibly have known.

The shipwreck scene introduces us to the villainous and worthless characters of the play. Shakespeare is concerned, naturally enough, with furthering his plot, but he must first define the villains, and in this scene he carefully sets them off against the figures of Gonzalo and the boatswain. The princely usurpers and idlers are useless in the emergency at hand and behave stupidly, whereas Gonzalo acts and speaks in a reasonable way, and the boatswain works competently and industriously. If we bring to the scene what we learn from the rest of the play, it is apparent that Shakespeare uses the progressive ideas and moral concepts of his day to define his heroes, and leaves his villains in a reactionary, or at least non-progressive, torpor. In this light, we see in the villains the representatives of the declining noble class who are concerned only with enjoying the feudal prerogatives they have inherited. They have nothing in common with Prospero, Gonzalo or simple workmen, whose actions and ideas anticipate the qualities of middle-class individualism and industriousness.

The first persons we encounter in the play are working people, acting out their professional roles in a responsible way. The master calls "Boatswain," and the boatswain answers: "Here, master; what cheer?" The master continues:

> Good, speak to the mariners: fall to't yarely, or we run ourselves aground: bestir, bestir.

We are quickly introduced to a situation structured by the needs of expedient work under conditions of utmost stress. The speakers address each other by means of their functional names. The way in which they speak to each other is that of workers getting on about their business; it could also be the way of a senior and a junior engineer. The chief gives an order, the boatswain responds, and the whole mood is relaxed, friendly and factual despite their predicament. We can imagine that two skilled pilots might behave in the same way if their plane were in trouble.

The master expresses clearly and simply the need for speed. His words invite comparison with those of Alonso, king of Naples, when, a few seconds later, he enters the scene and commands the boatswain to "play the men." The attitude of the king is that of the feudal lord to the lowest of his subjects. He does not understand the situation, and his relationship to the crew members is that of imperium and domination, not of reason.

The words of the shipmaster, however, are strictly geared to the understanding that exists among the crewmen of the purposes of the work at hand. It is interesting to note that he never again appears on the scene. He has given the plan of overall strategy and his general directions to the boatswain, who will from now on know what to do. Authority is not something continuously visible as it was in feudal times; it is ingrained in the productive processes themselves, and the captain can, therefore, disappear. As a matter of fact, the sailors and the boatswain have a hard time trying to get the feudal lords out of their way, so convinced are the latter that their visible authority is needed, and so useless is it, actually, to the workmen. The working men are on the job, doing efficiently what has to be done without undue fear or impatience.

As the scene progresses, the crew members come on deck and the boatswain speaks to them as follows:

Heigh, my hearts! Cheerly, cheerly, my hearts! Yare, yare! Take in the topsail! Tend to the master's whistle! Blow, till thou burst thy wind if room enough!

The boatswain reproduces the friendliness and simple efficiency of the master, although the tone is now somewhat more paternalistic. The distance between boatswain and sailors is patently greater than that between master and boatswain. Whereas the master has given general instructions about the main goal to the boatswain, the latter is more specific in his dealings with the less-skilled and less-educated group at his command. Nobody, however, uses harsh words except when the boatswain, in an ironical way, curses the elements. Here, as generally in modern literature, the irony expresses a feeling of limitation and constitutes an insight into the frailty of men; it is humility in non-theological clothing. What the boatswain is really saying is: We are doing all we can in our exchange with nature. We shall try to use nature for our purposes, but a wind can be stronger than a man's intelligence.

The feudal lords enter the scene at the very moment the boatswain has acknowledged the limitations of human power by shouting at the storm. Now, it is no longer merely

man against nature, but man against man: Shakespeare pits
the industrious professional and the workman against men
who are in power. Among those who appear are Alonso,
king of Naples, Antonio, usurper of the Dukedom of
Milan, and Gonzalo, a minister of the state of Naples.
(Ferdinand, the innocent young prince, who later will speak
in a most human way, remains silent.) The king says,

> Good boatswain, have care. Where's the Master? Play the
> men.

The remarks are not unfriendly, but they are condescend-
ing. The king wants the master, nobody else will do. He
can think only in terms of hierarchy. As we have seen, however, it is a hierarchy with which the master himself is
little concerned; the entire crew from the master on down
are interested merely in the matter at hand. The boatswain
does not respond to the words of the king; he continues to
behave rationally, and the only rationality possible at the
moment is to keep the deck cleared of passengers so that
the work of combating the storm is not impeded.

Antonio interrupts brusquely:

> Where's the master, bos'n?

Shakespeare introduces this character by showing in his
speech and, we may assume, in his gestures the relations between social usefulness and individual character. Antonio is
a criminal and a socially useless, irrational person. Interest-
ingly enough, the boatswain, who had nothing to say to the
king, answers Antonio: "Do you not hear him?" He
means, of course, the master. He then adds:

> You mar our labor; keep your cabins: you do assist the storm.

What Antonio is supposed to hear from the master
is his whistle. We are given here an interesting juxtaposi-
tion of the old and the new societies. The master is invisible. He is the unseen supreme authority whose presence is
mediated by the whistle, symbol of the rational ordering
and structuring of reality. In the light of the new, the

old order with its tradition, possession, and power—as
these were built up in the Middle Ages—now appears ridiculous. The boatswain uses the key word that separates the
two worlds when he speaks of "labor." Labor, along with
its organization, is the leading principle of the new society;
he who does not work, who has no useful function, is super-
fluous; he should disappear, he should go to the cabins.
Antonio is, like the storm, a hindrance that must be overcome, made innocuous.

Gonzalo, the counsellor, takes no issue with the boatswain's orders and is only concerned to pour soothing oil on
the human tempest that is brewing. "Nay, good," he says,
"be patient." The boatswain's answer is in the same tone
and appeals again to common sense: there can only be
patience if the situation permits the crew to work patiently;
because of "these roarers" there is unfortunately no time
for lengthy explanation. But the boatswain goes a step
further, and appeals, as it were, to the higher knowledge
of the counsellor by saying:

What cares these roarers for the name of king?

The boatswain now for the first time puts the issue quite
straight. Nature is stronger than men of any kind and, by
implication, he who knows how to master nature is superior
to a man who does not, regardless of social titles. Again,
as so often in Shakespeare, we encounter the stature and
the inner dignity of the man of the new society coming into
being in Elizabethan England; man is justified by his work,
and his character is formed by his function in society. The
feudal lords, impatient and useless, have nothing to do but
act out their impatience in complete separation from the
real situation.

Gonzalo agrees with the boatswain, but with a defensive
note:

Good, yet remember whom thou hast aboard.

The answer of the boatswain,

None that I more love than myself,

is one familiar enough in later statements of the egalitarian ethos: in our nature we are equal and are egotistic and altruistic at one and the same time; we all love ourselves but we overcome this self-love or raise it to a higher moral standing by useful work.

The boatswain then expresses the wisdom of the simple but experienced workman about the division of labor in society. He delineates the spheres of power and skill of those who work with their hands and those who work with their brains. "You are a counsellor," he says,

> If you can command these elements to silence and work the peace of the present, we will not hand a rope more; use your authority: if you cannot, give thanks you have lived so long, and make yourself ready in your cabin for the mischance of the hour, if it so hap.—Cheerly, good hearts!—Out of our way, I say.

The boatswain obviously takes Gonzalo seriously; as the scene develops it will become quite clear, in fact, that the two conceive of each other as colleagues of a sort. Neither is the source of authority; both are middlemen. They represent that middle station which the progressive forces of the new society are beginning to occupy. And not only professionally, but also in their basic character traits, they are removed from extremes. This motif of a middle station in life and in character is a theme that will come to the fore in subsequent literature, and will come increasingly to mirror the image that middle-class man has of himself.[1]

It is interesting to note that in the boatswain's speech death appears in a completely non-theological meaning. The speech is related to the sentiments of Shakespeare's sonnet LXVI; both deal with love and death and in both death is viewed not as a fulfillment but as a terminal point. The entire scene is, indeed, secular, except for the recourse to prayer at the very end. During the emergency, no one claims to be in the hands of God; safety and security are viewed within the framework of the developing modernism of the Renaissance, and the generally shared belief is that we have security only to the extent that we have reason and experience. The boatswain, we may say, speaks as if he had read Montaigne, and Gonzalo answers as if he were Montaigne.

For a moment the boatswain leaves the scene to check up, we assume, on the work of the mariners. Gonzalo then delivers the following monologue:

> I have great comfort from this fellow: methinks he hath no drowning mark upon him; his complexion is perfect gallows. Stand fast, good Fate, to his hanging! Make the rope of his destiny our cable, for our own doth little advantage! If he be not born to be hanged, our case is miserable.

Gonzalo slanders the boatswain *in absentia;* his curses are ironical—he is simply using his urbane wit and language to give himself comfort.

The boatswain enters the now empty deck and after having given instructions to the mariners, says, upon hearing a cry from the cabin:

> A plague upon this howling! They are louder than weather, or our office.

We assume that he, like Gonzalo, is giving himself comfort with his words; he curses when those he insults are not present to hear him. The curses of both Gonzalo and the boatswain are in marked contrast to those of the reappearing feudal lords, who now include in their group Sebastian, the brother of the king of Naples. (King Alonso and his son Ferdinand do not reappear; they obviously heed the instructions of the boatswain.) Sebastian brings the swearing to new heights:

> A pox o' your throat, you bawling, blasphemous, incharitable dog!

We can infer that this powerless individual, who envies his brother in power, must live out in words his phantasies of domination (which later jell into a plan to murder his brother). In response to his cursing the boatswain says simply:

Work you, then.

By his answer, the boatswain codifies the basic difference between the legitimate, well-organized rationale of ordered work and the parasitical, impotent, and decaying rationale of unprincipled domination. As if to prove the point, Antonio now joins in to call the boatswain a "cur," a "whoreson," an "insolent noisemaker," and in absurd fury indicts him as being more cowardly than themselves.

From now on, the lords abandon the scene, which the middlemen, Gonzalo and the boatswain, dominate. Gonzalo again acts as moderator, as a mediator who uses psychological methods to soften the shock for the despairing feudal lords and his king. The boatswain continues to give orders to the crew in accord with the changing situation of the ship, until the seamen enter shouting:

All lost! To prayers, to prayers! All lost!

In a way, the mariners are still living on a cultural level different from that of the boatswain and Gonzalo; the latter no longer find solace in religion, but only in themselves.

At the end of the scene, Gonzalo says:

Now would I give a thousand furlongs of sea for an acre of barren ground; long heath, brown furze, anything. The wills above be done! But I would fain die a dry death.

His speech is again urbane; even his invocation to the wills above seems ironic.

Throughout the scene it is apparent that the feudal lords are unaware of what is going on; they can only resort to vulgar behavior and direct personal abuse. Neither Sebastian nor Antonio realizes that the real issue is the relationship between skilled men and nature. Of course, the audience learns that the storm has been created by Prospero, but this does not alter their knowledge that the gentlemen lie and that the boatswain and his crew are neither incompetent nor drunk. The feudal lords emerge as stupid; they do not know what the relations of science, work, technology, and human skill really are. While the boat, so to speak, sails to the new world, the old lords are suffocating in an outmoded and completely senseless state of mind.

Notes

Chapter I. The Spanish Writers

1. Lope de Vega, *El Duque de Viseo,* Act II.
2. *Loc. cit.*
3. Spanish title: *Las Paces de los Reyes y Yudia de Toledo.*
4. *El Duque de Viseo,* Act I.
5. *Loc. cit.,* Act III.
6. Lope, *Las Paces de los Reyes,* Act II (translation by Edgar Rosenberg).
7. Shakespeare, *The One Hundred Fifty-Four Sonnets,* (Crowell, New York, 1944) p. 65.
8. Calderon, *The Mayor of Zalamea,* Act I, Scene 3. From *Rubaiyat of Omar Khayyam and Six Plays of Calderon,* translated by Edward Fitzgerald (Everyman's Library, No. 819, London, 1928, p. 260). All quotations from this book are reprinted by permission of E. P. Dutton & Co., Inc.
9. *Ibid.,* Act I, Scene 2, p. 254.
10. Lope de Vega, *Wise Man at Home,* quoted in Calderon's *Plays, loc. cit.,* p. 284.
11. Calderon, *op. cit.,* Act III, Scene 3, p. 277.
12. *Loc. cit.*
13. *Loc. cit.*
14. *Ibid.,* Act IV, Scene 5, p. 283.
15. See, Goethe, "Calderon's 'Daughter of the Air'" (1822) in *Goethe's Literary Essays,* ed. J .E. Spingarn (New York, 1921), pp. 208-211.

Chapter II. Cervantes

1. Cervantes, *Don Quixote* (Samuel Putnam edition, 2 volumes, Viking, New York, 1949) Vol. II, pp. 538-539. All quotations from this edition are reprinted by permission of the Viking Press, Inc.
2. John Donne, *"The First Anniversary,"* 11.205-18, in: *The Poems of John Donne,* ed. Herbert J. Grierson (2 vols., Oxford, 1912), I, pp. 23-38.
3. *Op. cit.,* Vol. II, p. 539.
4. *Loc. cit.*
5. *Ibid.,* vol. II, p. 540.
6. *Ibid.,* vol. II, p. 722.
7. The reader may recognize the technique in *Tristram Shandy,* a seminal example for English literature. The German romantic playwrights, notably Tieck, allow their characters similar licenses; most recently the

late novels of Mann rely for much of their irony on premising a narrator who is constantly weaving in and out of his own narrative, upon which he comments; Joseph and his brothers make it a point to remind each other that they are "in a story," and so forth. Again, the technique of suspending the conventional boundaries functions in a good deal of the post-World War I expressionistic drama, both in Europe and America, in the work of Pirandello, O'Neill, and Wilder; and the very device of allowing characters to trespass the physical confines of their dramatic sphere is now something of a commonplace in stage production.

8. *Ibid.,* Vol. I, p. 43.
9. *Ibid.,* Vol. I, pp. 424-425.
10. *Ibid.,* Vol. II, p. 723.
11. "The Man of Glass," in Cervantes, *Three Exemplary Novels* (Putnam edition, New York, 1950), p. 103. All quotations from this book are reprinted by permission of the Viking Press, Inc.
12. *Loc. cit.*
13. *Loc. cit.*
14. *Ibid.,* p. 104.
15. *Ibid.,* pp. 104-105. To be sure, the learned professions were satirized occasionally in medieval literature, but it is in Cervantes that they are subjected for the first time to social criticism.
16. *Ibid.,* p. 112.
17. *Ibid.,* p. 109.
18. *Loc. cit.*
19. *Ibid.,* Vol. II, p. 722.
20. *Loc. cit.*
21. *Ibid.,* Vol. II, p. 723.
22. *Loc. cit.*
23. This concept is pervasive throughout the works of Shakespeare. See especially, *All's Well that Ends Well,* Act II, Scene 3:

> . . . If she be
> All that is virtuous, save what thou dislikest,
> A poor physician's daughter, thou dislikest
> Of virtue for the name: but do not so:
> From lowest place when virtuous things proceed,
> The place is dignified by the doer's deed:
> Where great additions swell's, and virtue none,
> It is a dropsied honor. Good alone
> Is good without a name. Vileness is so:
> The property by what it is should go,
> Not by the title. . . .

24. *Ibid.,* Vol. II, p. 821. See our comparison of this episode with Calderon's treatment of a similar theme.
25. *Loc. cit.*
26. "Rinconete and Cortadillo," in Cervantes, *Three Exemplary Novels,* p. 52.
27. "The Little Gypsy," in *The Complete Works of Miguel de Cervantes in Twelve Volumes,* ed. by James Fitzmaurice-Kelly, Glasgow, 1902, vol. 7, p. 38.
28. *Loc. cit.*

29. *Ibid.,* pp. 38-39.
30. *Ibid.,* p. 38.
31. *Loc. cit.*
32. *Ibid.,* pp. 39-40.
33. *Don Quixote,* Vol. I, pp. 81-82.
34. *Ibid.,* Vol. I, p. 82.
35. *Ibid.,* Vol. II, p. 781.
36. *Ibid.,* Vol. II, pp. 781-782.

Chapter III. Shakespeare's *The Tempest*

1. See pp. 221-229.
2. It is difficult to imagine a Tudor poet acquiescing to any such doctrine as this. For a convenient summary of the theological view of learning we may go to *The Defense of Poetry.* Writing about 1582, Sidney, in a sentence often cited by the anti-secular scholars, holds it axiomatic that "this purifying of wit, this enriching of memory, enabling of judgment, and enlarging of conceit, which commonly we call learning, under what name soever it come forth, or to what immediate end soever it be directed, the final end is, to lead and draw us to as high a perfection as our degenerate souls, made worse by their clay lodgings, can be capable of." (Works, ed. Feuillerat, Cambridge, 1923, III, 11).

   This theological formulation applies to learning in all its manifestations. But it applies to each separate branch and condition of learning. When, for example, Walter Raleigh, in his *History of the World,* written as late as 1614, tells us that "This cruel king, Richard III, Henry the Seventh cut off; and was therein . . . the immediate instrument of God's justice," he is really echoing Augustine's justification for the study of history as a means of getting to know the whys and wherefores of divine punishment.

   Nor must it be thought that such a view automatically implies an adherence to medieval and Catholic functions and schemata. It is perfectly consistent in a great pedagogue like Roger Ascham to propose, in the Dedication to *Toxophilus,* "the continual setting forth of God's word and His glory," and two pages later to grumble, "These books . . . were made the most part in abbeys and monasteries, a very likely and fit fruit of such an idle and blind kind of living."

   This is not to say, of course, that in 1603, upon the accession of James, Shakespeare decided to adopt a view of the world associated with the Jacobean reign and the name of Francis Bacon, and to discard his Elizabethan allegiances and an outlook which united him to Hooker, Sidney, Spenser, and Raleigh. The man who wrote *The Tempest* under James (or, so we suppose) wrote (we are certain) *Henry V* under Elizabeth. Our contention here is that *The Tempest* bears witness to a view of learning far more akin to the Baconian than the Spenserian.
3. The passage presents some fairly difficult problems if we take it as seriously as, I think, it should be taken. How is such a political anarchism to be reconciled with the Renaissance view of order among its magistrates? The passage is directly indebted to Montaigne's "Of Cannibales," and has occasionally been interpreted as satirizing its source rather than as versifying it. This interpretation, by which Gonzalo would be made to

spout nonsense, is, so far as I know, no longer regarded as viable. As has been said, Gonzalo is always skirting the edge of absurdity by reason of his age and Polonian mellifluence. The difficulty with him, as with quite a few of Shakespeare's old men, is always with how something is said, rather than with what is said. Gonzalo makes excellent sense, but one might wish—with the nobles—that he were not such a "spendthrift of his tongue."

4. For an astute analysis of Shakespeare's uses of the verbal conventions, see Wolfgang Clemens, *Shakespeares Bilder* (1935), transl. *Shakespeare's Imagery* (1951) and J. Dover Wilson's "Introduction" to the latter. The whole question of Shakespeare's dramatic verbal technique is brilliantly discussed in Moody Prior, *The Language of Tragedy* (1947), Ch. 2.

5. The notion that music exercises peculiarly seductive and dangerous powers over irrational and anti-rational minds is very old. A fairly recent disquisition on the toxic effects of song, with a prophetic political moral, is to be found in the chapter entitled "Politically Suspect" in Mann's *Magic Mountain*. We also recall the punch-drunk street songs of the brownshirts—Caliban's political heirs. They, too, under the content analyst's magnifying glass (it needn't be a powerful one), reveal a decidedly high incidence of cursing.

6. Of the four, the nobles Sebastian and Antonio represent the vilest of the vile, since the advantage of their station makes all the greater their fall. In this respect, one of Caliban's functions in the play may be said to be that of providing a yardstick by which to measure the depravity of these nobles.

7. It is typical of Shakespeare's heroines that they are committed to one great love; love becomes so integral to their identity and their destiny that death alone can end it.

Chapter IV. The Classical French Drama

1. See Paul Hazard, *The European Mind: The Critical Years* (1680-1715), (Yale University Press, 1953), p. xv.
2. *Horace,* Act II, Scene 3.
3. *Ibid.,* Act V, Scene 3.
4. *The Cid,* Act V, Scene 7, in *Six Plays* by Corneille and Racine, The Modern Library, New York, 1931, p. 64. All the following quotations from Corneille and Racine are taken from this edition, by permission of Random House, Inc.
5. *Cinna,* Act V, Scene 2, p. 121.
6. *Cinna,* Act V, Scene 1, p. 115.
7. *Ibid.,* Act V, Scene 3, p. 122.
8. *The Cid,* Act III, Scene 5, pp. 38-39.
9. *Ibid.,* p. 39.
10. *Ibid.,* Act V, Scene 7, p. 64.
11. Leo Spitzer, "The Récit de Theramène," in *Linguistics and Literary History,* Princeton, 1948, p. 104.
12. *Phaedra,* Act I, p. 255.
13. *Ibid.,* p. 253.

14. *Ibid.*, Act II, p. 267.
15. *Ibid.*, Act I, p. 251.
16. *Andromache*, Act I, p. 128.
17. *Ibid.*, p. 130.
18. *Ibid.*, p. 139.
19. *Ibid.*, Act II, p. 141.
20. *Ibid.*, p. 145.
21. *Ibid.*, Act IV, p. 171.
22. *Phaedra*, Act IV, p. 291.
23. *Britannicus*, Act II, p. 201.
24. *Andromache*, Act III, p. 151.
25. *Phaedra*, Act III, p. 275.
26. *Ibid.*, Act II, p. 271.
27. *Ibid.*, Act III, p. 277.
28. *Ibid.*, Act II, p. 263.
29. *Ibid.*, Act. I, p. 252.
30. *Ibid.*, Act III, p. 282.
31. *Ibid.*, Act V, p. 294.
32. *Britannicus*, Act II, p. 200.
33. *Ibid.*, pp. 211-212.
34. *Phaedra*, Act I, p. 252.
35. *Britannicus*, Act V, p. 243.
36. *Phaedra*, Act III, pp. 275-276.
37. *Andromache*, Act I, p. 129.
38. *Phaedra*, Act III, p. 274.
39. *Britannicus*, Act II, p. 208.
40. *Ibid.*, Act V, pp. 237-238.
41. *Andromache*, Act I, p. 127.
42. *Ibid.*, p. 128.
43. *Ibid.*, p. 129.
44. *Ibid.*, p. 138.
45. *Andromache*, Act IV, pp. 172-173.
46. *Phaedra*, Act II, p. 271.
47. *Ibid.*, Act V, p. 301.
48. *Ibid.*
49. *Ibid.*, p. 303.
50. *Andromache*, Act III, p. 154.
51. *The Miser (L'Avare)*, Act I, Scene 1, *Plays* by Molière, Modern Library, New York, p. 286. All quotations from Molière are taken from this edition, by permission of Random House, Inc.
52. Pierre Gassendi, "Objection V to the Meditations," in: *The Philosophical Works of Descartes, in two volumes* (Dover Publ., New York, 1955), Vol. II, p. 203. This edition is published at $1.95 per volume. The quotation is reprinted by permission of Dover Publications, Inc.
53. See, *The School for Wives (L'École des Femmes)*.
54. See, *Tartuffe*.
55. See, *The Misanthrope*.
56. *Tartuffe*, Act V, Scene 1, p. 161.
57. *The School for Wives*, Act IV, Scene 8, p. 87.
58. *The Misanthrope*, Act I, Scene 1, p. 180.
59. *Tartuffe*, Act IV, Scene 3, p. 151.

60. *The High-Brow Ladies,* Act I, Scene 1, p. 18.
61. *Tartuffe,* Act V, Scene 7, p. 171.
62. *Ibid.,* Act II, Scene 3, p. 128.
63. *Ibid.,* Act I, Scene 6, p. 116.
64. *The Misanthrope,* Act I, Scene 1, pp. 178-180.

Chapter V. *From* Werther *to* Wilhelm Meister

1. Eckermann, *Conversations of Goethe,* March 28, 1827 (Everyman's Library), p. 180. (Quotations from this translation by John Oxenford are reprinted by permission of E. P. Dutton & Co., Inc.) The same adulation is expressed everywhere; see e. g., *Tag- und Jahreshefte* [*Diaries*], 1805 (*Werke,* Grossherzogin Sophie edition, V. 35, p. 189) ; also Goethe, *Briefe* [*Correspondence*], ed. Philipp Stein (Berlin, 1905), Vol. VIII, pp. 235-236 (July 26/27, 1828). (All translations from the German text of Goethe's writings, unless otherwise noted, are by Edgar Rosenberg.)
2. See his reviews of "Histoire de la vie et des ouvrages de Molière" and of "Richelieu ou la journée des dupes," *Werke,* Vol. 41, 2, pp. 335-338.
3. See Eckermann, *op. cit.,* p. 180.
4. Eckermann, pp. 38-39 (Feb. 15, 1824).
5. We might, to be sure, have included a fourth and last novel, the *Elective Affinities,* in our discussion, if only by way of anticipating some of the motifs which recur in the dramas of Ibsen, treated in the next chapter. But it seemed advisable to confine our remarks to the conflict in its widest application, between individualism and conformity, a conflict not really basic to the *Elective Affinities* except as it relates specifically to the problems of marital and extra-marital relationships.
6. The reader who is interested in both the dynamics and the mechanics of this literary genre is referred to Lionel Trilling's excellent essay on Henry James' "Princess Casamassima" in *The Liberal Imagination,* New York 1950, pp. 58-92.
7. Literally "The Sufferings." The title has been consistently mistranslated and the error, alas, is fundamental. Werther is not conspicuously addicted to *Sorgen,* but very much to *Leiden.*
8. Goethe, "Werther," in *Great German Short Stories,* Modern Library, p. 99. (Quotations from this translation are reprinted by permission of William Rose.) Goethe's friend Kestner reported that a copy of this drama was found on the desk of Karl Wilhelm Jerusalem, a young civil servant with strong philosophical and literary interests, whose unhappy life, ending in suicide, inspired Goethe's novel.
9. *Ibid.,* p. 3.
10. *Ibid.,* pp. 54 and 58.
11. *Ibid.,* p. 55.
12. *Ibid.,* p. 60.
13. *Ibid.,* p. 61.
14. *Ibid.,* p. 80.
15. *Ibid.,* p. 6.
16. To Zelter, on December 25, 1829, Goethe wrote, "It is not to be described what effect Goldsmith's *Vicar* had upon me just at the critical moment

of my mental development. That lofty and benevolent irony, that fair and indulgent view of all infirmities and faults, that meekness under all calamities, that equanimity under all changes and chances, and the whole train of kindred virtues, whatever names they bear, proved my best education: and in the end these are the thoughts and feelings which have reclaimed us from all the errors of life." (Goethe, *Briefe*, p. 287.)

17. Goethe, *Wilhelm Meister's Apprenticeship and Travels*, Two volumes. Translated by Thomas Carlyle (A. L. Burt, New York), Vol. 1, p. 91, ("Apprenticeship").
18. *Ibid.*, Vol. I, p. 261.
19. *Loc. cit.*
20. *Ibid.*, Vol. 1, p. 262.
21. *Ibid.*, Vol. 1, pp. 262-263.
22. *Ibid.*, Vol. 1, p. 263.
23. *Ibid.*, Vol. 1, p. 359.
24. *Ibid.*, Vol. 2, p. 50.
25. Eckermann, *op. cit.*, p. 108 (May 1, 1825).
26. Goethe, *Werke, op. cit.*, p. 335.
27. Eckermann, *op. cit.*, p. 127 (January 29, 1826).
28. Goethe, *Briefe, op. cit.*, p. 236 (July 26/27, 1828).
29. Goethe, *Werke, op. cit.*, p. 334.
30. *Ibid.*, p. 335.
31. Eckermann, *op. cit.*, p. 127 (January 29, 1826).
32. Goethe, *Faust* (Modern Library, p. 5).
33. *Loc. cit.*
34. Goethe, "Weimarisches Hoftheater," in *Sämtliche Werke,* Jubiläumsausgabe (Stuttgart and Berlin), Vol. 36, pp. 193-194.
35. Goethe, *Maximen und Reflektionen (Maxims and Reflexions)*, 1829.
36. *Loc. cit.*
37. Goethe in a conversation with Chancellor von Müller, October 12, 1823, in *Gespräche und Zeugnisse* (ed. by Ernst Beutler), Zürich 1950, Vol. II, p. 311.
38. Goethe, "Weimarisches Hoftheater," *op. cit.*, pp. 191-192.
39. Goethe, *Zahme Xenien, Sämtliche Werke,* Vol. 4, pp. 46-47.
40. *Der Briefwechsel zwischen Schiller und Goethe (The Correspondence between Schiller and Goethe)*, in three volumes (Leipzig, 1922), Vol. I, pp. 370-371 (August 9, 1797).
41. *Ibid.*, Vol. II, p. 5 (January 3, 1798).
42. Molière, *The Misanthrope, loc. cit.*, p. 177.

Chapter VI. Henrik Ibsen

1. Letters of Henrik Ibsen, tr. by J. N. Laurvik and Mary Morison (New York, 1905), p. 334 (6/16/80). All quotations from Ibsen's plays and drafts of plays are taken from the William Archer "Viking Edition," *The Works of Henrik Ibsen* (New York, 1911-1912) 12 Vols., by permission of Charles Scribner's Sons.
2. *When We Dead Awaken, Act II,* (Vol. XI, p. 429).

3. *Little Eyolf*, Act I, (Vol. XI, p. 49).

4. *John Gabriel Borkman*, Act III (Vol. XI, pp. 296-297).

5. *The Master Builder*, Act II (Vol. XX, pp. 350-353).

6. The plays referred to are *Pillars of Society, John Gabriel Borkman, The Master Builder,* and *When We Dead Awaken,* respectively.

7. We refer to *Hedda Gabler, Ghosts, The Wild Duck,* and *Little Eyolf,* respectively.

8. See, *The Master Builder, When We Dead Awaken,* and *The Wild Duck,* respectively.

9. *Little Eyolf*, Act I, (Vol. XI, pp. 61-63).

10. See *Pillars of Society,* Act IV (Vol. VI, p. 457).

11. *The Master Builder,* Act I, (Vol. X, p. 284).

12. See, for example, *The Master Builder,* Act I (Vol. X, p. 258), *When We Dead Awaken,* Act II (Vol. XI, p. 450), *Little Eyolf,* Act II (Vol. XI, p. 117).

13. *The Master Builder,* Act III (Vol. X, p. 402).

14. *Hedda Gabler,* Act II (Vol. X, p. 92).

15. *Loc. cit.,* pp. 92-93.

16. *Little Eyolf,* Act II, (Vol. XI, p. 117).

17. *The Lady from the Sea,* Act IV, (Vol. IX, p. 368).

18. *The Master Builder,* Act II, (Vol. X, p. 367).

19. *The Lady from the Sea,* Act V, (Vol. IX, p. 380).

20. "Notes for a Modern Tragedy" [Draft of *A Doll's House*], (Vol. XII, pp. 91-92).

21. *Little Eyolf,* Act III, (Vol. XI, pp. 140-141).

22. Draft for *Ghosts* (Vol. XII, p. 186).

23. *Letters,* p. 359 (8/8/82).

24. *The Master Builder,* Act III (Vol. X, p. 426).

25. *Rosmersholm,* Act IV, (Vol. IX, p. 183).

26. *Loc. cit.,* (pp. 184-185).

27. *Ghosts,* Act I, (Vol. VII, p. 255).

28. *Loc. cit.* (p. 256).

29. *The Master Builder,* Act II (Vol. X, p. 335).

30. *Letters,* p. 234, (4/4/72).

31. "Speech to the Workingmen of Trondhjem" (6/14/85). In: *Speeches and New Letters,* tr. by Arne Kildal (Boston, 1910), p. 54.

32. *The Lady from the Sea,* Act IV, (Vol. IX, p. 334).

33. Draft for *A Doll's House,* (Vol. XII, p. 91).

34. Ibsen, *Nachgelassene Schriften,* ed. by J. Elias and H. Koht (Berlin, 1909), Vol. I, p. 206.

34a. See *Letters,* p. 199 (10/28/1870).

35. *When We Dead Awaken,* Act II, (Vol. XI, pp. 447-449).

36. *Ghosts,* Act III (Vol. VII, p. 336).

37. "Speech at the Banquet in Stockholm (9/24/87)," *Speeches,* pp. 56-57.

38. *Letters,* p. 86 (9/12/65).

39. See, his letter of June 16, 1880, quoted on page 165.

40. *Letters,* p. 218 (9/24/71).

41. Goethe, *Der Sammler und die Seinigen. Sämtliche Werke,* vol. 33, p. 182.

42. *Hedda Gabler,* Act. II (Vol. X, p. 105).

Chapter VII. Knut Hamsun

1. In its original form the following study was written twenty years ago, some time before the political sympathies of Hamsun for the Hitler movement became public knowledge. It is presented here not only as a case of sociological prediction but as a documentation of the authoritarian character and his ideology. See, *Zeitschrift für Sozialforschung,* ed. by Max Horkheimer, vol. VI (1937), pp. 295-345.

2. We may remind the reader of our analysis of Spanish literature—another case of social marginality illuminating traits of social typicality.

3. *Hunger,* tr. by George Egerton (Knopf, New York, 1920), p. 1. Whenever possible we have quoted from the American editions of Hamsun. Where these have been unavailable, German translations have been used as a basis for quotations. Quotations from American translations are reprinted by permission of Alfred A. Knopf, Inc.

4. *Ibid.,* p. 266.

5. *The Last Joy, (Die letzte Freude), Gesammelte Werke,* 12 Vols., German tr. ed. by J. Sandmeier (Albert Langen, München, n.d.), Vol. V, p. 291.

6. In connection with one of his eulogies of the natural strength of youth, Hamsun criticizes the aged who "have mollycoddled it [youth] with hymns and rot about peace eternal . . . If some one smites it on one cheek it turns the other accommodatingly, and keeps its fists in its pockets with admirable self-control." (*Shallow Soil,* tr. by C. C. Hyllested, Knopf, New York, 1914, p. 120.) Brutal resentment is much more apparent here than in the sentimental dress of the quotation in the text.

7. *The Last Joy, op. cit.,* p. 376.

8. *Pan,* tr. by W. W. Worster (Knopf, New York, 1921), p. 130.

9. *The Last Joy, op. cit.,* p. 289.

10. *Ibid.,* p. 293.

11. *Ibid.,* pp. 301-302.

12. *Ibid.,* p. 376.

13. *Mysteries,* tr. by A. G. Chater (Knopf, New York, 1927), p. 67. See also, *Pan,* p. 130: "This silence murmuring in my ears is the blood of all Nature seething; it is God weaving through the world and me."

14. *Pan, op. cit.,* p. 15.

15. *The Last Joy, op. cit.,* p. 310.

16. Kant, *Critique of Aesthetic Judgment,* tr. by J. D. Meredith (Oxford, 1911), p. 110. Kantian idealism, it should be remarked, received its most winning, and perhaps most profound, application to public affairs in the teachings of Thoreau and other New England Transcendentalists, who in turn, of course, influenced Tolstoi and Gandhi.

17. Kant, pp. 110-111.

18. *Pan, op. cit.,* pp. 10-11.

19. *The Last Joy, op. cit.,* p. 311.

20. See, for example, *Pan, loc. cit.,* pp. 23-24: "I pick up a little dry twig and hold it in my hand and sit looking at it, and think my own thoughts; the twig is almost rotten, its poor bark touches me, pity fills my heart.

And when I get up again, I do not throw the twig far away, but lay it down, and stand liking it; at least I look at it once more with wet eyes before I go away and leave it there."

21. *Wanderers,* tr. by W. W. Worster (Knopf, New York, 1922), p. 320.

22. *The Road Leads On,* tr. by Eugene Gay-Tifft (Coward-McCann, New York, 1934), p. 46.

23. *The Ring is Closed,* tr. by Eugene Gay-Tifft (Coward-McCann, New York, 1937), p. 152.

24. *Vagabonds,* tr. by Eugene Gay-Tifft (Coward-McCann, New York, 1930), p. 448.

25. *Cf. Growth of the Soil,* tr. by W. W. Worster, in two volumes (Knopf, New York, 1921), Vol. I, p. 7; Vol. II, p. 120; *Vagabonds,* p. 47.

26. *Growth of the Soil,* Vol. II, p. 120.

27. *Op. cit.,* Vol. II, p. 246; also *cf. Rosa,* tr. by A. G. Chater (Knopf, New York, 1926), p. 18: " 'What are you sitting here for?' 'Ah, young man,' he said, holding up the palm of his hand. 'What am I sitting here for? I sit here keeping pace with my existence. Ay, that's what I'm doing.' "

28. *Pan,* p. 164.

29. *Growth of the Soil, loc. cit.,* Vol. I, p. 99.

30. *Ibid.,* Vol. II, pp. 243-244.

31. *Loc. cit.*

32. *Loc. cit.*

33. *Chapter the Last,* tr. by A. G. Chater (Knopf, New York, 1929), pp. 266-267.

34. *Vagabonds,* p. 47.

35. *Growth of the Soil,* Vol. I, p. 122.

36. *Ibid.,* Vol. II, p. 179.

37. *Ibid.,* Vol. I, p. 42.

38. *August,* tr. by Eugene Gay-Tifft (Coward-McCann, New York, 1931), p. 149.

39. *Chapter the Last,* p. 4.

40. *Vagabonds,* p 540.

41. See *ibid.,* pp. 537-538.

42. *Ibid.,* p. 539.

43. *The Women at the Pump,* tr. by A. G. Chater (Knopf, New York, 1928), p. 316.

44. Hamsun is factually mistaken here. Primitive people often revere old age. The elders frequently enjoy the highest status in their societies.

45. *The Last Joy,* p. 351.

46. *Ibid.,* p. 318.

47. *Shallow Soil,* p. 74.

48. *Growth of the Soil,* Vol. I, p. 211.

49. *The Road Leads On,* p. 409.

50. *The Last Joy,* p. 298.

51. *Children of the Age,* tr. by J. S. Scott (Knopf, New York, 1924), p. 82.

52. *Mysteries,* p. 51.

53. See, *Mysteries,* p. 121.

54. See, *Pan,* p. 169.

55. *Rosa,* p. 55.

56. *Pan,* p. 132.

57. *Mysteries*, p. 276.
58. *The Ring is Closed*, p. 254.
59. *Growth of the Soil*, Vol. II, p. 92.
60. *Pan*, p. 34.
61. *Chapter the Last*, p. 177.
62. *Ibid.*, p. 102.
63. *Wanderers*, p. 317.
64. *Cf. Chapter the Last*, pp. 105-107.
65. *Segelfoss Town*, tr. by J. S. Scott (Knopf, New York, 1925), p. 299.
66. *Growth of the Soil, loc. cit.*, Vol. II, p. 220.
67. *Ibid.*, Vol. II, p. 253.
68. *Wanderers, loc. cit.*, p. 312.
69. *Growth of the Soil*, Vol. II, p. 9.
70. *The Last Joy*, p. 344. It is consistent with his concept of women that "the greatest thing" in which Hamsun participated was his struggle against the lenient treatment of infanticide. ("Barnemord" [Infanticide], *Morgenbladet* for March 6th, 1916, cited from Walter A. Berendsohn, *Knut Hamsun*, Albert Langen, München, 1929, p. 104.)
71. *Vagabonds*, p. 143.
72. See, for example, *Segelfoss Town*, p. 27; *The Women at the Pump, loc. cit.*, pp. 193-194; *August*, p. 342.
73. See, *Children of the Age*, pp. 81-82, 216; *Segelfoss Town*, pp. 166-168, 314-315; *August*, p. 230; *The Road Leads On*, p. 167.
74. *Cf.* his contempt for positivism in *Mysteries*, p. 157: "I am a fact!" See also, *The Last Joy*, p. 329; *The Women at the Pump*, p. 120.
75. See, *Chapter the Last*, pp. 80-81, 107.
76. See, for example, *The Last Joy*, p. 291.
77. See, *Mysteries*, p. 66; *Chapter the Last*, p. 15.
78. See, *Mysteries*, pp. 89-90.
79. *Growth of the Soil*, Vol. II, p. 245.
80. See, *The Last Joy*, p. 337.
81. *Ibid.*, p. 328.
82. *Wanderers*, p. 207.
83. *August*, p. 351.
84. *Segelfoss Town*, p. 27.
85. See *The Last Joy*, p. 362.
86. See, *Mysteries*, p. 157; *The Last Joy*, p. 329; *The Women at the Pump, loc. cit.*
87. See references enumerated in footnote 72.
88. *Children of the Age*, pp. 81-82.
89. *Ibid.*, pp 82-83.
90. *Segelfoss Town*, pp. 167-168.
91. *Wanderers*, p. 189.
92. *Ibid.*, p. 215.
93. *The Ring is Closed*, p. 191.
94. *Children of the Age*, pp. 79-80.
95. *Segelfoss Town*, p. 337.
96. *The Women at the Pump*, pp. 144-145.
97. *Ibid.*, p. 147; *cf. Segelfoss Town*, pp. 10 and 21.
98. *Mysteries*, p. 200.

99. *Ibid.*, pp. 187, 201.
100. *Ibid.*, p. 201.
101. *The Last Joy*, p. 337.
102. *Mysteries*, p. 49.
103. *Hunger, loc. cit.*, p. 22.
104. *Redakteur Lynge*, German translation ed. by J. Sandmeier (Albert Langen, München, 1922), p. 31.
105. *Pan*, p. 157.
106. *August*, p. 342.
107. *Wanderers*, p. 314.
108. *Ibid.*, p. 291.
109. *The Last Joy*, p. 317.
110. *Rosa*, p. 99.
111. *Wanderers*, p. 312.
112. *Ibid.*, p. 314.
113. *The Women at the Pump*, p. 138.
114. *Ibid.*, p. 5.

Appendix

1. See, our analysis of the intermediaries in Racine (pp. 110-112) and Molière (pp. 126-127).

Index